Browne and Beyond

IOEPress

The Bedford Way Papers Series

A full list of Bedford Way Papers, including earlier books in the series, can be requested by emailing ioepress@ioe.ac.uk

Browne and Beyond

Modernizing English higher education

Edited By Claire Callender and Peter Scott

Institute of Education Press
Bedford Way Papers

First published in 2013 by the Institute of Education, University of London,
20 Bedford Way, London WC1H 0AL

www.ioe.ac.uk/ioepress

British Library Cataloguing in Publication Data:
A catalogue record for this publication is available from the British Library

ISBNs
978-1-78277-026-8 (paperback)
978-1-78277-058-9 (PDF eBook)
978-1-78277-059-6 (ePub eBook)
978-1-78277-060-2 (Kindle eBook)

Typeset by Quadrant Infotech (India) Pvt Ltd
Printed by CPI Group (UK) Ltd, Croydon CR0 4YY

Cover: Eric Crama/Shutterstock

Contents

List of figures and tables

Claire Callender and Peter Scott

Acknowledgements

Our thanks go to all the contributors and colleagues at the Institute of Education and other institutions who made this book possible – and to our families, who put up with our constant chatter about the white paper, higher education, and student funding.

About the authors

Ronald Barnett is Emeritus Professor of Higher Education at the Institute of Education, University of London. For the last thirty years, he has been developing a social philosophy of the university and higher education, endeavouring to identify resources for advancing the educational, epistemological, and human potential of the university in a complex and challenging world. His books include *The Idea of Higher Education, Realizing the University in an age of Supercomplexity, Higher Education: A critical business, Beyond All Reason: Living with ideology in the university,* and *Being a University.* His latest book is *Imagining the University* (Routledge, 2013).

Claire Callender is Professor of Higher Education both at the Institute of Education and at Birkbeck College, University of London. Her research and writing has focused on student finances in higher education and issues related to the topic. She has been commissioned to undertake research for the most significant committees of inquiry into student funding in the UK. She gave evidence to the 2010 Independent Review of Higher Education Funding and Student Finance headed by Lord Browne and to various House of Commons Education Select Committees. She was awarded a Fulbright New Century Scholarship for 2007–08 and spent time at the Harvard Graduate School of Education. She has recently completed a longitudinal study of just under 4,000 part-time students and is currently conducting research, funded by the Nuffield Foundation, on parents' access to higher education. She is about to start another ESRC funded study on undergraduate students' attitudes to debt.

Joel Mullan is Research and Policy Adviser at the 1994 Group. He was previously Education and Skills Manager at the think tank Policy Connect, where he acted as lead researcher to the Higher Education Commission's inquiry into postgraduate education.

Michael Shattock is a Visiting Professor of Higher Education in the Centre for Higher Education Studies at the Institute of Education, a former registrar of the University of Warwick and author inter alia of *Managing Successful Universities, Managing Good Governance in Higher Education* and *Making Policy in British Higher Education 1945–2011* (McGraw-Hill/Open University Press) and some 80 articles and book chapters. He was educated at Oxford and holds honorary degrees from the

Universities of Aberdeen, Leicester, Reading, and Warwick. He is well known for his high-profile advisory work on institutional and system management and governance, and chaired the 2003 OECD Review of Irish Higher Education.

Peter Scott is Professor of Higher Education Studies at the Institute of Education, University of London. He is Chair of the Behavioural Sciences section of the Academia Europaea and a member of the Academy of Social Sciences. He was Vice-Chancellor of Kingston University London from 1998 until 2010 and a member of the board of the Higher Education Funding Council for England from 2000 until 2006, chairing two of its strategic committees. Previously he was Pro-Vice-Chancellor and Professor of Education at the University of Leeds and editor of *The Times Higher Education Supplement* (now the *Times Higher Education*) from 1976 until 1992. Among his previous books are *The Meanings of Mass Higher Education* and, with other authors, *The New Production of Knowledge: The dynamics of science and research in contemporary societies,* and *Rethinking Science: Knowledge and the public in an age of uncertainty.*

Paul Temple is Reader in Higher Education Management at the Institute of Education, University of London, and Co-Director of its Centre for Higher Education Studies, where he co-directs its MBA programme in higher education management. He was formerly head of the federal University of London's planning division, and before that worked on college and polytechnic planning in London. He edited *Universities in the Knowledge Economy* (2012) in Routledge's International Studies in Higher Education series, and is currently working on a book on how the physical form of the university affects its life and work. He is editor of the *London Review of Education.*

Anna Vignoles is Professor of Education at the University of Cambridge. Her research interests include issues pertaining to equity in education, school choice, school efficiency and finance, and the economic value of schooling. She has published widely on the impact of school resources on pupil achievement, on the socio-economic gap in pupil achievement and in particular on issues relating to widening participation in higher education and the economic value of higher education. Anna is a Research Fellow at the Institute for Fiscal Studies and a Visiting Professor at the Institute of Education. She has advised numerous government departments, including the Department for Education, the Department of Business, Innovation and Skills, and HM Treasury. She also provided advice to the Browne Review of Higher Education Funding, the House of Commons Education and Skills Committee's investigation of higher education funding, the House of Lords Economic Affairs Select Committee, as part of their inquiry into education and training opportunities for young people, and Lord Leitch's Review of Skills. Anna is the economist member of the NHS Pay Review Body.

David Watson has been Principal of Green Templeton College and Professor of Higher Education at the University of Oxford since October 2010. He was Professor of Higher Education Management at the Institute of Education, University of London, from 2005 to 2010, and Vice-Chancellor of the University of Brighton between 1990 and 2005. His most recent books are *Managing Civic and Community Engagement* (2007), *The Dearing Report: Ten years on* (2007), *The Question of Morale: Managing happiness and unhappiness in university life* (2009), *The Engaged University* (2011), and *The Question of Conscience: Higher education and personal responsibility* (2014). He has contributed widely to developments in UK higher education, including as a member of the Council for National Academic Awards (1977–93), the Polytechnics and Colleges Funding Council (1988–92), and the Higher Education Funding Council for England (1992–6). He was a member of the Paul Hamlyn Foundation's National Commission on Education (1992–3), and the National Committee of Inquiry into Higher Education, chaired by Sir Ron Dearing (1996–7). He was the elected chair of the Universities Association for Continuing Education (1994–8), chair of the Longer Term Strategy Group of Universities UK (1999–2005), and President of the Society for Research into Higher Education (2005–12). He is a Trustee of the Nuffield Foundation (since 2005), a Companion of the Institute of Management (2000), and a National Teaching Fellow (2008). He chaired the national Inquiry into the Future for Lifelong Learning, and co-authored its report *Learning through Life* (2009). He was knighted in 1998 for services to higher education.

Geoff Whitty was director of the Institute of Education, University of London, for over ten years from 2000 to 2010, and currently holds visiting professorships at the universities of Birmingham and Bath. Earlier in his career, Geoff taught in primary and secondary schools before working at higher education institutions in Britain and the USA. He was President of the British Educational Research Association in 2005–07 and has been an adviser to successive House of Commons' select committees on education since 2005. He was a member of the Higher Education Commission, which produced a recent report on the future of postgraduate education.

Gareth Williams is Emeritus Professor at the Institute of Education, University of London. He founded its Centre for Higher Education Studies in 1985 and its MBA in Higher Education Management (with Michael Shattock) in 2001. An education economist, he has worked mainly on higher education policy and finance since the publication of *Changing Patterns of Finance in Higher Education* (1992). He is a past chairman of the Society for Research in Higher Education and was director of its Leverhulme project on the future of higher education in the early 1980s, which foresaw the likely direction of many of the changes of the 1980s and 1990s.

Gill Wyness is a Research Officer at the Centre for Economic Performance (CEP), London School of Economics, where her specialism is in the economics of higher education. Her work involves evaluating the impact on university participation of the UK government tuition fee and higher education finance policies of the last two decades. Her recent research includes a randomized control trial that aimed to find out what school students know about the costs and benefits of going to university – and what would be the impact on their knowledge and aspirations of an 'information campaign' focused on the costs and returns to higher education. She is also currently researching the impact of higher education bursaries on performance and drop-out rates of university students. Gill joined CEP from the Institute of Fiscal Studies. She obtained her PhD from the Institute of Education, University of London, in 2010.

Chapter 1

Introduction

Claire Callender and Peter Scott

The expansion and growing importance of higher education in England over the past 50 years, especially since the 1980s, have prompted numerous developments aimed at reshaping and restructuring the sector and its funding. In turn, these events reflect higher education's changing ideological, economic, and social functions. The reforms introduced in 2012/13 in England are arguably the most radical and have far-reaching consequences, both intended and unintended. At their heart lies the question of how to pay for the increasing demand for higher education. These reforms are the focus of this book. They were informed by the Independent Review of Higher Education Funding and Student Finance, chaired by Lord Browne, and the subsequent 2011 White Paper – *Higher Education: Students at the heart of the system* (BIS, 2011).

The book seeks to unpack what has driven and underpinned the 2012/13 reforms while locating them in a broad historical, ideological, and policy context. It looks both back at the factors that prompted and informed them as well as forward to what they mean for the higher education sector, how it is managed, its future, and the policymaking process.

To help contextualize the book the first part of this chapter provides a descriptive account of the contents of the *Browne Report* and the 2011 White Paper. The second part summarizes the other chapters.

Independent Review of Higher Education Funding and Student Finance 2009

The Independent Review of Higher Education Funding and Student Finance, chaired by Lord Browne, was launched on 9 November 2009 with full political party support. It arose from the Labour Government's commitment, made during the Commons stages of the 2004 Higher Education Bill, to review the operation of variable tuition fees for full-time students after three years. Thus initially, the Review was not prompted by a need for reform, but by a desire to assess the 2004 Higher Education Act. The Browne Review was 'tasked with making recommendations to government on the future of fees policy and financial support for full and part-time undergraduate and postgraduate students' (BIS, 2009) and was to report after the General Election of May 2010. The highly contentious and vote-losing issue of resolving student finances was consequently wiped off the General Election agenda, and left to the incoming government: the Conservative–Liberal Democratic Coalition. Such a defusing strategy had also been used by the Conservatives: when they launched the 1996 National Committee of Inquiry into Higher Education, chaired by Sir Ron (later Lord) Dearing, and in the publication of the *Dearing Report* after the 1997 election.

The Browne Review's final report – *Securing a Sustainable Future for Higher Education: An independent review of higher education funding and student finance* – was published on 12 October 2010. Its case for reform focused on three issues (IRHEFSF, 2010: 23). First, the need to increase higher education participation because demand exceeded supply. In addition, low-income students and under-represented groups were not going to the most prestigious universities, so 'fair access' had not been achieved while access to part-time study was hampered by a lack of government financial support. The second focus was on improving quality: students lacked the skills employers wanted to improve productivity and higher education institutions needed more money to upgrade their courses and also lacked incentives to enhance the 'student experience'. The third issue concentrated on the desire to create a sustainable system of higher education funding and to alter the balance of private and public contributions to the higher education sector. This had not changed since 2006. Tuition fees of £3,000, introduced by the 2004 Higher Education Act, had generated more income for universities, but the government was spending more on student financial support. Consequently, higher education remained overly reliant on public funding, and if subject to public expenditure cuts would be unable to attract additional funds.

The economic context within which the Review's recommendations operated was one of the global recession and unprecedented cuts in public expenditure (HM Treasury, 2010). This is paramount for understanding its recommendations – and the Coalition's response to them. So, too, are the political context and the Coalition's ideology.

The Report's key recommendations were as follows:

The Student Finance Plan

1. Most of the money higher education institutions receive from the government for teaching undergraduate courses should be withdrawn, but government subsidies for science, technology, engineering, and mathematics courses should continue at a reduced level. This lost income would be replaced by higher tuition fees.
2. The government-set cap of £3,290 on undergraduate tuition fees should be removed.
3. Higher education institutions charging tuition fees over £6,000 should be subject to a levy. Higher education institutions would keep a diminishing proportion of any fees charged above £6,000, and the levy returned to government to help fund the national student financial support system, so avoiding the need to restrict or cut student numbers.

4. All full-time students would continue to receive student loans to pay all their tuition fees, including those attending private higher education institutions, and for the first time, part-time students also should qualify for tuition fee loans.

5. All full-time students would carry on receiving student loans for maintenance but these should no longer be means tested. Full-time low-income students also would still qualify for maintenance grants that would be increased to compensate for the proposed abolition of statutory bursaries.

6. The terms and conditions of student loans repayment should change. The point at which graduates start to repay their loans should increase from £15,000 to £21,000, and all outstanding debt should be forgiven after 30 years – previously 25 years. Consequently, graduates would pay 9 per cent (unchanged) of their income above £21,000 until they had repaid all their student loan debt, with any outstanding debt written off after 30 years.

7. The interest paid on the loans for graduates earning above £21,000 should be equal to the government's cost of borrowing (inflation plus 2.2 per cent), and this income threshold should no longer rise automatically in line with inflation.

8. Potential students should be provided, primarily by higher education institutions, with more information and careers advice about courses and their outcomes, so they can make informed higher education choices.

9. Entitlement to student finance should be determined by a minimum higher education entry standard, based on UCAS tariff points agreed annually.

The Higher Education Council

10. The four bodies regulating the higher education sector – the Higher Education Funding Council for England (HEFCE), Quality Assurance Agency (QAA), Office for Fair Access (OFFA), and the Office of the Independent Adjudicator (OIA) – should be combined into one: the Higher Education Council. It would take a more targeted approach to regulation, with greater autonomy for higher education institutions, and have five areas of responsibility: investment, quality, equity of access, competition, and dispute resolution.

Other provisions

11. Increase in student numbers of around 10 per cent over the next three years.

The Coalition Government's response to the *Browne Report*

2010 government Spending Review

On 20 October 2010 the Chancellor, George Osborne, presented the government's Spending Review. The 25 per cent reduction by 2014–15 of the Department for Business, Innovation and Skills' resource budget hit higher education the hardest of all. Two-thirds of the savings were to be delivered by reforming the funding of higher and further education (BIS, 2010), while the overall higher education resource budget, excluding research funding, was cut by 40 per cent – or £2.9 billion – and reduced to £4.2 billion by 2014–15 (BIS, 2010). Such measures were inextricably linked to the Browne Review's recommendations and the withdrawal of government funding for most undergraduate courses.

The government's formal response to the *Browne Report* came in two stages: in a statement by David Willetts, Minister for Universities and Science, in the House of Commons on 3 November 2010 (Hansard, 2010) and in their publication on 28 June 2011 of the White Paper *Higher Education: Students at the heart of the system* (BIS, 2011) – which reiterated the announcement of November 2010. The government accepted some of Browne's proposals while rejecting others. They also introduced some new mechanisms in the White Paper while supporting the ideological thrust of the *Browne Report* for a more marketized higher education sector with students as consumers at the heart of the system.

Announcement by David Willetts in the House of Commons on 3 November 2010

All the changes Willetts pronounced on 3 November 2010 came into force for new higher education entrants in 2012/13. The government:

- endorsed Browne's recommendation to withdraw most of higher education institutions' teaching funds (see 1 above)
- rejected Browne's suggestion that the tuition fees cap should be abolished (2). Instead, the existing cap of £3,290 per annum for full-time courses was increased to a maximum of £9,000, and for the first time, a cap of £6,750 was put on the fees for part-time undergraduate courses
- abandoned the idea of a fees levy (3) – but higher education institutions charging more than £6,000 were to be subject to 'a tougher regime' to ensure they met their widening participation and fair access responsibilities
- approved the extension of tuition fee loans to part-time undergraduates (4), but continued to partially means-test maintenance loans for full-time students (5)
- allowed maintenance grants for low-income students to be increased (5) but limited eligibility to partial grants to students whose family annual income was between £25,000 and £42,000
- agreed with Browne's earnings threshold for loan repayments and the extended period of debt forgiveness (6)
- introduced higher interests rates on loans (7). Both graduates from part-time and full-time study will not start repaying their loans until earning £21,000 a year, when the interest on their loan will be limited to inflation. Graduates earning between £21,000 and £41,000 will be charged interest on a sliding scale up to a maximum of inflation plus 3 per cent when annual earnings exceed £41,000
- supported more information for students (8)

- announced a National Scholarship Programme, co-funded by the government and higher education institutions, as a sop to the Liberal Democrats in the Coalition. This support for low-income students, worth at least £3,000, was not an entitlement: higher education institutions determine who receives help and what they get.

Significantly, both Browne and the government recognized the importance of a comprehensive student support system to safeguard higher education participation. Consequently, the overall structure and type of student financial support available to full-time students remain largely unchanged, mirroring the provision introduced in 2006. However, students will graduate with much higher student loan debt, which it will take graduates far longer to pay off.

2011 White Paper: *Higher Education: Students at the heart of the system*

The 2011 White Paper (BIS, 2011) primarily repeated, albeit in more detail, the statement Willetts had made in November 2010 but also sought to deal with HEI's responses to that announcement, especially the higher than expected fees higher education institutions planned to charge – all within an ideologically driven vision of a higher education sector whose purpose and role were to be defined by the market.

The White Paper mirrors the *Browne Report*'s case for reform:

> Our reforms tackle three challenges. First, putting higher education on a sustainable footing. We inherited the largest budget deficit in post-war history, requiring spending cuts across government. By shifting public spending away from teaching grants and towards repayable tuition loans, we have ensured that higher education receives the funding it needs even as substantial savings are made to public expenditure. Second, institutions must deliver a better student experience; improving teaching, assessment, feedback and preparation for the world of work. Third, they must take more responsibility for increasing social mobility.
>
> (BIS, 2011: 4)

The White Paper established mechanisms to reduce higher education institutions' tuition fees (and the government's student loan bill), and to create more competition between providers in an environment of constrained student numbers by 'liberating student number controls' (BIS, 2011: 48). It introduced 'core and margin' full-time student places. Higher education institutions were allowed to recruit as many students as they liked scoring the equivalent of AAB or above at A-level, while 20,000 places were reserved for higher education providers whose average tuition fee, after fee waivers, was £7,500 or below. These places were removed from the national pot of government-allocated student places and a higher education institution's core allocation, which led to a reduction in core allocations in 2012–13. Over time it was anticipated that the number of 'core' places would decline further, while the number of competitive 'margin' places would increase. However, there was to be no increase in total student numbers.

The government also sought to create greater provider competition by simplifying the regulations for obtaining and renewing degree-awarding powers to make it easier for new providers to enter the sector and by reviewing the use of the title 'university'. However, they rejected Browne's idea of a single regulatory body but said that they would 'put in place a new regulatory system that protects standards and quality, gives power to students to trigger quality reviews where there are grounds for concern, yet cuts back the burden of review for high performing institutions' (BIS, 2011: 6). The measure required new legislation – and as Peter Scott shows in chapter 3, there was little political appetite for that.

Outline of the book

This book contributes to an understanding of these reforms and their initial impact on higher education institutions, students, and society as a whole. The volume has two sections. The first provides a history and a context to the 2011 White Paper while the second examines particular issues and themes arising from it.

Chapter 2 by Michael Shattock describes the historical, economic, and fiscal background to the budgetary decisions about higher education taken in the 2010 Comprehensive Spending Review (CSR) and later incorporated into policy in the White Paper (BIS, 2011). Like most policy decisions taken in higher education, Shattock argues that their roots extend far back in time. They were heavily conditioned by government policymaking machinery first established in the 1960s and by policy assumptions about the relationship between higher education and public expenditure dating back to the Thatcherite approach to reducing the latter in 1979–80. The CSR decision to cut higher education government funding by 40 per cent was not newly minted in 2010. It reached back to policy tools first considered in 1961–2 but which, rejected by Robbins in 1963 and by the Tory Government in the mid-1980s, were reactivated by New Labour, as part of their 'Third Way' politics, under Tony Blair in 2003. While not wishing to exaggerate the continuities in government decision-making, the decisions outlined in the CSR perhaps reflected a final stage in the Treasury's search for a fiscal mechanism that would reconcile the key policy drivers of higher education's post-war history: the increasing demand for places and the question of how to pay for them.

The next chapter, by Peter Scott, explores in more depth the policymaking process. Scott argues that the Browne Review and the subsequent White Paper represent a 'new model' of policy formation, one which had its origins in the 1980s under Thatcher and which was reinforced by New Labour from 1997. In contrast to the twentieth century's more rationalist models of policymaking, this new model has four characteristics: a heightened degree of ideological dogmatism, a distrust of traditional forms of professional expertise, a more pressurized 24/7 politics where presentation counts for more than implementation, and a focus on policy delivery at the expense of policy formation. The 'new model' has had a significant impact on higher education. It has contributed, firstly, to the increasing pace of policymaking and the frequency of policy interventions; secondly, to the decline of 'grand narrative' inquiries and the substitution of short-term political agendas – which helps account for why the *Browne Report* seems somewhat lightweight in comparison to the reports produced by the Robbins and Dearing Committees; thirdly, to the subordination of higher education policy to wider policies concerning innovation, industry, and employment; and finally, to more detailed intrusions into higher education under the guise of better management and improved accountability. As a result, policymaking focuses more on 'on (ideological) message' policy interventions that are brisker in their process, briefer in their presentation, and which reflect a number of trends such as the shift from the welfare to the market state, the development of a knowledge-based global economy, the rise of the audit society, and even the foreshortening of time itself.

Compared with the *Dearing* and *Robbins Reports*, Scott argues that the *Browne Report* fits this new model of policy formation well. However, while the *Dearing* and *Browne Reports* were received very differently by the higher education community, in their policy narratives are considerable continuities and a shared political consensus: that some sort of cost-sharing was necessary to deliver additional income to the higher education sector to maintain high-quality provision; that investment in higher education was justified in offering economic returns to both individuals and the state; and that enhancing learning and teaching, improving the student experience, and empowering students were all desired aims. Scott suggests that the *Browne Report* and 2011 White Paper may have bent, but certainly did not break, this strong political consensus.

Continuing to describe and critique the contents of the *Browne Report* and 2011 White Paper, Scott's conclusions are twofold. First, there was no inevitability to the policies implemented by the Coalition Government. Rather, they reflect the contingency of policy formation. Second, the most dramatic changes in higher education may not result directly from the 2009–11 reforms but from the unintended impacts of other discrete, and uncoordinated, policy changes that together produce a 'perfect storm' in English higher education. These policies include: the recruitment of international students, the future shape of research (and innovation) policies, reforms in English schools, and the long-term consequences of devolution. Both conclusions – the contingency of policy formation and the gathering of a 'perfect storm' – reinforce the plasticity of policy.

Central to both the Browne Review and the 2011 White Paper, as we have seen, was the desire for a more market orientated higher education system with greater provider competition and user choice. As Scott argues, 'market' discourse has now been irreversibly lodged in mainstream policy thinking. In chapter 4 Gareth Williams shows how this has come about and provides an economic critique of the limits of higher education's marketization. He chronicles the shift in the sector's funding and suggests there are two basic ways in which higher education can be organized: as a publicly provided service free at the point of delivery with its profile determined by politicians and planners, or a service provided by the market, which decides how much is provided and who reaps the benefits on the basis of choices by individual consumers. In practice, all higher education systems are a combination of the two but the balance between them changes over time. In the UK the public service model was dominant until the late 1980s. But the past 20 years have seen a move towards market-based provision. In the UK, this change was prompted by pressures brought about by 'massification' and radical ideological changes in ideas about how public services are best provided. However, the 2011 White Paper marks a major step towards a fully marketized higher education system in England. While the system has the potential to bring some benefits, especially in reducing the cost of provision by weakening the monopolizing power of providers, the so-called commodification of higher education also has many potential weaknesses.

Considering these weaknesses, Williams asks whether, from an economic perspective, there are, or should be, limits to higher education's marketization. He suggests that the idea of profit making by universities is a bridge too far. He argues that there are two central weaknesses to markets as mechanisms for the strategic allocation of resources. First, their tendency to prioritize short-term decision-making and second, their lack of concern with how the outcome of the large number of individual decisions that make up a market, distributes costs and benefits. Such weaknesses can contribute in turn towards, for instance, greater inequalities in access to higher education, a more stratified and hierarchical system of higher education, greater risks of corruption, increased managerialism and regulation, and a more intense audit culture. Williams maintains that it is possible to overcome these weaknesses but at a cost. However, he concludes that all the risks associated with market behaviour are likely to become more apparent the nearer higher education comes to being a service provided on an entirely financially transactional basis.

The second part of the book examines issues and themes emerging from the 2011 White Paper. Here, it is useful to distinguish between policy aims – what the policy is supposed to achieve – and policy goals – the outcomes of policies and whether their aims are being achieved (Spicker, 2006). As discussed, the White Paper had three main policy aims: creating a financially sustainable higher education system, improving the student experience, and increasing social mobility. As Scott discusses in chapter 3 and the concluding chapter, along with Watson in chapter 11, there is considerable doubt as to whether these changes will lead to a more financially stable higher education sector. In the short- to medium-term public expenditure on higher education will rise, as will public sector debt in the first half of the century.

What about the student experience (whatever this term really means[1]) – is this likely to improve? The main driver in the 2012/13 reforms for improving the 'student experience' is the development of a higher education market that will lead, in theory, to better quality provision, drive down prices, and put *'students at the heart of the system'*. However, as Ron Barnett concludes in chapter 5, the student experience is likely to get worse as a result of the 2011 reforms. Barnett explores the marketization of higher education in relation to students. He probes the tacit idea of the 'student' informing the White Paper which, in line with the notion of higher education's marketization, assumes that the 'student', in advance of her studies and with the aid of documents and data, can know what she wants from higher education, make rational choices about what to study, and can capture her educational experience and engagement in her course of study. A genuinely higher education, however, and all that is significant about higher education, Barnett argues, cannot be transparent and explicit in the way the White Paper requires. Indeed this search for transparency produces a process devoid of spontaneity, unpredictability, difficulty, challenge, and wonder while undermining higher education's transformatory potential. Barnett illustrates his argument by interrogating the assumptions underpinning the White Paper. For instance, he calls into question its demand for 'well-informed students driving teaching excellence' (BIS, 2011: 25) and for 'a better student experience and better-qualified graduates' (BIS, 2011: 33). By dissecting the ideas bolstering such demands, Barnett highlights the White Paper's narrow and regressive visions of the student and of learning. Ultimately, the reforms are likely to change the pedagogical relationship between students and their institutions to one that mirrors a market relationship and is thus *self-undermining*. In doing so they will impair the student experience rather than improve it.

Another important dynamic of a higher education market is the number of student places. Contrary to the Browne Review's recommendation, the Coalition reforms have reduced the overall number of places, making admissions a zero-sum game. If some universities expand others must contract. If the number of institutions increases with new entrants, the average size of each must fall. Without greater student numbers, demand will continue to outstrip supply, constraining competition on quality and limiting student choice. Thus for some would-be students there will be no 'student experience' to improve. However, as Gill Wyness discusses in chapter 6, the government attempted to overcome such issues and to put a downward pressure on tuition fees by introducing an awkward quasi-market. They abolished quotas for full-time students with A-level (or equivalent) grades of AAB or better and reserved 20,000 places for higher education institutions whose fees were less than £7,500 a year. Wyness explores some initial consequences of these changes and how they have had a strongly unequal impact on different types of higher education institutions and students. She suggests that under the government's new system, the universities most likely to be affected negatively are those charging over £7,500 without many AAB+

students. Russell Group universities, by contrast, were relatively protected, although some had unfilled places in 2012/13. Further education colleges were meant to be winners but they, too, failed to fill many of their newly allocated places. Wyness's analysis helps explain full-time enrolment patterns in 2012/13, which she recognizes may be atypical of future years. While there were very few changes in student enrolment by family background or in terms of the courses students applied for, there were differential decreases in application rates and volumes among students of different age groups. The number of 19-year-olds applying in 2012/13 decreased in particular, a reduction likely to affect Russell Group universities especially since they tend to recruit a greater proportion of younger students. Applications from older students were also down in 2012/13, which strongly affected further education colleges as well as mid- to low-tier universities. Whilst applications amongst such students may recover in future years, Wyness suggests that a permanent fall in mature students – and a fall in student numbers in general – could have serious consequences for certain institutions and be a major threat to the government's reforms. Looking ahead, Wyness concludes that the somewhat awkward quasi-market will prevail. The government's announcement to remove the cap on students with ABB as well as AAB is likely to have a similar affect to the reforms of 2012/13. Student deferrals, however, are likely to be less of an issue since Russell Group and other prestigious universities will be protected, while participation falls are more likely to affect medium and low tariff institutions and academically weaker students.

In chapter 7 by Anna Vignoles, we turn to the White Paper's ambitious policy aim of increasing social mobility, which seeks both to increase the chances of someone from a lower socio-economic background going to university and to increase their chances relative to their more advantaged peers. Should this happen it implies a decline in the relative chance of students from middle and high socio-economic groups gaining entrance into university. Vignoles reminds us of the importance of widening participation as a means for achieving social mobility. She shows that despite the fact that more people are participating in university, the socio-economic gap in participation is substantial and she continues to explore some of the reasons for this. In suggesting that the new system of student financial support mostly protects poorer students from the potentially deterring effect of higher tuition fees, Vignoles largely rejects the argument that poor students are unable to access university because it is unaffordable. Instead she argues that poorer students are less likely to go to university because they have lower levels of prior educational attainment, which in turn is associated with their family characteristics. Consequently, as the White Paper recognizes, the policy effort needs to focus on improving poorer children's achievement in school and on providing better resourced careers advice for all children. However, some responsibility for widening participation rests with higher education institutions. The National Scholarship Programme, in its current form, is unlikely to be of much assistance in this regard. Using contextual data in admissions might help at the margins, as might the Office for Fair Access' (OFFA) enhanced role. More outreach would be beneficial too – especially to encourage those poorer students who are qualified to enter university but choose to pursue non-degree options – as would assessing the overall effectiveness of outreach activities.

One of the policy goals of the White Paper was to open up access to higher education, particularly through part-time study. The government sought to achieve this goal by providing enhanced financial support for part-time undergraduate students, introducing, for the first time, loans for their tuition fees. Following this change, however, there has been a 40 per cent fall in part-time undergraduate entrants since 2010/11. Chapter 8 by Claire Callender focuses on part-time students and provides a critique of the reforms of part-time student finances. Far from remedying the longstanding injustice in support for adult learners, Callender argues that the new loans for part-time students are likely to re-enforce or perpetuate them. The loans' very restrictive eligibility criteria mean that the majority of part-time undergraduates do not qualify for them, and yet are faced with far higher tuition fees that they have to pay upfront, and out of their own pocket. Callender suggests that these policies were designed for the 'typical student and graduate': a young school leaver who studies full-time and who, on graduation, enters the labour market for the first time. They fail to acknowledge the distinctive characteristics of the part-time student population, who consequently miss out most on the loans or choose to shun them. In their present form, Callender contends, the loans are an inappropriate tool of student support for many part-timers. Both the lower financial private returns to part-time study and the wide ranging non-pecuniary benefits students reap from their studies together justify larger government subsidies to encourage demand for part-time study. Callender proposes that the government, at a minimum, should rethink the eligibility criteria of loans so that more students qualify for them. She concludes that unless there is the political will both within the higher education sector and the government to tackle the challenges posed by part-time study, demand and supply is likely to continue to fall, contrary to the government's intentions.

Another way the government has sought to open up access to higher education and to increase student choice and provider competition is through encouraging new entrants – including private providers and further education colleges – into the sector. Such new entrants are integral to the government's vision of a well-operating higher education market. In Chapter 9 Paul Temple discusses aspects of UK private higher education. He describes the difficulty of neatly classifying the UK system into the public or private sector, arguing that UK universities have always been private, non-profit institutions but with important links to the state. The post-war expansion of higher education was seen as the state's responsibility, as was providing generous state support for students, which made UK higher education an international anomaly: a public–private partnership relying on public funds. Very few universities in the UK are completely private, namely, institutions that receive no direct public financial support. Encouraging greater private sector involvement in higher education – crucially, by making it easier to gain a university title and by removing the legal impediments to private companies buying existing universities – is something the White Paper sought to remedy. However, as Temple argues, the White Paper provides no clear rationale for the growth of private provision and its benefits, nor does it give well-honed arguments as to why private sector providers should compete on equal terms with the public sector. Temple thus concludes that increasing the number of private providers was an ideological goal, and a policy framework was put together to support such an objective. He ends by suggesting that the ecology of the UK higher education is changing, with expanding private for-profit and non-profit sectors gaining degree-awarding powers. Looking ahead he sees a more complex pattern of higher education developing, with intersecting fields of public and private provision and a wider range of overlapping institutional types. Ultimately this brings into question the extent to which we can still speak of a single higher education 'system' or 'sector'.

Unlike previous higher education White Papers, the 2011 White Paper is very narrowly drawn, focusing exclusively on the undergraduate economy, especially student funding, while failing to locate higher education within a broader context or addressing other higher education concerns. Overlooked and forgotten topics include postgraduate education, research, innovation, and knowledge exchange. Chapter 10 by Geoff Whitty and Joel Mullan focuses on postgraduate education. The authors point out that not all government funding has been withdrawn from postgraduate courses, unlike most undergraduate courses. For the time being, existing levels of core funding for postgraduate teaching in higher cost subjects has been maintained. Longer-term solutions to the funding of postgraduate courses and students are required, however, because, as Whitty and Mullan show, postgraduate education matters for the long-term health of the higher education sector, the economy, the nation's culture, the professions, and for social justice and access including social mobility. Despite their importance, however, the majority of home postgraduates on taught courses receive no financial help with their tuition fee costs, nor do those undertaking part-time postgraduate research. Whitty and Mullan, in response, present a range of possible approaches to funding postgraduate study – including loans, long-term private bonds, alumni borrowing, and tax incentives for employers – and highlight a range of recommendations from the Higher Education Commission. To ensure against iniquities in the higher education system that have so far been neglected in the funding debate, they conclude that measures urgently need to be put in place before the first cohort of undergraduates paying £9,000 in tuition fees graduate in 2016.

It is clear that the reforms are creating considerable instability in the sector. In chapter 11 David Watson discusses how higher education institutions can weather the storm of national policy confusion, funding uncertainty, and diminished public confidence arising from the White Paper. Watson looks at two key themes in recent literature on UK higher education management: the limits of institutional autonomy and the freedom of choice of strategic direction. He begins with a historical analysis of 'mission choice' by UK higher education institutions since the Conservative Government came to power in 1979, setting this in a context of changes in sectorial organization and funding including those contained within the 2011 White Paper. From there he derives a pattern of actual and potential constraints on whole-institution actions related to policy, markets, inherited and accumulated resources (of all kinds), performance (including of leadership and governance), and reputation. He then develops the concept of an institution's 'zone of freedom of action' based on the interplay of opportunities, constraints, and resources, a process that reviews a series of techniques and objectives for institutional self-study. He concludes with a prognosis of possible and likely institutional trajectories.

In the concluding chapter Claire Callender and Peter Scott explore firstly how best to interpret the 2011/12 reforms – in terms of continuity or rupture? Secondly, they examine the reform's collateral effects, or unforeseen and unintended consequences, in relation to student demand, access and equity, part-time study, postgraduate education, and new providers. They suggest that so far the reforms have failed to produce the changes ministers desired, but they may achieve their overall objective to change the culture of the English higher education system. The 'market' university may not have emerged but the 'managerial' university is likely to develop, changing both institutional priorities and organizational cultures.

Note

[1] Given the diversity of the student population, it is highly questionable if we can really talk about a monolithic 'student experience'.

References

BIS (Department for Business, Innovation and Skills) (2009) Press Release. Online. http://hereview.independent.gov.uk/hereview/press-release-9-november-2009/ (Accessed 9 November 2009).

—(2010) *The Department for Business, Innovation and Skills Spending Review Settlement.* Online. http://nds.coi.gov.uk/content/Detail.aspx?ReleaseID=416110&NewsAreaID=2 (Accessed 20 October 2010).

— (2011) *Higher Education: Students at the heart of the system.* London: Stationery Office.

Hansard, series 5 HC (2010) 'Higher Education Funding', vol. 517, no. 64, col. 924–46, 3 November. Online. www.publications.parliament.uk/pa/cm201011/cmhansrd/cm101103/debtext/1011030001.htm#10110358000003 (Accessed 8 July 2013).

Her Majesty's Treasury (2010) *Spending Review.* Cm 7942. London: Stationery Office.

IRHEFSF (Independent Review of Higher Education Funding and Student Finance) (2010) *Securing a Sustainable Future for Higher Education: An independent review of higher education funding and student finance.* Online. www.independent.gov.uk/browne-report (Accessed 12 October 2010).

Claire Callender and Peter Scott

NCIHE (National Committee of Inquiry into Higher Education) (1997) *Higher Education in the Learning Society.* London: HMSO.

Spicker, P. (2006) *Policy Analysis for Practice: Applying social policy.* Bristol: Policy Press.

Chapter 2

Public expenditure and tuition fees: The search for alternative ways to pay for higher education
Michael Shattock

Introduction

This chapter describes the historical, economic, and fiscal background to the budgetary decisions about higher education taken in the 2010 Comprehensive Spending Review (CSR) and later translated into policy in the White Paper: *Higher Education: Students at the heart of the system* (BIS, 2011). Like most policy decisions in higher education, their roots extend far back in time. While I do not claim that they were an inevitable culmination of economic and demographic pressures, I do argue that they were heavily conditioned by government policymaking machinery first established in the 1960s and by policy assumptions about the relationship between higher education and public expenditure, which extended back to the Thatcherite approach to reducing the latter in 1979–80. The CSR decisions were not newly minted in 2010. They reached back to policy tools first considered in 1961–2 but which, rejected by Robbins in 1963 and the Tory Government in the mid-1980s, were reactivated by Labour, as part of their Middle Way policies to higher education, under the Blair Government in 2003.

While it might have been draconian, the decision in the CSR to cut government funding for higher education by 40 per cent only extended the decision – and essentially used the same machinery – made since the period when Sir Keith Joseph had been secretary of state in the mid-1980s to determine higher education on fiscal and economic grounds. This is not to say it is impossible to exaggerate the continuities in government decision-making – political decisions are inevitably influenced by circumstances (the economic downturn, the need to react to the Browne Review) and political relationships (the Coalition, the dominance of the Chancellor's commitment to reduce public expenditure). But the CSR decisions also reflected perhaps a final stage in the Treasury's search for a fiscal mechanism that would reconcile the key policy drivers of higher education's post-war history: the increasing demand for places and the question of how to pay for them.

Michael Shattock

The nationalization of higher education

The inter-war years were a period of sluggish economic growth, concerns about the labour market, and, until investment in rearmament began to take place, falling production. There was no government policy towards the universities, which funded themselves approximately one-third through tuition fee income, one-third through endowment income, appeals to the local community, and grants from local authorities, and one-third from recurrent grants from the University Grants Committee (UGC). The UGC's grant was calculated on a deficiency basis arising out of the shortfall in necessary funding from the first two funding sources. It was made on a quinquennial basis and the approval of institutions' quinquennial plans provided the UGC with machinery to influence institutional development. This responsibility it exercised sparingly, however, being most concerned to assess bids on the level of financial rather than academic criteria. The UGC was a committee of the Treasury, staffed by civil servants seconded from the Treasury, and its quinquennial bid for funding represented not much more than a bundling up of the bids submitted by the universities themselves. Apart from isolated occasions such as the imposition of 'the Geddes axe' on departmental expenditure, the Treasury, confident in the efforts of its staff at the UGC to control unnecessary expenditure, was able to meet the UGC's applications for support. During the war grant levels were maintained in spite of sharp falls in student numbers and the recruitment of many staff into war service.

However, universities emerged from the war into a new world. The Beveridge Report and the growth in the state's power in the intervening years had predisposed government against the laissez-faire approaches of the 1930s, which led to the Labour Party's promise in its 1945 manifesto *Let Us Face the Future* that planning would supersede a reliance on price mechanisms. In the spring of 1944, following the recommendation made by Lord Hankey's Inter Departmental Committee on Further Education and Training that the number of university places would need to be doubled from the figures for 1938–9, universities were immediately faced with the pressures of demobilization and the admission of ex-servicemen under the Class B priority scheme (Gosden, 1983). Moreover, various government departments launched inquiries aimed at meeting future professional manpower requirements – specifically, in higher technological education, scientific manpower, medical education, dentistry, agriculture, oriental, Slavonic, eastern European and African languages, and in social and economic research – which led to earmarked grants to the UGC to implement the various recommendations. Such demands came at a time when the universities were themselves struggling with the depredations of war, bomb damage, the occupations of their premises by the military or the Ministry of Works (the University of London and its colleges were moved out of London in 1939–40), and a lack of maintenance and refurbishment since the war had started.

It was clear that the pre-war funding mechanisms for universities had to change. There was little alternative but to turn to the state: pre-war endowment income had been decimated by the war, local authority contributions were limited by the new economic demands being imposed on them, and an increase in tuition fees was out of the question for demobilized armed forces. The universities, through their representative body, the Committee of Vice-Chancellors and Principals (CVCP), appealed to the Chancellor in two significant documents: a Memorandum dated 5 January 1945 and a public document *A Note on University Policy and Finance in the Decennium 1946–56*, which set out the case for increased funding and recognized the implication that UGC funding would need to grow from around 30 per cent to around 75 per cent of university budgets (Shattock, 2012). The state was generous in its response, resulting effectively in a nationalization of the university system: by 1949–50 the state contribution through the UGC had risen to 64 per cent from 34 per cent in 1935–6 and the tuition fee contribution – mostly paid, in any case, by individual local authorities – had fallen from 32 per cent to 18 per cent. By 1979–80 the contribution – including tuition fees, which were now paid by the state through local authorities – had risen to 80 per cent.

At the same time the government reformed the UGC, which gave it stronger terms of reference to plan the university system and reinforced its membership but left it firmly located under the Treasury. The universities may have effectively been nationalized, but the authority of the UGC, operating as Carswell, a former UGC secretary, described it 'as a collective minister' (Carswell, 1985) under the financial umbrella of the Treasury, gave the universities who dominated the UGC's membership an independence from government that served as a guarantee against any direct intervention from external political interests. Of course, the UGC had still to secure from the Treasury sufficient resources to run the university system satisfactorily. Three factors were important. The first was the close relations between staff in the Treasury and staff seconded to the UGC. Edward Playfair, at the time in charge, within the Treasury, of the financing of universities, emphasized to a Parliamentary Select Committee on Estimates the special position of the UGC compared to the Ministry of Education: 'The situation is not quite the same with the UGC who are in our minds part of the Treasury. Their job is to do our job ... we regard them as being our agents and trustworthy agents' (Select Committee on Estimates 1951–2, in Shinn, 1986). Keith (later Lord) Murray, chairman of the UGC from 1953–63, buttressed this relationship by dining with the permanent secretary every month. The second factor was the Treasury's obvious pride in the cultural significance of its responsibility for the universities (it was also responsible for funding museums and galleries). In 1956 the financial secretary to the Treasury greeted a delegation from the CVCP with the words:

> From the Treasury point of view, of course, it is one of the redeeming features of the lives of Treasury ministers that we have this contact with the universities. I feel that very keenly myself. We have to be constantly dealing with figures and saying 'No' to colleagues in the government and yet here is something of a warm and young and constructive character into which we can throw ourselves.
>
> (CVCP, 1956)

The third factor was the government's political desire to avoid being accused of denying the opportunity of entering higher education to those qualified to benefit from it. Initially this was most obviously associated with the population's sufferings during the War. Gardner argues that an informal social contract was forged in London during the Blitz: 'People who "took it" should be entitled to "get it" – if "it" meant better housing, a fairer education system, more job opportunities' (Gardner, 2011). But the improvement of educational opportunity, as exemplified in the 1944 Education Act, lay at the heart of progressive post-war thinking. Entry to higher education represented a key element in this programme – as the public response to the decision not to support the UGC's forecast of need for additional places in 1962 (see below) amply demonstrated – and was fuelled by comparison with the much higher proportions of students entering higher education in the United States.

The post-war expansion reached its peak at 85,000 students in 1949 and fell to 80,000 in 1953, after which demand began to rise again. The UGC was the first to identify the components of the likely growth: the 'bulge' arising from the return of demobilized servicemen and the 'trend' for increasing proportions of school children to stay on in the sixth form. Such was the pressure to meet demand that when existing universities proved reluctant to expand, the Treasury found the funding for the UGC to establish seven new universities. Forecast growth rates of 5 per cent p.a. had to be raised to 7.5 per cent by the 1957–62 quinquennium and the target accepted by the Chancellor of 124,000 places by the mid-1960s had to be raised to 136,000. The UGC also forecasted the need for 170,000 places by the early 1970s. Already there were tensions in government about the growth of public expenditure. While the general national mood was optimistic and Macmillan had won the 1957 General Election with the famous words 'most of our people have never had it so good. Go round the country, go to the industrial towns, go to the farms and you will see a state of prosperity such as we have never had in my lifetime – nor indeed ever in this country' (Hennessy, 2006), in December of that year his Chancellor, Thorneycroft, together with two Treasury ministers, Enoch Powell and Nigel Birch, resigned because they could not secure a £48 million reduction in public expenditure to reduce the 1958–9 estimates to the level of 1957–8. By contrast, the universities were given an 8.3 per cent increase in the 1957–62 quinquennium settlement, and when the CVCP complained about its inadequacy the UGC's chairman responded that the universities were being protected from cuts imposed on other departments and should consider themselves as being in 'a privileged position' (CVCP, 1957).

However justified the CVCP comment may have been in the light of the prospective expansion, the fact was that the UGC's relationship with the Treasury ensured the universities' budget was 'top sliced' and not subjected to the same competitive pressures for funding as other areas of public spending. Murray might have had to have two separate meetings with the Chancellor himself to secure the quinquennial settlement, but it remained within the Treasury's gift: the universities were indeed in a privileged position – they had an inside track.

The introduction of the Public Expenditure Survey (PES)

As the Thorneycroft resignation testifies, there were already concerns in the 1950s about the growth of public expenditure. Hennessy quotes a memo from Brooke, a senior Treasury official (later Sir Norman Brooke, secretary to the Cabinet) to Bridges, the head of the civil service, expressing his surprise that 'the great increase in public expenditure and the substantial change in its pattern, which has come about in the last five years in consequence of their [government] policies in the field of social services', had not been accompanied by a review of the longer term implications (Hennessy, 2006). In 1958, the Select Committee on Estimates prompted the Plowden Committee, whose Report, *Control of Public Expenditure* (HM Treasury, 1961), suggested a radical change in the way government estimates of future expenditure were arrived at. The essence of the Report was the recommendation that a formal process be introduced for assessing the public expenditure implications of policies five years ahead. Implementation brought a wholly new rigour into the establishment of priorities. First, it established a committee, the Public Expenditure Survey Committee (PESC), to control the process; second, it recommended the establishment of a Cabinet-level minister in the Treasury, the chief secretary, to take charge, under the Chancellor, of public expenditure; third, it laid down that the beginning of the process was a Cabinet decision which set a public expenditure target against which individual bids for new expenditure had to be judged; and finally, it established the mode of a departmental bidding process. Over the years the ceiling against which this bidding took place was normally fixed at between 40 per cent and 42 per cent of national spending: in 2008–09 it had risen to 43.2 per cent (Crawford *et al.*, 2009).

The prime architect of the PESC machinery was Sir Richard (Otto) Clarke, the civil servant responsible for public expenditure in the Treasury and for the universities' budget. At its meeting in January 1962 Clarke addressed the UGC, congratulating it on the scope and thoroughness of its quinquennial report but warning that 'the scale of university finance was now such that decisions could no longer be taken by Treasury ministers on their own but had become the responsibility of the government as a whole' (UGC, 1962). This was a coded message that the special relationship with the Treasury was at an end. Now the arbiter of public expenditure in a new competitive process, the Treasury could no longer itself be the budget holder and, by implication, the advocate in a bidding exercise. Almost overnight it had become the impartial inquisitor of higher education expenditure and the relentless proponent of devices to restrain departmental spending within a pre-decided public expenditure target.

The institution of the new PESC machinery cut across negotiations the UGC had been having with the Treasury since 1960 about the need to accept an expansion of student numbers to 170,000, and dealt with the recurrent and capital grant implications. The timing of capital grants was particularly important to ensure building starts to accommodate increased numbers in 1962 and 1963. By January 1961 the UGC had secured some improvement in capital grant for 1962–5 but no acceptance of student number targets beyond 150,000 at the end of the 1962–7 quinquennium. In his address Clarke warned that the government was facing enormous demands from the health services and the roads programme, that GDP would not rise above 2.5 per cent annually, and that any increase in public expenditure above between 40 and 45 per cent of national expenditure (the Cabinet fixed the PESC target at 42.5 per cent) could only be paid for by politically unpopular tax increases. In March, the Chief Secretary to the Treasury, Henry Brooke, reported to the House of Commons that 'considerations of economic policy, which are, of course, right outside the scope of the [UGC's] responsibility, have made it necessary to depart from the Committee's recommendations' (Berdahl, 1962). Although the actual settlement for recurrent resource up to 1967 was only a little less than the UGC's bid, the crucial issue was that the 170,000 figure had been deferred until 1973–4, a year later than the end of the following quinquennium. The public response was immediate, prompting debates in both Houses of Parliament. In the Commons Gaitskell, the leader of the Labour Opposition, described the government's action as 'discreditable in substance, dishonourable in presentation and deplorable in its consequences', while Lord Longford, the Opposition spokesman in the Lords, called for the removal of Treasury control over the universities (Berdahl, *ibid*). For a government already in political difficulty, what was most damaging was the fact that many of the speakers against the decision were from the Tory party. In response it quietly reversed its decision later in the year and transferred Henry Brooke in a reshuffle. More significant about the event, however, was the fact that the universities' budget was no longer ring fenced, that it now had to fight its corner with other national needs, and that a new powerful piece of policymaking machinery – which could superimpose its decisions, unless overturned in Cabinet, on the aspirations of whatever authority, whether the UGC or, later, secretaries of state for education – had been introduced.

The *Robbins Report* and the future financing of higher education

The violence of the political reaction to the government's failure to support the UGC's forecast of demand was to have a long-term impact. In part it reflected a view that the government had appeared to foreclose an area of policy – namely the rate and pattern of higher education's expansion that the Robbins Committee had been set up to recommend on only a year previously – and in part it was a genuine reaction against those who were qualified for university entry being denied the opportunity. The political scars from the episode were to determine the government's reaction to the Robbins recommendations. In the meantime two other important developments had taken place. The first was a growth in higher education outside the universities, recognized in the 1956 Technical Education Act by the identification of colleges where such growth might be encouraged, and by the creation of a group of standard bearers for the local authority sector called Colleges of Advanced Technology, which were to be permitted to award a degree-equivalent Diploma in Technology. The second was the decision following the *Anderson Report* to finance tuition fees and student maintenance centrally, as an automatic right consequent on entry to higher education rather than being solely based on the judgement of local education authorities. Both decisions had clear long-term financial implications.

The Robbins Committee, though chaired by a leading economist, was much more concerned to present forecasts of the potential rate of expansion than to dwell in detail on how it was to be paid for. In this respect the waters had been particularly muddied by the decision to implement the *Anderson Report* in 1961. At the time the Anderson recommendations seemed like an entirely straightforward rationalization of provision, previously under the control of LEAs, and it was only in the 1980s that the Treasury compounded automatic student maintenance costs with the costs of student number expansion to create a single combined 'pot of gold' on which economies could be imposed. The Robbins Committee, forecasting a growth in student numbers from 216,000 in 1962–3 to 558,000 in 1980–1, had a unique opportunity to offer recommendations as to how this expansion (which implied more than a doubling of the public expenditure bill) could be financed – but chose not to do so. The chapter headed 'The financial and economic aspects of our proposals' comprised no more than 17 of the Report's 296 pages (CHE, 1963) and relied on a generalized human capital argument – that 'communities that had paid the most attention to higher studies have in general been the most obviously progressive in respect of wealth and income' (*ibid*: para 626) – to justify the additional investment the expansion required.

The Robbins approach to the finance issue was the more surprising because it tacitly rejected the evidence presented by the Treasury. An examination of the various drafts of the Treasury evidence held in the National Archive (HM Treasury, 1961–2) show that while the Treasury was fully in support of a policy of expansion, and of the economic and social gains to be derived from it, it was very concerned about how it was to be paid for. Reviewing a range of options as to how non-state moneys could be injected into the system, tuition fees, it noted, now amounted to only 12 per cent of total income: did not higher education bring private as well as public benefit? Was it not inequitable that the minority receiving its benefits should be supported by the majority who were not? Were loans to cover fees not justifiable? What was the justification for paying the fees of international students? Should consideration be given to two-year degrees? Such were to be the perennial questions in the next 30 years. The Treasury offered two possible models within a target expansion to 500,000 students by 1980–1: an Alpha model that envisaged an even split between university and non-university higher education students, in which universities would receive a 10 per cent improvement in staffing, with two-thirds of their students in residence; and a Beta model in which universities would be capped at 170,000 student places in 1973–4, the figure already approved, while the rest of the expansion took place in non-university sectors. It projected the total costs of these scenarios as representing 1.90 per cent and 1.72 per cent of GNP respectively, as compared with the 1959–60 percentage of 0.92 per cent. The Treasury pointed out that even Beta represented a doubling of the proportion of GNP and that this had to compete in Education alone with improving primary education and abolishing class sizes of over 40, improving secondary schools and extending the leaving age to 16, and extending part-time technical education – all against a projected increase of GNP of no more than 2.5 per cent. It concluded by saying that:

> There is likely to be a large expansion of public expenditure in the next decade and it can reasonably forecast that governments will continue to limit the rate of growth of each service in order to keep the aggregate within tolerable limits. The development of all publicly financed services is therefore bound to depend upon the government's choice of priorities between a large number of objectives, all desirable in themselves but not simultaneously practical.
>
> (CHE, 1963: para 58)

The Robbins Committee ignored the implied warning. Its 1980–1 forecast was for 558,000 students, not 500,000, of whom 346,000 would be in universities and 212,000 in non-university higher education, the former a much higher proportion than even the Alpha model envisaged. It accepted the point about tuition fees but recommended that they be raised to 20 per cent but continue to be paid by the state. It also argued against loans, though conceded that they might have to be addressed in the future. Even more significantly it accepted the forecast of the National Economic Development Committee (NEDC), a body set up by Macmillan shortly before his resignation, whose Report, *Growth of the UK Economy to 1966* (NEDC, 1963), had forecast a growth in GNP of 4 per cent rather than the Treasury's 2.5 per cent. In answer to the rhetorical question it posed to itself – 'Is this extra proportionate call on the national income likely to cause undue strain on the resources of the future?' (CHE, 1963: para 634) – it replied: 'In the last resort, public money is spent on what people want; and if they want more higher education then, on the estimates we have made it should be possible to finance it without imposing intolerable strains on the budget or the economy' (CHE, 1963: para 636).

The Report's recommendations generated enormous popular momentum and it was here that the impact of the 1962 decision kicked in. The government, facing a General Election, could not afford to be seen denying opportunity to enter higher education and within 24 hours issued a statement accepting Robbins's student number forecasts. It did so in such a way, however, as to lay down a policy imperative which lasted until 1980–1. The paper the chief secretary addressed to the Cabinet accepted the Robbins forecast numbers up to 1973–4, a ten-year programme, stating that it represented a growth in GNP from 0.80 per cent to 1.3 per cent within an assumed GNP growth rate of 4 per cent per annum. Not only was the chief secretary resiling from the Treasury's previous evidence to Robbins on the economy, of which he was party to, but the GNP figures for 1963 and 1964 were both the product of Chancellor Maudling's 'dash for growth' and no more than a blip on the 2.5 per cent p.a. average growth rate that actually went on to occur between 1964 and 1980. The decision was taken on the basis, soon to be forgotten, that 'this additional charge can be accepted if it is regarded as having priority both within the educational field and indeed over other proposals for public expenditure' (Cabinet Office, 1963). It represented a crucial commitment that was to last in effect until the public expenditure decisions of 1980 and 1981. Robbins could be said to have lost a once and for all opportunity to recommend a sustainable approach to financing an expansion everyone wanted to see. Instead the Tory cabinet connived under the pressure of political necessity by fudging the figures.

Higher education funding 1963–77: The breakdown of the Robbins system

Despite student numbers continuing to grow, the period from 1963 to 1997 reflects the gradual breakdown of the Robbins financial settlement and the failure both of successive governments and the PES process to reform it. In the first half of the period a number of factors combined to protect higher education. Although, formally, the government's decision in 1963 only guaranteed the Robbins figures until 1973–4, Robbins's forecasts for 1980–1 were, in practice, politically sacrosanct and it was only the failure of student demand that legitimized their revision downwards. The PES process, until its reassessment after the 1973–4 oil crisis and its inflationary consequences, was based on volume planning, so Robbins's forecasts provided the essential backdrop to PES negotiations. The transfer of the UGC to the new

Department of Education and Science (DES) facilitated this by locating the universities (though not local authority based higher education, which was still funded through the Department of the Environment) under a main line spending department. In 1972 the new secretary of state, Margaret Thatcher, signed her Department up to the Programme Analysis Review (PAR) system, which further entrenched student numbers in any bidding process. Nevertheless attempts were made around the edges to reduce the rise in the higher education bill: in 1966 a differential was introduced for the first time in the level of tuition fees charged for home and international students (Crosland being offered a choice in the PES round of additional payments by international students or introducing charging for school meals); Shirley Williams's 13 points, which included a Treasury favourite, two-year degrees (repeated yet again in the 2011 White Paper), made suggestions for economies in 1969; capital grants for student residences were discontinued and institutions were encouraged to turn to loan finance; and the quinquennial funding system for universities collapsed under the strains of the oil crisis.

The most significant change, however, was the end of volume planning as a basis for PES resource allocation and its replacement in April 1976 with 'cash limits', a move intended to curb inflation. The change meant the end of what the then permanent secretary of the Treasury called 'funny money at constant prices' (Pliatzky, 1975) or, in higher education terms, an inflation-proofed student unit of resource. In 1980–1 'cash limits' were replaced by 'cash planning', which ensured all PES three-year expenditure decisions were based on firm cash targets that offered no flexibility if inflation outran estimates. 'Cash planning' represented a key element in the Thatcher Government's approach to the control of public expenditure and was 'at the heart of Britain's present difficulties', as the public expenditure White Paper of 1980–1 said. Public spending, it went on to say, had been increased 'on assumptions about economic growth which have not been achieved. The inevitable result has been a growing burden of taxes and borrowing' (HM Treasury, 1980). The arrival of the Thatcher Government coincided with the last year of the protection provided by the Robbins student number forecast. For the Thatcher Government the first priority was the reduction of public expenditure: higher education was simply part of a bigger picture. The first casualty of the 1980 cuts was the subsidy implied by the less-than-full-cost tuition fees charged to international students. This produced a saving of £100 million, thus realizing in full the issue raised in the Treasury evidence to Robbins. The next was a sweeping cut of 8.5 per cent across public expenditure, from which higher education was not exempted. One important structural consequence was the creation of the National Advisory Body for Public Sector Higher Education (NAB), ostensibly to manage the capping of the Advanced Further Education 'pool' from which local authority higher education was funded, but which in practice was a first step towards bringing it under direct DES control.

The new situation with the two sectors, brought together under one department, offered the prospect of greater central planning and, with the continued expansion of demand, greater influence from the Treasury through PES. In practice there was little increase in central planning but a considerable increase in the impact of PES on the struggle to control the costs of expansion. Four broad approaches can be discerned. The first was to meet demand by permitting, and even encouraging, expansion in the local authority (public) sector – where unit costs were some 25 per cent lower – and restraining growth in the universities. In 1980–1 the breakdown of full-time student numbers between the two sectors was as follows: university 269,000 and public sector 146,000. By 1986 the numbers were broadly equal and as demand expanded very rapidly in the late 1980s, the figures quoted for full-time equivalents in the 1991 White Paper (DES, 1991) recorded 317,000 in the universities and 510,000 in the public sector. However, 1992 saw a further extension of the policy as the two sectors merged and the student unit costs across them were rationalized, which capitalized on the reduction of costs from the expansion of the polytechnics and concentrated research spending through the RAE mechanism. The success of this approach, from the Treasury's point of view, was the Dearing Committee's calculation that demand had been met but only by a 45 per cent reduction in unit costs between 1976 and 1995 (NCIHE, 1997).

A second approach was to call for more efficiency in the management of higher education institutions. The universities were persuaded to join the Rayner-driven Financial Management Initiative for the public services, which led to the *Jarratt Committee Report* (CVCP, 1985). The detailed studies by the Jarratt efficiency team threw up only marginal savings. A parallel study for the public sector was derailed by the decision to abandon the NAB compromise and transfer local authority control to the DES. Sir Keith Joseph called for universities to generate more non-state income, increase efficiency in financial management, rationalize small departments, and introduce staff appraisal, a process concluded by the chairman of the CVCP and the UGC signing up to an action plan. The implementation of such measures set the tone for the 1980s but, in themselves, made only marginal contributions to reducing costs – and much less than the imposed 'efficiency gains' required by successive PES spending reviews.

A third approach was to uncouple the linkage between student numbers and a fixed unit of resource. Right up to the 1980–1 cuts the Treasury seems to have broadly accepted that any growth in university student numbers had to be accompanied by resources at a standard rate. The across-the-board reduction in public expenditure imposed by the Thatcher Government in 1980 and 1981 took no cognizance of a desirable student unit of resource and it was the UGC that cut student numbers in an attempt to preserve it. Within Whitehall it was obvious that the idea of a fixed unit of resource had to be abandoned if student demand was to be met (Shattock, 2012). As Kenneth (now Lord) Baker claims in his autobiography (Baker, 1993), however, it was his decision to give priority to the need to match student demand over the need to retain a given unit of resource. This may be a *post hoc* rationalization, as John Major, writing of his time as Chief Secretary of the Treasury, when he was in charge of the PES process, provides an unflattering account of Baker's performance in PES negotiation over the costs of increased numbers (Major, 1999). There is no doubt that Baker was personally committed to an expansion of numbers and in a speech at Lancaster he argued that the then age participation rate of 18.5 per cent needed to be raised in the next 25 years to 33 per cent. Baker's solution to the public expenditure dilemma was to encourage a form of marketization where institutions were encouraged to expand at marginal costs. While enthusiastically implemented by the new Polytechnics and Colleges Funding Council (PCFC), the suggestion was resisted by the universities, who formed a cartel to negate the introduction of competitive pricing for increased numbers. Baker's difficulty, as he spelt it out to the CVCP, was how this growth was to be achieved within a planned limit in public spending of 40 per cent of GDP and when spending demands from other parts of the public sector had such high priority; spending on the NHS, for example, would need to increase by 1 per cent p.a. simply for demographic reasons. He said he could not imagine that the growth in higher education would justify a tax increase (Baker, 1986).

Baker's difficulty was exacerbated by the failure of the one radical attempt, launched by his predecessor, Sir Keith Joseph, to introduce a new approach to funding higher education. Joseph was already facing the 'pot of gold' argument from the Treasury – namely that the higher education budget, institutional costs, and student support for maintenance and tuition fees needed to be addressed together as a total budget item – and had responded by restricting the rise in student support costs to annual increases lower than inflation. In 1984, wishing to invest another £20 million into the science budget, he obtained approval from the Treasury for a scheme that would abolish the minimum level of maintenance grant and make tuition fees means tested, making it possible that wealthier parents might have to pay £520 p.a., the fee level at that time for undergraduate programmes. The Tory backbenches exploded: half the parliamentary party signed an early day motion opposing the proposals and at a meeting of the 1922 Committee a proposal that the whole idea should be withdrawn was greeted with cheers and desk banging (Denham and Garnett, 2001). Their constituents, they believed, would not wear it. The incident was to foreclose any prospect of significant change in funding mechanisms while the Tories remained in power. In 1991 at a dinner in Downing Street, John Major made it clear to the CVCP that the government would actively oppose any campaign in support of 'top up' fees. The issue was not especially a Party one: when Jeff (now Lord) Rooker, the Labour higher education minister, publicly proposed a graduate tax, he was promptly sacked by the Leader of the Labour Party, John Smith. The only alternative source of saving was the student maintenance grant which, deprived of inflation proofing, was gradually reduced and would soon be replaced by a loan scheme. The decline in the unit of resource only increased and in December 1995 the CVCP, now representing both the pre- and the post-1992 universities, formally endorsed a proposal for universities to levy 'top up' fees of £300 p.a. on the 1997 student entry. In March 1996, with the support of the Labour Party, the secretary of state announced the establishment of the Dearing Committee to defuse the issue before the General Election.

The accelerating march to 2010

The Dearing Committee's prime task was to produce a solution to the problem of paying for a higher education system that was expanding faster than the growth of GDP and against a background of huge pressure for increased resources from other parts of the economy's public sector. Its Report can be said to have broken the logjam on the introduction of private contributions to the costs of the system but with hindsight it offered only a palliative. It recommended tuition fees be introduced, calculated at about 25 per cent of the average costs of a non-medical first degree (about £1,000), which would be paid directly by the student on an income contingent basis backed up by a loan scheme and the reintroduction of maintenance grants. An essential element was that the tuition fee payment was to constitute new and additional income to current government funding levels. However, the incoming Labour Government had already committed, with the next Comprehensive Spending Review due in 1998, to adhere to its predecessors' spending plans for its first two years of office – which included a further efficiency gain cut in higher education. The effect, therefore, of accepting the Dearing recommendation with effect from 2000 was simply to absorb the efficiency gain in the increased income. Blunkett, the new secretary of state, argued that he had secured a favourable settlement by achieving increased funding for an additional 97,000 student places for 1999–2000 and 2000–01. However, this did nothing to alleviate the fall over the previous decade of 35 per cent in the unit of resource (Taggart, 2004). Although the next spending review produced some increase in the unit of resource, most of the additional money was earmarked for Blunkett's own priorities – research, widening access, the disastrous E University, and foundation degrees – and the grant letter committed the system to a 50 per cent age participation rate (DfES, 2000).

A change was to come, however, from outside the Department but from the prime minister's office. Lobbied by Lord Jenkins as Chancellor of Oxford, and advised by Andrew (now Lord) Adonis, Blair was already sympathetic to higher education's position – but from a different point of view. While Dearing was concerned over the funding of the system, Blair's concerns related to the funding and international ranking of individual universities. The turning point was a meeting with key members of the Russell Group in late 2001. In Blair's own words, prompted by the meeting:

> I looked at the top fifty universities in the world [presumably as described
> in the Shanghai Jaio league table] and saw only a handful in the UK, and
> barely any in mainland Europe. America was winning this particular race
> with China and India coming up fast behind. The point about the US was
> telling. Their domination in the top fifty – and top one hundred for that
> matter – was not by chance or dint of size; it was plainly and inescapably
> due to their system of fees. They were more entrepreneurial; they went
> after their alumni and built up endowments; their bursary system allowed
> them to attract poorer students; and their financial flexibility meant they
> could attract the best academics. Simple as that.
>
> (Blair, 2010)

Two years were to elapse between the meeting with the Russell Group and the publication of the 2003 White Paper *The Future of Higher Education* (DfES, 2003), occupied by dispute between the prime minister and his Chancellor of the Exchequer over the way forward. It was a further three years before the White Paper's recommendation of a variable tuition fee of up to £3,000, underpinned by income-contingent loans, could be implemented, and even then it was only with the backing of the narrowest majority in the House of Commons. In the end the fees could hardly be described as variable – only two universities decided not to charge the full £3,000 – but the die had been cast, much more significantly than by Dearing, that the solution to the problem of paying for further expansion would be through an injection of private funding.

In 2006 higher education's funding looked surprisingly like the income balance of the 1930s, with one-third derived from fees, one-third from the state recurrent grant, and one-third from other sources including research grants and contracts. However, built into the legislation was a commitment to review the impact of the new funding structure by an independent commission in three years' time. The commitment was intended to reassure MPs that the new structure did not act as a disincentive to widening participation, as indeed the application figures for 2006 and 2007 proved, and as the legislation's terms of reference made clear its primary task was to review the fees policy with the unspoken expectation that its recommendations would feed into the 2010 Comprehensive Spending Review.

The denationalization of higher education in England

One might have expected the Review to have contented itself with endorsing the charging principles agreed by Parliament in 2004, and perhaps to have raised the tuition fee cap to, say, £5,000 or even £7,000 p.a. to attempt to recapture the concept of variability, and perhaps also to have extended the loan scheme to part-time courses, for which there was much public pressure. In fact, the Browne Review went much further than this: it proposed that the fee cap be removed altogether – leaving universities to charge what they liked according to the cost of the degree subject – with a levy, to be paid back to the government, imposed on fees of £6,000 and above, rising to approximately 25 per cent when the tuition fee level reached £12,000. The Review went on to propose removing the cap on student numbers, first introduced on demand by the Treasury in 1994 as a way of controlling an open-ended budget, to allow student choice and institutional selection policies to determine the size of the system and institutions, subject only to the creation of an entry tariff based on A-level scores (IRHEFSF, 2010).

Such proposals might have looked plausible to New Labour market enthusiasts in 2004 – when the economy was expanding – but in 2010, when the economic downturn was in full swing and Lehmans Bank had collapsed, they offered far too many hostages to fortune for the Treasury to stomach. Certainly they offered a long-term theoretical solution to financing expansion by appearing to remove higher education's dependence on public expenditure, but the upfront costs to the state in transferring to the new funding model and the uncertainties implicit in the implementation – in particular, the practical difficulties of designing an effective tariff – presented too many risks to a Comprehensive Spending Review charged with making fundamental and long-term reductions to public expenditure.

The decisions that emerged from the 2010 CSR and the subsequent White Paper of 2011 – particularly those relating to 'the core and margin' – bear the clear imprint of the Browne Review's thinking: the teaching function of higher education had essentially been privatized. While the Treasury still had to bear the costs of the loan arrangements, the PES round was relieved of a substantial element of future public expenditure costs. If the government's primary strategy was to eliminate a line of public expenditure fraught with political problems, it had succeeded. In a very real sense the decisions reached by the 2010 CSR represented the culmination of thinking that can be said to have begun in discussions inside the Treasury as it was preparing its evidence to Robbins some half a century earlier. Denationalization may be an overstatement because research continues to be state funded but there can be no doubt that 2010 marked a significant shift of higher education into the private sector.

For as long as it has had to compete for resources to teach expanding numbers of students against public expenditure priorities within a predetermined public sector ceiling, higher education was bound to be vulnerable. But it could also be said that the changes were only introduced after the horse had bolted; the time to have introduced student paid fees and loans would have been before expansion took off. If Robbins had grasped the nettle of thinking through the public expenditure implications of expansion, it might have mitigated the shock generated by the last decade's drastic changes. It is rumoured that the Treasury later viewed the expansion beyond an age participation rate of 30 per cent as demanding the introduction of cost sharing, but any move at that point was frustrated by Tory backbenchers' reactions to Joseph's 1985 proposals. What is not clear is whether the 2010 policy will be sustainable over a decade of continued austerity: imposing such heavy debts on the graduate output may have unanticipated effects on a range of economic and social policies. What is clear, however, is that it is hard, under any fiscal scenario, to envisage a return to Robbins's publicly funded system. For the present we can compare the futures of Scotland and England, the former with no fees, the latter effectively with full-cost fees, to see how the modern state manages the funding of the transfer from elite to near universal higher education. We cannot assume that either approach will be stable over the next decade.

References

Baker, K. (1986) Speech at CVCP residential conference, 23 September. CVCP files. London: Universities UK.

—(1993) *The Turbulent Years: My life in politics.* London: Faber and Faber.

Berdahl, R.O. (1962) *University–State Relations Re-examined.* (Sociological Review Monographs, no. 7) Keele: Sociological Review Monographs.

BIS (Department for Business, Innovation and Skills) (2011) *Higher Education: Students at the heart of the system.* London: Stationery Office.

Blair, T. (2010) *A Journey.* London: Hutchinson.

Cabinet Office (1963) Paper C (63) 173. (I am grateful to Gareth Williams for showing me this paper.)

Carswell, J. (1985) *Government and the Universities.* Cambridge: Cambridge University Press.

CHE (Committee on Higher Education) (1963) *Higher Education: A report by the committee appointed by the Prime Minister under the chairmanship of Lord Robbins, 1961–63 (The Robbins Report).* London: HMSO.

Crawford, R., Emmerson, C., and Tetlow, G. (2009) *A Survey of Public Spending in the UK.* IFS briefing note, BN43. London: Institute for Fiscal Studies.

CVCP (Committee of Vice-Chancellors and Principals) (1956) Report of a meeting with the financial secretary to the Treasury, 22 November. CVCP Archive, vol. 12, *MSS* 399. Modern Records Centre, University of Warwick. (Accessed 1 January 2012).

—(1957) Minute of a meeting on 25 October with the chairman of the UGC. CVCP Archive, *MSS* 399. Modern Records Centre, University of Warwick.

—(1985) *Report of the Steering Committee for Efficiency Studies in Universities (The Jarratt Report).* London: CVCP.

DfES (Department for Education and Skills) (2000) Grant letter from the secretary of state to the chairman of the HEFCE. London: HMSO.

—(2003) *The Future of Higher Education.* London: HMSO.

Denham, A. and Garnett, M. (2001) *Keith Joseph.* Chesham: Acumen.

DES (Department for Education and Science) (1991) *Higher Education: A new framework.* London: HMSO.

Gardner, J. (2011) *The Blitz.* London: Harper Collins.

Gosden, P.H.J. (1983) *The Education System Since 1944.* Oxford: Martin Robertson.

Hennessy, P. (2006) *Having It So Good: Britain in the Fifties.* London: Allen Lane.

HM Treasury (Her Majesty's Treasury) (1961) *Control of Public Expenditure (The Plowden Report).* London: HMSO.

—(1961–2) NA T 227/1768.

—(1980) *The Government's Expenditure Plans 1980–81*. London: HMSO.

IRHEFSF (Independent Review of Higher Education Funding and Student Finance) (2010) *Securing a Sustainable Future for Higher Education*. Online. www.independent.gov.uk (Accessed 20 October 2010).

Major, J. (1999) *The Autobiography*. London: Harper Collins.

NCIHE (National Committee of Inquiry into Higher Education) (1997) *Higher Education in the Learning Society (The Dearing Report)*. London: HMSO.

NEDC (National Economic Development Committee) (1963) *Growth of the United Kingdom Economy Up To 1966*. London: HMSO.

Pliatzky, L. (1975) *Getting and Spending*. Quoted in Hennessy, P. (1990) *Whitehall*. London: Fontana Press.

Select Committee on Estimates (1951–2) *Fifth Report*. Quoted in Shinn, C.H. (1986) *Paying the Piper*. Lewes: Falmer Press.

Shattock, M.L. (2012) *Making Policy in British Higher Education 1945–2011*. Maidenhead: Open University Press.

Taggart, G.J. (2004) 'A Critical Review of the Role of the English Funding Body for Higher Education in the Relationship between the State and Higher Education in the Period 1945–2003'. ED thesis, Bristol University.

UGC (University Grants Commission) (1962) NA UGC 1/8 Minutes 17 January.

Chapter 3

The Coalition Government's reform of higher education: Policy formation and political process

Peter Scott

Introduction

When Lord Browne, chair of the Independent Committee on Student Fees and Funding, introduced its report in October 2010, he announced confidently that it set out a blueprint for 'a new paradigm in [English] higher education'. The Conservative–Liberal Democrat Coalition Government, elected six months earlier, published an immediate response, the core of which was to reject the Committee's central recommendation that there should be no upper cap on tuition fees. But it took the Department of Business, Innovation and Skills a further nine months to publish a White Paper in July 2011 revealing the policies the government planned to adopt to implement the Committee's other recommendations and produce a workable system for a new funding regime. The contrast between the urgency, extravagance even, of the *Browne Report*'s launch and the government's initially knee-jerk and then faltering responses was striking.

One reason for the contrast was the political flux that succeeded the General Election's indecisive result in May 2010. The election's outcome brought to an end 13 years of New Labour rule and led to the formation of the first peacetime Coalition Government since the fall, almost 90 years earlier, of David Lloyd George's administration in 1923. Two parties, the Conservatives and the Liberal Democrats, with incompatible policies on higher education, came together to form the new government. The Conservatives had been largely silent on higher education in the run-up to the election, although they had voted against the previous Labour Government's decision to increase fees to £3,000 in 2005 in what was widely regarded as an opportunist, even cynical, manoeuvre. The Liberal Democrats, by contrast, had made a high-profile pledge in their manifesto not only to vote against any further tuition fee increases but, if it lay in their power, to abolish fees entirely. Since the *Browne Report* recommended that there should be no upper limit on fees, some degree of ambivalence at Westminster and turbulence in Whitehall was an inevitable consequence of such political confusion.

However, perhaps a second – and more significant – reason accounts for the hiatus between the *Browne Report* and the White Paper's respective publications, one that was a consequence of a 'new model' of policy formation. The 'new model' had its origins in the 1980s during Margaret Thatcher's time as prime minister and was reinforced when New Labour came to power in 1997. To some degree it is an analogue of the more celebrated 'New Public Management'. The 'new model' had – and continues to have – a number of characteristics. The first is a heightened degree of ideological dogmatism that reflects the decay of the so-called post-war settlement (and the political consensus that had sustained it), although some argue that a broadly social democratic settlement/consensus has simply been replaced by a neo-liberal one. The second is a distrust of traditional forms of professional expertise grounded in fear of so-called 'producer capture'. The third is the greater pressures of a 24/7 politics in which (short-term, if not instantaneous) presentation counts for far more than (medium and long-term) implementation (Maarten, 2009).

However, the 'new model' also has a fourth characteristic: a focus on policy delivery at the expense, perhaps, of policy formation. The ideological 'line' having been pre-set, consideration of different policy options appears to be less urgent. To the extent that such options still need to be developed the primary role appears to have shifted to 'on message' think tanks broadly, if unofficially, aligned with political parties. Also the predetermined orchestration of the views of 'stakeholders' is now managed through contrived 'consultations' in which genuine expressions of opinion are sometimes shouted down by the aggressive lobbying of organized stakeholder groups. But increasingly policymaking appears to be dominated by issues of delivery – even if the delivery of the government's reforms of higher education since the publication of the *Browne Report* has been anything but smooth. Greater use is now made of management consultants, more attuned perhaps to the private sector's commercial culture, for policy development but, to an even greater extent, for policy delivery. In addition, policy delivery now tends to be defined in terms of (relatively) short-range timelines and immediate objectives rather than of longer-term structural change, which may help to partly explain the government's difficulties over implementing the *Browne Report* and its own White Paper.

This chapter is divided into three main sections:

- A review of the policy processes underlying earlier episodes of major reforms of higher education – notably the *Robbins Report* of 1963 and the *Dearing Report* of 1997 – and a (continuation of the) discussion of these overarching changes in policy formation at Westminster and in Whitehall.
- An account of how policies were developed from 1997 onward (though already apparent from the second half of the 1980s as Margaret Thatcher's government

gained ideological traction) as part of a drive to 'modernize' higher education, of which the current reforms are the culmination.

- An analysis of, and critical commentary on, continuing processes of policy formation designed to implement the new funding and regulatory regime that has emerged as a result of these reforms.

'The past is another country'

The 'new model' of policymaking that has developed since the mid-1980s has little in common with the twentieth century's more rationalist models (Lindblom and Woodhouse, 1992), even in modified forms (Parsons, 2002; Birkland, 2011). It has had a significant impact on higher education which has been felt in a number of ways: firstly, in the increasing pace of policymaking and the frequency of policy interventions; secondly, in the decline of 'grand narrative' inquiries and the substitution of short-term (and presentation-driven) political agendas; thirdly, in the subordination of higher education policy to wider policies concerning innovation, industry, and employment; and finally, in increasingly more detailed intrusions justified in terms of better management and improved accountability. I discuss each of these four dimensions in turn.

At a conservative estimate there have been 11 major policy interventions in higher education since 1960 – major reports, White Papers, and significant pieces of legislation. These were, in chronological order:

- The *Robbins Report* of 1963 that so magisterially endorsed student expansion (CHE, 1963)
- The 1966 White Paper that established the polytechnics and formally articulated the binary system (DES, 1966)
- The 1972 White Paper *A Framework for Expansion* – although overridden to some degree by changes in public expenditure that heralded the collapse of universities' guaranteed quinquennial funding (DES, 1972a)
- The 1987 White Paper and subsequent Education Reform Act that led to the incorporation of the polytechnics (i.e. their removal from the control of local education authorities) and the abolition of the University Grants Committee (DES, 1987)
- The 1988 White Paper *Top-Up Loans for Students* and subsequent Education (Student Loans) Act, which ended the grants system established by the *Anderson Report* the year before Robbins (DES, 1988)
- The 1991 White Paper that led to the abandonment of the binary system, the 'promotion' of the polytechnics to university status, and the creation of a single higher education funding council in England (DES, 1991)

- The 1998 *Dearing Report* that aspired to be a second *Robbins Report* and in the process perhaps lost focus (NCIHE, 1997)
- The 1998 Teaching and Higher Education Act which, incidentally, laid the foundations of the current system of student support and established the Student Loans Company
- The 2003 White Paper *The Future of Higher Education* that opened the door to higher fees and the subsequent 2004 Higher Education Act (DfE, 2003)
- The 2010 *Browne Report* that recommended there should be no cap on the fees institutions should be allowed to charge (IRHEFSF, 2010)
- The 2011 White Paper *Higher Education: Students at the heart of the system* that is the subject of this chapter (and book) (BIS, 2011).

In addition there have been a larger number of other important policy interventions: Green Papers; 'letters of guidance' to funding agencies; Select Committee reports; enquiry reports – whether commissioned by government, such as the 1972 *James Report* on teacher education (DES, 1972b), or by other agencies, such as the 1985 *Jarratt Report* on university efficiency commissioned by the then Committee of Vice-Chancellors and Principals (CVCP, 1985); and planning papers on student numbers. A significant number of reports have also been produced on Scottish and Welsh higher education, both preceding the establishment of devolved administrations and subsequently published by these administrations. Finally, intermediate agencies – beginning with the UGC and the National Advisory Body (for public sector higher education), continuing with the Universities Funding Council and Polytechnics and Colleges Funding Council, and most recently including the Higher Education Funding Council for England (HEFCE) (as well as the Scottish Funding Council and Higher Education Funding Council for Wales) – have made regular policy interventions, in the form of circular letters, consultation documents, and annual reports.

An observer might well conclude that higher education has been drowning in policy. Indeed, the velocity of policymaking has certainly been increasing: nearly half of the major policy interventions – five out of 11 – have been in the past decade. But the major increase has been in other policy interventions, many of which have been necessary to implement the proposals made in the major policy interventions, notably White Papers. A second group has reflected the increasing number of single-ticket initiatives – whether widening participation, enterprise and links between higher education and industry or sustainability and the 'green' agenda. A third group has spoken of the development of more elaborate regulatory cultures reflecting a wider phenomenon: the rise of the 'audit society' (Power, 1999) and the drive to create a 'market' in higher education (notably in terms of more detailed disclosure of information to students and other stakeholders). The final group, of course, have arisen from the system's operational requirements such as the provision of student data, research assessment returns, financial forecasts, and the like. The result has been an accretion of policy interventions that have required universities in turn to invest in sophisticated management systems, establish planning units, and create more elaborate lobbying and influencing capacities.

The second effect of policymaking's 'new model' has been a sharp reduction in 'grand narrative' inquiries. The age of Royal Commissions – and the 'Blue Books' of the nineteenth century, which were themselves formidable contributions to social science – is finally and firmly over. The only, partial, exceptions are judge-led inquiries on topics of the highest political sensitivity: Saville on 'Bloody Sunday' (Saville, 2010), Hutton on the 'sexed-up' intelligence dossier justifying the Iraq invasion (Hutton, 2004), or Leveson on phone hacking (Leveson, 2012). However, it may be significant that action groups have copied some of the operating methods once employed by 'grand narrative' inquiries, the most recent of which has been the re-examination of the evidence concerning the Hillsborough disaster (HIP, 2012). While government may have abandoned such inquiries – deeming them too ponderous, not sufficiently political, or, perhaps, too revealing even – civil society organizations appear anxious to adopt them.

It is important to resist nostalgia, however. The Robbins Committee, although it behaved like a Royal Commission, had in fact been established by the prime minister of the day, Harold Macmillan. The *Dearing Report* had been commissioned by the then Secretary of State for Education. The *Browne Report* was established by Peter Mandelson, who possessed the grand title of first secretary (and headed the recently created Department of Business, Innovation and Skills). So the differences between Robbins and Dearing on the one hand and Browne on the other did not arise from their formal status. They arose instead from the latter's modes of operation and publication, which partly reflected choices made by Lord Browne and his colleagues and were partly the result of policymaking's 'new model'.

The Browne Committee engaged with stakeholders and other interested parties in two ways: firstly, as Robbins and Dearing had done, by soliciting views and evidence on student fees and funding and secondly, by organizing hearings, or public sessions, at which a selection of these views were presented and during which the Committee could interrogate those who were speaking. These sessions were also 'broadcast', in the sense that they were put on the web. Two influences appear to have helped shape Browne's mode of operation. First, the parallel with the inquisitorial hearings characteristic of judge-led inquiries appears to have been deliberate. Second, the establishment of the Browne Committee had, in one sense, been the next stage in the 'debate' about the future of higher education previously initiated by John Denham (see the next section of this chapter). It therefore naturally maintained a similar degree of participation.

But the Browne Committee, unlike its two predecessors, did not commission a significant body of new research. The contrast is stark – and with the Robbins Committee in particular. Under the leadership of its research director, Claus Moser, it commissioned a volume of research that bears comparison with the evidence collected for the 'Blue Books' of the nineteenth century. The National Commission, chaired by Ron Dearing 35 years later, also generated a significant but more modest amount of research. Less of the research commissioned by Dearing was empirical (or quantitative) and more was synoptic (or qualitative) – surveys of opinion for example, were heavily relied upon. Browne's, by contrast, was a research-lite report. It did not commission, or otherwise generate, any significant body of new research. Much of the 'evidence' it did collect came from interested stakeholders rather than disinterested researchers.

One reason for such an absence was the inquiry's much shorter time scale. The Committee had been established only months before the General Election's due date. Its report could not be delayed for several months after the formation of the new government if it was to have much impact, and its recommendations were closely related to impending, urgent, and necessary decisions about public expenditure. Another, more general, explanation was the reduced role of commissioned research in policymaking's 'new model' and the fact that evidence-based policy (despite the headline rhetoric) had been abandoned – which inevitably led, therefore, to a reduction in capacity to undertake public policy research.

Timescales are also more significant generally. It has been argued that we now live in the 'extended present', in which the past has been forgotten and the future tamed by sophisticated forecasting and risk management systems. As I've already said, the nature of policymaking has been transformed by the mass media's more intense and immediate (even instantaneous) intrusion into politics. Policies have shrinking shelf lives, measured in days and weeks rather than months or years. Most recently print and (conventional) electronic media have come under pressure from so-called 'social networking' sites that enable instantaneous and real-time comments to be posted and interventions made. Time has become ever more scarce. The impact on research practice has also been pronounced. As timescales have been foreshortened, research has been squeezed into even tighter time frames.

Whatever the causes, the result is that the *Browne Report* stands or falls on its recommendations. In contrast, the *Robbins* and *Dearing Report*s have a significance that does not depend so much on how acceptable are their recommendations. In fact, as I discuss in the next section, although Robbins's overall endorsement of student expansion had a powerful influence on higher education's future, its detailed policy prescriptions were largely rejected. Instead the polytechnics were established and an explicitly binary division created. While Dearing's recommendations were not dismissed so categorically, its proposals for the (re)introduction of fees were substantially changed. Yet both remain landmark reports, their authority resting on the dispassionate research evidence and detailed statistical analyses they either commissioned or mobilized. Higher education scholars researching the state of UK higher education in the early 1960s or at the end of the twentieth century will always be in debt to Robbins and Dearing. Their successors are less likely to feel the same debt towards Browne.

The third and fourth effects of policymaking's 'new model' are the subordination of higher education policy (and other policies) to overall strategies for innovation and economic development and the strengthening and elaboration of accountability regimes. The former can be attributed to the emergence of the 'knowledge society', in its neo-liberal interpretation at any rate. The provision of 'knowledge' goods and services – in the shape of research products and a highly skilled workforce – is now regarded as crucial to wealth generation, and wealth generation is also regarded as closely related to economic liberalization, whether through the creation of a more flexible workforce or the removal of trade barriers. The latter can be attributed to two factors: first, the advance of the 'audit society' – in which rituals of verification and the management of risk have assumed more important roles – and second, the shift of emphasis from policy development to policy delivery.

Both factors have had an ambiguous impact on higher education's development. However, both can be observed in the policies recommended in the *Browne Report*. Here, the instrumentalist justification of higher education is sharply etched – as it always has been. However, this justification is now more often expressed indirectly – in terms of individual investment by graduates in terms of their employment prospects and earning potential (which thus provides the basis for the affordability, and appropriateness, of higher fees and large loans) – rather than directly in terms of state investment in research and development (which was more characteristic of the New Labour era). The accountability to stakeholders, and importance of delivery, are reflected in the new information regime proposed by Browne, designed to power informed student choice (and which builds on earlier consumer-oriented initiatives such as the National Student Survey).

In summary, the 'new model' of policymaking is characterized by a preference for more focused policy interventions that are 'on (ideological) message', brisker in their process, and briefer in their presentation – a stark contrast to the more capacious, more ideologically detached 'grand narrative' inquiries of the past. Browne fits this new model, unlike the *Dearing* and *Robbins Reports*. In turn, this 'new model' of policymaking reflects a number of trends such as the shift from the welfare to the market state, the development of a knowledge-based global economy, the rise of audit society, and even the foreshortening of time itself.

Modernizing higher education

The government's reforms of higher education in England can be described in terms of two narratives: a macro narrative of the wider modernization of mass higher education systems and a micro narrative describing the English system's particular evolution.

The first, therefore, is a broad based account of the modernization of higher education, embracing elements such as the growth of mass systems (Scott, 1995), the development of new modes of research (Gibbons *et al.*, 1994), the evolution of more entrepreneurial models of the university (Clark, 2004), and the increasing impact of internationalization (and globalization) (King *et al.*, 2011). This process of modernization is perhaps part of an even larger narrative: the erosion of the post-war welfare state, with its strong sense of social purpose, and the corresponding rise of the market state with a more pronounced 'market' orientation, the emergence of new forms of society – variously labelled 'risk', 'audit', or 'information' – and the growth of new forms of individualized identities moulded by consumer culture and expressed through so-called 'social media'.

The second narrative is more particular. It focuses on the evolution of higher education policy in the United Kingdom – and, more specifically, England – from the (partial) implementation of the *Dearing Report* in the early years of New Labour, through the 2003 White Paper and substantial increase of tuition fees in 2006, to the publication of the *Browne Report* and the 2011 White Paper. However, this second narrative has a long backstory. The establishment of the polytechnics by Anthony Crosland, a Labour Secretary of State for Education, in the mid-1960s was perhaps the first occasion when politicians seriously dissented from the academic-led direction of higher education development, even if the primary motive was to promote a local authority-led sector. This level of dissatisfaction sharply increased during the Thatcher period when university budgets were savagely cut in 1981 and the UGC itself, that much celebrated 'buffer' between universities and the state, was abolished five years later.

The first narrative is sometimes overlooked because of policymakers' reluctance to take the long view – which, to be fair, is difficult to do in a world where politics is given a 24/7 media coverage, if through the lens of an ideologically inspired determinism. In other words the massification of higher education has inexorably fuelled demands for modernization that have, inevitably, demanded some degree of marketization. But the first narrative cannot be reduced to an endorsement of a 'single path' of higher education development. The rapid expansion of higher education systems since 1960 has certainly raised issues of funding in more acute and urgent forms. But it has also stimulated greater intervention by the state for two broad reasons. First is the growing need to coordinate these expanding higher education systems (and, in particular, determine more formally issues of differentiation and stratification – or their opposites). Second is the need to align higher education's 'outputs' with perceived national needs, whether skilled graduates and impactful research in the economic domain or access and equity in the wider social domain. It is the latter, increasing state intervention, rather than the former, funding dilemmas, that has dominated this first narrative, not only in the UK but in many other developed (and developing) countries also.

Both higher education and the state have been transformed. In the former's case elite systems with participation rates of less than 15 per cent of the eligible population have been transformed into mass systems enrolling 40 per cent or more of school leavers. Previously unrelated components of post-secondary education – traditional universities, higher professional and vocational education institutions, and specialist teacher or nurse training schools – have been aggregated into coordinated higher education systems, whether binary or unified in structure. The research mission of higher education has also intensified, both in terms of the drive for research excellence – so-called 'world-class' research – and of wider notions of knowledge generation and dissemination – the growing emphasis on so-called 'Mode 2' knowledge. Both are now seen as key inputs into competitiveness in the global knowledge economy.

Equally transformative transitions can be observed if we consider the state. The post-war 'welfare state', animated by collectivist values and ambitious to provide a wide range of services to its citizens, has been gradually – though not entirely – superseded by a 'market state' characterized by more individualistic values and a commitment to 'shrink' the state through the direct provision and funding of services and via its new and intrusive roles as regulator, auditor, and champion of the claims made by its citizen–customers. At the same time the nation state's influence has been compromised by the advance of globalization – in the form of a tightly integrated world economy in which financial markets and credit agencies play a more powerful role, of regional blocs such as the European Union, and of truly transcendent issues such as global warning and enduring conflicts.

This chapter is not the place to further explore this first narrative. But it is important at least to register this deep background: the transformations of higher education and the state and, in particular, the synergies and dissonances between them. For example, the affordability of mass higher education would have been a less urgent issue had the 'welfare state' persisted: its urgency is derived to a large extent from the unwillingness, or impossibility, of maintaining high levels of personal taxation. Also, within a framework of civil society, higher education's openness and autonomy would have been easier to sustain if the 'market state' had not taken on its more intrusive roles as regulator and auditor. Equally, if mass higher education had not evolved, its overall cost would have been lower – and perhaps below the political 'radar' – and its trust relationships might have been more easily maintained (reducing the regulatory and audit pressures). The second, and more familiar, narrative – the more particular process of modernization undergone by UK (and English) higher education – therefore needs to be considered in this broader, general context.

The backstory – the efforts to modernize higher education between the 1960s and early 1990s – has already been briefly sketched; a fuller account is contained in Shattock's study of the making of higher education policy between 1945 and 2011 (Shattock, 2012). The natural starting point for a more detailed account of the process of modernization that culminated in the *Browne Report* and the 2011 White Paper is the *Dearing Report* of 1997. Like the Independent Committee on Student Fees and Funding (Browne), the National Commission on the Future of Higher Education (Dearing) was established by one government and reported to another. In Dearing's case, Conservative and Labour governments; in Browne's, a Labour administration and a Conservative–Liberal Democrat coalition. Both, therefore, were planned as bi-partisan initiatives. While Browne's provoked greater political 'fuss' than Dearing's, despite the – abject? – acquiescence of university leaders, this may have disguised the existence of a comparatively robust political consensus. Certainly the continuities of national policy through the Major, Blair, Brown, and now Cameron Governments are at least as striking as the ruptures.

Indeed the main difference between how the *Dearing* and *Browne Report*s were received was the contrast in the higher education community's response to them. The former they deemed broadly acceptable, while the latter was met with widespread antagonism. One possible explanation why the *Dearing Report* met with greater acceptability was the National Commission's mode of operation – engaging stakeholders, consulting widely and commissioning extensive background research – which helped to bind in the political and academic communities. The *Browne Report*, by contrast, offered a more superficial – and perhaps token – engagement.

Four phases of policy can be identified following the publication of the *Dearing Report*:

- The first phase began with the new (New) Labour Government's decisions about which of the National Commission's recommendations to implement, and extended to the development of a strong widening participation and lifelong learning agenda under Labour's first Secretary of State for Education, David Blunkett. Dearing's proposal to introduce fees was accepted – but in a modified form that perhaps owed as much to Whitehall pressures, in particular from the Treasury, as to left-wing political anxieties. Many other of Dearing's recommendations were also accepted, notably the establishment of the Higher Education Academy to give a stronger focus to learning and teaching in higher education. But closer to Blunkett's heart were widening participation and lifelong learning. The former was incorporated within the HEFCE's funding methodology in the form of earmarked allocations. The latter was the subject of a neglected report by Bob Fryer, former principal of the Northern College and a fellow member of the South Yorkshire Labour establishment (Fryer, 1997)

- The second phase coincided with the tenure of Blunkett's successor, Charles Clarke. It began with a White Paper and culminated in the decision to substantially increase fees. The decision was one of the most hotly contested taken by the Blair Government; the increase was approved by the House of Commons in a wafer-thin majority (more Labour MPs voted against the introduction of higher fees than the invasion of Iraq). To win the vote Clarke promised to establish a review of the effects of higher fees within three years, the genesis of the later Browne Committee. The increase to a ceiling of £3,000 (initially) was justified by the need to secure additional resources for higher education that could not have been achieved as easily by increasing direct grants to institutions through the HEFCE. By and large the promise of 'additionality' was kept. An equally significant decision was to replace the existing Research Assessment Exercise (RAE) with a Research Excellence Framework (REF) that would attempt to measure 'impact' as well as assess 'quality'

- The third phase was characterized by two important initiatives. The first was to establish a separate Department for Universities, Innovation and Skills (DIUS) and strip the Department of Education, also renamed, of responsibility for higher education. Reversing the integration of all levels of education under a single department, dating back four decades to 1964, sent a clear signal of the importance attached to universities and research within an increasingly knowledge-based economy. But it also communicated their subordination to innovation and economic imperatives. The second initiative was the debate about higher education's future launched by the new secretary of state, John Denham. Although this debate never got off the ground fully, a number of working groups were established to offer advice on a range of topics. To a large degree, however, the Denham debate was an attempt to produce greater coherence – and perhaps also to differentiate between universities' mission statements to favour an elite of research intensive universities – within the mass higher education system that had been developed – almost – in a fit of absent-mindedness. The issue of fees, and any need to increase them further, appears to have been deliberately sidestepped

- The final phase began in the dying days of the Labour Government when Denham's successor, Peter Mandelson, was made responsible for the Department of Business, Innovation and Skills (BIS) – a reconfiguration that, whether deliberately or not, distanced higher education even further from its old home in a department of education and reinforced the links with improving economic performance. The new first secretary also established the Independent Committee on Student Fees and Funding under Lord Browne, in fulfilment of the promise made by Charles Clarke five years earlier. The Committee subsequently reported to the new Conservative–Liberal Democrat Coalition Government. Its key recommendations – that there should be no cap on fees institutions could charge but an increasing proportion of fees of more than £9,000 should be paid into a fund to pay for scholarships – were swiftly rejected.

This brief chronological account already reveals substantial continuities and perhaps a more limited number of discontinuities:

1. The first, and most high-profile, continuity is the growing conviction that some degree of cost-sharing between taxpayers and students/graduates is necessary to deliver the additional resources a high-quality higher education system needs (in the New Labour period) and/or to protect higher education from the worst of the cruel-but-necessary cuts in public expenditure required to reduce the deficit (since the Coalition Government came to power)

2. A second continuity, almost as important, is the belief that investment in higher education is predominantly justified in terms of enhanced lifetime earnings (in the case of individuals) and improved economic performance (in the case of the state). The increasing focus on research excellence and impact is the best example of this belief – as is the consequent need to identify more clearly and protect elite universities. But other examples include the growing emphasis on employability

3. A third, perhaps more ragged, continuity is a commitment to policies designed to enhance learning and teaching, improve the student experience, and empower students. A number of policies have been developed to these ends: National Teaching Fellows, the Higher Education Academy, Centres of Excellence in Teaching and Learning, the National Student Survey and now Key Information Sets (KIS). The continuity is more 'ragged' as it is unclear whether the increasing emphasis on the student as the 'customer', particularly pronounced under the Coalition Government and celebrated in the title of the 2011 White Paper, is a driving cause or justificatory effect of the shift towards cost-sharing.

In contrast, discontinuities have been less apparent. Perhaps the most significant has been the declining emphasis on widening participation – from its high point under Blunkett in the early years of the Blair Government, through the establishment of the Office of Fair Access and the rise and fall of lifelong learning partnerships, to the its current low under the Coalition Government in which the favouring of conventionally qualified entrants with high grades amounts to a blatant form of discrimination. Other discontinuities either regard second-order issues or are attributable to differences of emphasis and rates of change, rather than to any fundamental differences of opinion. It is difficult, therefore, to escape the conclusion that over the last decade and a half – and most probably much longer – there has been a strong political consensus that the *Browne Report* and 2011 White Paper may have bent but did not break.

Implementing the White Paper

The *Browne Report* was the victim of – or accomplice in? – mission creep. What began as a limited intervention – the promised review of what impact Charles Clarke's decision to triple full-time fees to a maximum of £3,000 had had – ended up a wide-ranging report on English higher education, to the extent that, as I have already said, Lord Browne himself claimed it was proposing a 'new paradigm', despite the much narrower remit of his Committee. Browne's claim may have been difficult to sustain in light of important gaps, the most important of which was postgraduate education. Nor did the Report address key issues such as the future structure of the system, the potential impact of higher fees for the governance and management of institutions, the implications for learning and teaching or quality and standards, and the impact of research capacity (linked, of course, to its silence on postgraduates).

The pattern of mission creep established by the Browne Committee's open interpretation of its terms of reference was continued with the White Paper. While perhaps not a deliberate attempt to emulate the grand reforms of the past, broadening the reform agenda came about following the need to deal with the implications of higher fees (for example, the rebalancing of the HEFCE's funding, the requirement to revise the existing regulatory regime, and, in particular, the necessity to limit overall expenditure and therefore to cap total student numbers). In the period since the White Paper, as other agendas have been incorporated, the pattern of mission creep has extended further. A good example is the decision to allow a 'free market' for candidates with better entry qualifications (initially those with AAB grades at A-level or their equivalent and later those with ABB), a move that clearly mirrors the government's school reforms.

In this section I consider the evolution of policy in two phases: the recommendations made by the Browne Committee – and the government's immediate response – and the proposals made in the White Paper ten months later, together with subsequent developments as new agendas have been added and new constraints have become apparent. However, a common thread running through both phases has been the need to respond to levels of uncertainty and turbulence that almost certainly exceeded the intentions of evolving policy – Donald Rumsfeld's (actually J.K. Galbraith's description of the Great Depression of the 1930s) 'knowns, known unknowns and unknown unknowns'.

Browne and the government's immediate response

The Browne Committee reported in October 2010. Its recommendations provoked a storm of controversy – largely perhaps because the Liberal Democrats, the junior partners in the new Coalition Government, had gone into the General Election six months earlier with a manifesto promising not only to not increase tuition fees but to abolish them entirely. The *Browne Report* recommended that there should be no overall cap on the level of fees universities could charge. While only one strand in the Report, and by no means the most important, the Liberal Democrats' broken election promise focused public attention on the likely level of tuition fees in the future. The result, inevitably, was a public debate on Browne that generated more heat than light.

It is important to go back to what the *Browne Report* actually said, which is in danger of almost being forgotten. Browne's recommendations were grounded in an analysis of the weaknesses of the current system of fees and funding. The report listed six such weaknesses:

1. There was an insufficient number of places to meet student demand (it is important to remember that the Browne formula was intended to fund expansion)
2. The existing system, because of its dependence on (direct) public funding, was vulnerable to future reductions in public expenditure (again, it is important to recognize that the Browne Committee's hands were tied by the new government's non-negotiable decision to cut public expenditure – fast)
3. There had been limited progress on access, a surprising (but not unfair) conclusion in light of the previous New Labour Government's high-profile commitment to widening participation
4. The existing system provided inadequate support for part-time students
5. It was not sufficiently responsive to the changing skills required by the economy, a conclusion that could have been – and was – reached by almost every post-war government (and one that, for example, had been used to justify the establishment of the polytechnics by Anthony Crosland in 1966)
6. There had been only limited improvements in the student experience – perhaps the shakiest of the Report's conclusions given the absence of a consensus on what constitutes the student experience (although a key one for Browne in that it helped to justify the Report's reliance on student choice as the primary means for improving quality).

Having made a diagnosis of what was wrong Browne then established a number of key principles that must apply in any new system. Again, there were six: first, that more investment was needed in higher education; second, that there should be greater student choice; third, that everyone with the potential should be able to benefit (a restatement of the venerable Robbins principle); fourth, that no student should be expected to make any financial contribution to the cost of their higher education before they were in work; fifth, that any payments they did make should be affordable; and finally, that part-time students should be treated in the same way as full-time students.

In order to dissipate some of the heat generated by the immediate reaction to it and judge its recommendations fairly, it is important to recognize the *Browne Report's* conceptual furniture. Perhaps too much attention has been concentrated on Browne's commitment to student choice as the driver of any funding system – and the corresponding belief that this was also the mechanism most likely to drive improvements in quality. This commitment and belief have been widely criticized as displaying either an unquestioning acceptance of neo-liberal ideology or a view that higher education's value must be assessed in largely instrumental terms (higher earnings for individuals and enhanced competitiveness in the global economy) – or both. Two points perhaps need to be made in Browne's defence: firstly, these were commonplace views held by wide sections of the political establishment, including the previous Labour Government, and secondly, Browne offered a broader analysis of the existing system's weaknesses regarding funding and also set out a number of key principles, none of which were especially controversial.

The *Browne Report*'s detailed recommendations can be divided into three groups: student support/graduate contributions, institutional funding, and regulation of the proposed new system:

- Regarding the first group, Browne recommended that no students should be required to make any financial contribution to the cost of their higher education until they were in work – and earning at least £21,000, a threshold the Committee recommended should be periodically reviewed (in other words, increased). Interest rates should be low – the rate of inflation plus 2.2 per cent was the Report's suggested figure – and any outstanding payments should be written off after 30 years. Finally, all full-time students should be entitled to receive a non-means tested loan of £3,750 to help with their living expenses, while those from poorer homes would receive an additional grant of £3,250

- Regarding the second group, Browne recommended that institutions should be free to set their own fees. If they decided to charge more than £6,000, however, they should be expected to pay an increasing proportion of the additional tuition fee income back to the government to fund the Committee's proposals on student support. Institutions charging £9,000 would thus receive only 85 per cent of the proceeds, while those charging £12,000 would receive only 73 per cent. Such an ingenious proposal for a 'fees taper' had a number of advantages: the freedom of institutions to set their own fees was respected, there would be a disincentive to charge very high fees, and the pot of money for student support would be topped up – and would thus save expense on the part of the Treasury

- Regarding the third group, Browne recommended that a Higher Education Council should be established, combining the responsibilities of the HEFCE, the Quality Assurance Agency, the Office for Fair Access, and the Office for Independent Adjudication. The Committee concluded that the advantages of having a simpler and less cluttered regulatory environment outweighed the difficulties of combining in a single organization potentially conflicting responsibilities for investment (i.e. directly funding institutions), guaranteeing quality, monitoring access, and dealing with student complaints.

The Committee believed their recommendations would create scope for higher education to expand – although it recognized that there might need to be some cap on overall student numbers and recommended that the government should be given the power to annually set a minimum A-level points tariff to determine eligibility; that they would encourage institutions to compete, though Browne envisaged that such competition would be primarily expressed through students' access to transparent and reliable information on institutional performance – including, crucially, employment rates – rather than through a crude 'price war' by setting variable fees; and that they would allow necessarily more tightly rationed public investment in higher education to be more clearly targeted – and therefore, perhaps, more easy to defend against future cuts.

So what went wrong?

The White Paper

The White Paper was published nine months later in the summer of 2011. Its timing was itself significant: the government had originally promised it would be published 'before Christmas' (2010) and its publication was delayed on three subsequent occasions. A number of reasons appear to account for such postponements. The first, and most significant, was that the original timescale was almost certainly too optimistic. The Browne Committee itself had substantially widened its remit beyond the promised review of the student fees and funding system introduced by the previous Labour Government. Understandably perhaps, in light of the incoming government's far tougher approach to reducing the deficit (which required much deeper, and faster, cuts in public expenditure), Lord Browne and his colleagues came to the conclusion that a more systematic review was required. Of course, the stretched remit still excluded key areas of policy, most notably, perhaps, with regard to postgraduate education. In the same way the government was obliged to write a more comprehensive White Paper, partly to provide a more detailed justification of the decision to charge higher fees but partly also to knit together other strands of policy – notably, the emphasis on students as empowered customers, which then gave the White Paper its title.

A second reason for the delay in publishing the White Paper can be attributed to the difficulties all governments face in taking office. Broad-brush ideological and policy preferences must be translated into workable policies; it takes all new governments time to penetrate the Whitehall machine. In the past these difficulties have sometimes been seen as the Civil Service's predilection for a status quo it has itself constructed, combined perhaps with a resistance to novelty and innovation. Such suspicions were famously articulated by Richard Crossman in his diaries when he joined Harold Wilson's Cabinet in 1964 (Crossman, 1975–7). However, less dramatic – paranoid? – explanations are possible. For example, the effective exclusion of the HEFCE from the Browne Committee's development of its recommendations – which, as a result, could not be rigorously tested for their practicability – is largely explained by the focus of the Committee's original remit on areas, notably student fees, for which the HEFCE was not responsible. It was only when the remit widened through a process of 'mission creep' that the failure to involve sufficiently early in the policy process the agency with hands-on experience of managing the system became a significant liability. However, its decision to keep out the National Union of Students, which was denied even an advance copy of the final report, is more difficult to explain.

The White Paper's proposals were grouped around three themes. The first, commanding the other two, was the need to secure a sustainable system of funding for higher education which began, of course, with an assumption that had to be taken as a 'given': that there was no alternative to the new government's deficit reduction strategy. However, from that non-negotiable starting point, the White Paper was frank about the options available to ministers: to reduce student numbers, to cut funding per student (the so-called unit-of-resource), or to adopt a harsher, and less progressive, repayment system for student loans.

The second theme was the need to improve the student experience. Again, it was framed by a 'given': that the student experience was unsatisfactory in ways that remained unspecified. In fact most of the proposals grouped under this theme, accounting for the majority of the proposals made in the White Paper, were designed not so much to improve the student experience but to promote a more dynamic system:

1. The most significant was to 'move away from tight number controls that constrain individual higher education institutions' (BIS, 2011). To achieve this a pool of so-called 'contestable' places would be created, consisting of approximately 65,000 students with entry qualifications equivalent to A-level grades of AAB, and 20,000 places for which institutions charging fees of less than £7,500 on average would be able to bid

2. A second important proposal was to promote a greater diversity of institutions by making it easier for smaller institutions with more restricted course portfolios to acquire 'university' titles, by allowing more private providers to enter the market, and by encouraging further education colleges to offer more higher education programmes. Also floated was the idea that degree awarding might be uncoupled from teaching by encouraging universities to award degrees for programmes taught in other institutions – which, of course, already happened on a significant scale through franchising arrangements

3. The third important proposal was to require all institutions to publish much more detailed information in the form of 'key information sets' on a course-by-course basis about a wide range of indicators including average entry grades for newly recruited students and employment rates among graduates. Much of this data, of course, was already available from bodies like the Higher Education Statistics Agency (HESA) and others and used to construct newspaper league

tables but new measures were proposed to make it more transparent and more comprehensive. Institutions would also be required to publish summary reports of their own internal student evaluation surveys.

The third theme around which the White Paper's proposals was grouped was the need to increase social mobility. These proposals reflected in particular the views of the junior members in the Coalition Government, the Liberal Democrats. First, the White Paper 'endorsed' the Robbins principle that higher education should be available to all those willing and able to benefit from it. Second, the government's decisions about the repayment of student loans, which had previously been announced, were further commended and reinforced. Third, full grants for living expenses would be available to students from families with income of less than £25,000 per year. Finally, a National Scholarships Programme was established, though it would not reach its target of £150 million until 2014. This programme would supplement the scholarships and bursaries awarded by individual institutions as a condition of their agreements with the Office for Fair Access if they had decided to charge fees of more than £6,000 (in practice, virtually all institutions).

The White Paper was less clear about the detailed mechanisms required to implement such proposals. The Browne Committee's recommendation that a single Higher Education Council should be established by merging the HEFCE, the Quality Assurance Agency, the Office for Fair Access, and the Office for Independent Adjudication had already been rejected by the government, partly on the grounds that it would create serious conflicts of interest. Such conflicts were not entirely avoided by the proposals in the White Paper, however. It announced that the HEFCE would be given an 'explicit remit' as the overall regulator of the sector to 'protect the interests of students' and to 'promote competitiveness'. To that end it announced that there would be legislation to allow the HEFCE to attach conditions to grants. At the same time the HEFCE would continue to be responsible for distributing the remaining (direct) grant for teaching, specifically to support specialist institutions, widening participation, knowledge exchange, and those subjects that would continue to cost more than the maximum £9,000 tuition fee (science, engineering, and medicine). In addition, although not mentioned in the White Paper, the HEFCE would continue to distribute QR (quality research) funding.

The White Paper appeared to be 'work in progress'. It is best seen as a snapshot of where the Department for Business, Innovation and Skills had got to in its efforts to implement the government's new funding system, while coping with its collateral consequences, in the summer of 2011. But policy continued to evolve, and a number of issues remained intractable: the development of a lighter-touch, risk-based quality regime and the 'level playing field' for existing higher education institutions, further education colleges, and new private providers, on both of which progress has been slow. There was little evidence that colleges had a significantly increased appetite to offer higher education programmes: seven private providers were granted the power to award degrees – for taught courses not research degrees – and ten smaller institutions were allowed to use 'university' titles, which hardly amounted to the substantial extension in the system's institutional base promised, implicitly, by the White Paper. Meanwhile, the HEFCE's primary efforts have been focused on managing the transition to the new high-fee regime and reducing the teaching grant without destabilizing institutional finances. The development of a stable system for the allocation of teaching funding to science, technology, engineering, and medicine (STEM) and strategic and vulnerable subjects remains a longer-term objective, although consultation has begun.

However, the most important changes following the White Paper have been the effective abandonment of the idea of 'contestable' places for which institutions can bid and the effective reduction in student numbers. Both reflect significant deviations from the policies set out in the White Paper:

1. The number of 'contestable' places has been reduced from 20,000 to 10,000 and in future will be distributed formulaically instead of as a result of an active bidding process (HEFCE, 2012). To some degree this change has recognized reality: many of the places awarded remained unfilled, especially in further education colleges. But it may also reflect an ideological shift. It has been decided that students with qualifications equivalent to A-level grades of ABB are now to be removed from institutions' student number controls (which were reduced pro rata). The focus has shifted from encouraging lower-cost provision to privileging highly qualified students, whose choice, therefore, is now being enhanced at the expense of their less qualified peers

2. There are also signs that the overall size of the English higher education system is likely to shrink as a result of the Coalition Government's new funding system – which is significant because the White Paper justified the government's decision to increase fees as an alternative to reducing student numbers. Yet this appears to have been its effect. The number of full-time applications to higher education for entry in 2012, the year in which the higher fees came into effect, fell by 7 per cent (UCAS, 2012); actual acceptances fell by a greater percentage. The reduction was not altogether unexpected: a similar, although smaller, decline had taken place when the previous Labour Government had increased fees to £3,000. In the early stages of the UCAS cycle for 2013 entry there were further precipitate falls in applications, although they had recovered by the January Census date and ended up slightly ahead of the total at the equivalent time 12 months before (UCAS, 2013). But unless there is a dramatic rebound in demand, overall student numbers will decline as the large intakes from 2010 and 2011 work their way through the system. In addition, the number of young adults in the overall population will continue to decline for more than a decade (Thompson and Bekhradnia,

2012b). The prospect in the coming years, therefore, is of a significant shortage of graduates.

Like all White Papers, the 2011 Higher Education White Paper was composed of an unstable combination of ideological preferences and pragmatic prescriptions. It is not my purpose to argue with the former, although the extent to which the new funding regime has been able to – or can ever – promote student choice is open to doubt. This is only partly because of the weaknesses in the construction of that regime – for example, the failure to recognize that individual institutions suffer few, if any, market disadvantages from charging higher fees, even if the system as a whole experiences a decline in demand. Combined with the substantial failure to widen the system's institutional base, that could be said to constitute 'market failure'. Some will conclude that the remedy is to redouble efforts to create a higher education market; others that the nature of higher education – notably its role as a positional and long-term good – mean that such efforts are destined to fail.

Of greater significance is the paradox at the heart of the government's higher education policy. By its own admission the total of publicly provided resources flowing into higher education would increase by more than 10 per cent by the middle of the decade, which is difficult to reconcile with its overriding determination to cut the deficit by reducing public expenditure – except in the narrowest accounting terms (Thompson and Bekhradnia, 2012a). Such an outcome is the direct result of the government's own, commendable, decision to introduce a less onerous repayment system, making it likely that a substantial minority of graduates will be able to pay back their student loans in full. In practice, higher education's contribution to reducing the deficit can probably only be achieved by reducing student numbers. Such a measure would undermine all the efforts to promote social mobility by providing sufficiently generous terms to ensure that students from poorer homes are not discouraged and disadvantaged.

Finally, even if this central paradox is overlooked, there remain detailed issues of implementation that were not resolved by the White Paper and continue to be unresolved. For example, the government decided against introducing further legislation despite its promise in the White Paper to do so. Their choice has had three consequences. First, the HEFCE (and other agencies responsible for the delivery of the new funding system) have been denied the legal tools they need. Not only is it unclear how the HEFCE will be able to discharge its designated role as, if not a formal regulator then a de facto overseer of the system, it will lack the means even to enforce the detailed funding decision it – with the encouragement of ministers – has taken. Secondly, no effective mechanisms have been proposed to coordinate the actions (and effects) of decisions taken by a range of separate agencies – notably the HEFCE and the Student Loans Company. The threads of coordination will be held by ministers who will always be subject to short-term political pressures and brief tenures of office. Finally, the degree of uncertainty within the system has been substantially increased. The risks of dysfunctional behaviour, with ill anticipated collateral effects, have also increased. As a result the system could be reshaped in perverse but difficult to reverse ways over the next decade.

Conclusion

The reform of higher education (and student) funding by the Coalition Government that came to power in 2010 has already been characterized as a watershed moment in the development of English higher education. First, it is said to represent a fundamental ideological shift: competition is now entrenched as the major dynamic for improvement and more active (and informed) student choice is the instrument of securing it. While such a view of higher education is hardly novel – and to some extent informed policy choices made by the previous Labour Governments under Tony Blair and Gordon Brown in their efforts to 'modernize' higher education – 'market' discourse has now been irreversibly lodged in mainstream policy thinking. A tipping point has been reached.

Secondly, the process of implementing this reform is now causing far-reaching changes in institutional behaviour as colleges and universities seek to modify not only their management systems but also their strategies and even their organizational cultures to cope with the new funding environment. The fact that this process has been incremental, unpredictable, and even chaotic has intensified the sense of transition: from a policy landscape that, in its essentials, had prevailed certainly for more than two decades since the abolition of the binary system and the creation of the HEFCE – and, some would argue, since the 1960s, when the first steps towards the creation of a mass higher education system were taken in the United Kingdom – to an unfamiliar, and still unknowable, policy landscape.

Of course, a contrary position can be taken: that core institutional values and behaviours are likely to survive the imposition of the new fees-led funding system without fundamental modification. Universities have proved themselves to be remarkably resilient institutions in the past and are likely to remain so – rightly, many will add, because they are key institutions within the space of a 'civil society' that mediates between the state and the market and, as such, should not be subject to ceaseless 'reforms'. Also the process of policy implementation will inevitably require a series of, perhaps increasing, accommodations with existing practice. As such accommodations accumulate, it could well erode some of the radical potential of the original headline reforms – as is already evident in the (inevitable) survival of student number controls. Indeed the legal failure to specify the HEFCE's regulatory responsibilities under the new funding regime might, in effect, increase its informal influence over institutions.

However, these are matters that cannot yet be determined. All that is possible at present is a provisional assessment, one that might emphasize two broad conclusions:

The contingency of policy formation

The first is that contingency always plays an important role in policy formation. All policy, of course, is formed by a mixture of structural determinism, the *longue durée* in the phrase made famous by the French historian Fernand Braudel, and political contingency, his *histoire evénémentielle*. But the mix has varied. In this case the (perceived) need to reduce the deficit as an urgent and overriding priority, and the determination to do so by reducing public expenditure rather than increasing taxes, lent an urgency to the deliberations of the Browne Committee and the development of the White Paper. If this need had been seen as less urgent, or a different balance between cuts and taxes had been preferred, the package of reforms might have taken a different shape. Although the long-term drift of higher education policy, common ground between all major political parties and many developed countries, had been towards increasing reliance on 'user payments' to fund institutions, the detailed proposals made by Browne and modified by the White Paper were not an inevitable outcome.

Another contingency was that the government formed in 2010 was a coalition between Conservatives and Liberal Democrats, who had pledged in their election manifesto to abolish student fees entirely and were consequently deeply embarrassed by the *volte face* forced upon them. Two elements in the package of reforms can safely be attributed to the Liberal Democrat influence: the more generous repayment schedule and the emphasis on social mobility. While the latter can be dismissed as window-dressing, the former has had important consequences – not least the sharp reduction in price sensitivity among students and the consequent failure on the part of institutions to produce the kind of variable tuition fee structures a genuine market requires.

An illuminating comparison can be drawn with the debates historians have about the causes of the First World War. In the 1960s a group of radical German historians came to argue that Germany in 1914 embraced war as a means of ensuring, and enhancing, its dominance in Europe (and beyond) and quickly devised ambitious war aims. According to their analysis the (in)famous 'war guilt' clause in the Versailles treaty was amply justified (Fischer, 1967; 2007). More recently gentler and more nuanced analyses have tended to prevail. While the dangers of militarism were real, it was not inevitable that a local conflict in the Balkans would rapidly explode into a world war. Like previous – and actually more threatening – Balkan conflicts, it could have been contained given slightly changed circumstances (Clark, 2012). There was perhaps no similar inevitability about the shape taken by the reform of higher education funding in England between 2009 and 2011. It, too, was shaped by events, sometimes transitory, and contingencies that imposed their own constraints.

Peter Scott

A 'perfect storm'

If indeed the 2009–11 reforms come to be seen as a revolution in English higher education, the second conclusion is that this may be due not solely (or even mainly) to their direct consequences but rather to the unintended impacts of other policy changes. The combined effect of discrete, and uncoordinated, policy strands could be to produce what might be termed a 'perfect storm' in English higher education. Certainly their unstable combination is a major ingredient in the turbulence and uncertainty currently affecting England's universities and colleges, which might have been able to adjust more comfortably to the proposals made in the White Paper.

Four developments may be particularly significant: the recruitment of international students, the future shape of research (and innovation) policies, reforms in English schools, and the long-term consequences of devolution. First, given the importance of internationalization strategies in the future development of higher education, the chilling effect of the new visa regime imposed by the Coalition Government – the direct result of the Conservatives' pledge to reduce immigration – could well have a greater impact on both the future shape of the English higher education system and the fortunes of individual institutions than the shift towards a high-fee funding regime. At the very least new rules on visas will compound the consequences of this new funding regime. Secondly, the abolition of regional development agencies in England has also had a significant effect on patterns of funding for applied research and development. Decisions yet to be taken on the distribution of QR funding following the outcomes of the 2013 Research Excellence Framework (REF) could also have far-reaching consequences. The current – and perhaps complacent – assumption that the REF will be a re-run of previous Research Assessment Exercises (RAEs) ignores its different origins and architecture.

Thirdly, the effective abandonment of comprehensive secondary education – and its replacement by a variety of school types such as academies and free schools – and the continuing uncertainty about the future of the General Certificate of Secondary Education (GCSE), first abandoned and then reprieved, as the foundational qualification in schools, are likely to have important consequences for demand for higher education. The establishment of a comprehensive secondary school system – and, in particular, the introduction of the GCSE – were key stimuli for the development of the current mass higher education system. Finally, the fracturing of higher education in the United Kingdom into three (or four) 'national' systems has been accelerated by the decisions of the Scottish and Welsh governments not to follow the English lead by charging high fees but to persist with funding regimes more dependent on public expenditure. Such decisions have produced centrifugal forces that may be difficult to contain and a number of 'interface' difficulties that may prove intractable.

Both conclusions – the contingency of policy formation and the gathering of a 'perfect storm' – tend to reinforce the plasticity of policy. Painstaking analysis of the stately progress of committee reports, White Papers, and (although absent in this particular phase of higher education reform – so far) legislation may convey a misleading impression of order and regularity. In fact, policy formation remains a chaotic business. Indeed a historical survey of the development of higher education policy may even suggest that, as policy interventions have become more intrusive (in the sense that the political will to meddle has become less constrained and ideological considerations have become more pronounced), they have also become more chaotic, as the growing difficulties regarding their implementation and the greater impact of unintended consequences and collateral policies reflect.

References

Birkland, T. (2011) *An Introduction to the Policy Process: Theories, concepts and models of public policy making.* 3rd ed. Armonk, NY: M.E. Sharpe.

BIS (Department of Business, Innovation and Skills) (2011) *Higher Education: Students at the heart of the system.* London: HMSO.

CHE (Committee on Higher Education) (1963) *Higher Education: A report by the committee appointed by the Prime Minister under the chairmanship of Lord Robbins, 1961–63 (The Robbins Report).* London: HMSO.

Clark, B. (2004) *Creating Entrepreneurial Universities: Organizational pathways of transformation.* Maidenhead: Society for Research into Higher Education/Open University Press.

Clark, C. (2012) *The Sleepwalkers: How Europe went to war in 1914.* London: Allen Lane.

Crossman, R. (1975–7) *Diaries of a Cabinet Minister.* London: Hamish Hamilton and Jonathan Cape.

CVCP (Committee of Vice-Chancellors and Principals) (1985) *Report of the Steering Group for Efficiency Studies in Universities (The Jarratt Report).* London: CVCP.

DES (Department for Education and Science) (1966) *A Plan for Polytechnics and Other Colleges.* London: HMSO.

—(1972a) *Education: A framework for expansion.* London: HMSO.

—(1972b) *Teacher Education and Training (The James Report).* London: HMSO.

—(1987) *Higher Education: Meeting the challenge.* London: HMSO.

—(1988) *Top-Up Loans for Students.* London: HMSO.

—(1991) *Higher Education: A new framework.* London: HMSO.

DfE (Department for Education and Skills) (2003) *The Future of Higher Education.* London: Stationery Office.

Fischer, F. (2007) *Germany's Aims in the First World War.* Originally 1967. New York: W.W. Norton.

Fryer, B. (1997) *Learning for the Twenty-first Century: First report of the National Advisory Group for Continuing Education and Lifelong Learning.* London: NAGCELL.

Gibbons, M., Limoges, C., Nowotny, H., Scott, P., Schwartzman, S., and Trow, M. (1994) *The New Production of Knowledge: The dynamics of science and research in contemporary societies.* London: Sage.

HEFCE (Higher Education Funding Council for England) (2012) *Student Number Controls for 2013–14: Next steps.* Circular 32 2012. Bristol: HEFCE.

HIP (Hillsborough Independent Panel) (2012) *The Report of the Hillsborough Independent Panel* (*The Hillsborough Report*). London: HMSO.

Hutton, J.B.E., Baron Hutton (2004) *Report of the Inquiry into the Circumstances Surrounding the Death of Dr David Kelly CMG* (*The Hutton Report*). London: HMSO.

IRHEFSF (Independent Review of Higher Education Funding and Student Finance) (2010) *Securing a Sustainable Future for Higher Education* (*The Browne Report*). London: Department for Business, Innovation, and Skills. Online. www.bis.gov.uk/assets/biscore/corporate/docs/s/10-1208-securing-sustainable-higher-education-browne-report.pdf.

King, R., Marginson, S., and Naidoo, R. (eds) (2011) *Handbook on Globalization and Higher Education*. Cheltenham: Edward Elgar.

Leveson, B.H., Lord Justice Leveson (2012) *Inquiry into the Culture, Practices and Ethics of the Press* (*The Leveson Report*). London: HMSO.

Lindblom, C. and Woodhouse, E. (1992) *The Policy-making Process*. 3rd ed. London: Prentice-Hall.

Maarten, M. (2009) *Authoritative Governance: Policy-making in the age of mediatization*. Oxford: Oxford University Press.

NCIHE (National Committee of Inquiry into Higher Education) (1997) *Higher Education in the Learning Society* (*The Dearing Report*). London: HMSO.

Parsons, W. (2002) 'From "muddling through" to "muddling up" – evidence-based policy-making in the modernisation of British government'. *Public Policy and Administration*, 17 (3), 54–60.

Power, M. (1999) *The Audit Society: Rituals of verification*. Oxford: Oxford University Press.

Saville, M.O., Baron Saville of Newdigate (2010) *Report of the Bloody Sunday Inquiry* (*The Saville Report*). London: HMSO.

Scott, P. (1995) *The Meanings of Mass Higher Education*. Buckingham: Open University Press.

Shattock, M. (2012) *Making Policy in British Higher Education 1945–2011*. Maidenhead: McGraw-Hill/Open University Press.

Thompson, J. and Bekhradnia, B. (2012a) *The Cost of the Government's Reforms of the Financing Higher Education*. Oxford: Higher Education Policy Institute.

—(2012b) *The Impact on Demand of the Government's Reforms of Higher Education*. Oxford: Higher Education Policy Institute.

UCAS (University and College Admissions Service) (2012) *End of Cycle Report 2012*. Cheltenham: UCAS.

—(2013) *2013 Cycle Applicant Figures – January deadline*. Cheltenham: UCAS. Online. www.ucas.com/documents/stats/2013_applicantfigures_jan

Chapter 4

A bridge too far: An economic critique of marketization of higher education

Gareth Williams

Prologue

> *Practical men, who believe themselves to be quite exempt from any intellectual influences, are usually the slaves of some defunct economist. Madmen in authority, who hear voices in the air, are distilling their frenzy from some academic scribbler of a few years back.*
>
> (Keynes, 1936)

The evolution of policy on the financing of higher education, and the changing public sentiment about the payment and financing of tuition fees and living costs by students in particular, provides a good example of how research findings and scholarly interpretations can eventually find their way into policy and practice. As with much in modern economics, recent ideas about higher education's financing were conceived in the mind of Adam Smith. In the little read Appendix 1 to Book 5 of the *Wealth of Nations* (Smith, 2010) Smith comments on the effects of different ways of financing and regulating universities in England, France, and Scotland. Speaking of the first he says that guaranteed income from property ownership and endowments, as at Oxford, led to sloth and corruption; of the second, that state finance and regulation were a bureaucratic nightmare; and of the third, that a system of finance based on fee-paying students produced universities that were responsive to the needs of their clients, up to date, and efficient.

The *Robbins Report* – Lionel Robbins was a distinguished economist – considered it was desirable for academic freedom that universities receive their income from several different sources, including fees from students, but made the proviso that it was appropriate for the state to continue to meet most of the costs until the practice of attending university was more deeply entrenched in British culture.

> On balance I do not recommend immediate recourse to a system of financing students by loans. At a time when many parents are only just beginning to acquire the habit of contemplating higher education for those of their children, especially girls, who are capable of benefiting from it, I think it probable that it would have undesirable disincentivising effects. But if, as time goes on, the habit is more firmly established, the arguments of justice in distribution and of the advantage of increasing

individual responsibility may come to weigh more heavily and lead to some experiments in this direction.

(CHE, 1963: para 647)

However, the Committee recommended that student fees, even if subsidized, should not cover more than about a quarter of the costs of courses. In a very prescient remark they said that:

if fees were at a high level ... it is highly probable that the level of fees rather than broad questions of educational policy would become the focus of public discussion; and if this were so the problem of preserving academic freedom would present itself in a new form.

(CHE, 1963: para 653)

It was after the publication of the *Robbins Report* in 1963 and the establishment of the Unit for Economic and Statistical Studies in Higher Education, set up by the LSE to continue the groundbreaking statistical analyses inaugurated by Claus Moser and Richard Layard for the Report, that the economics of education – and higher education particularly – became part of mainstream economics in the United Kingdom. At the heart of its analysis were the theory and the measurement of 'human capital'. Mark Blaug wrote a decade later:

The birth of human capital theory was announced by Theodore Schultz in 1960 (in his presidential address to the American Economics Association). The birth itself may be said to have taken place two years later when the *Journal of Political Economy* published its October 1962 supplement volume on 'Investment in Human Beings'. This volume included ... the preliminary chapters of Gary Becker's 1964 monograph 'Human Capital' which has, ever since, served as the locus classicus on the subject.

(Blaug, 1970: 12)

Human capital theory was attractive to economists for several reasons. It appeared to offer a solution to one of the puzzles presented by economic growth theory. For over a hundred years economic expansion in the West had been more rapid than could be explained simply by the accumulation of physical capital (Denison, 1962; 1968). Increases in knowledge had clearly made an important contribution. It was in the public's interest for governments to maximize the investment in knowledge creation and dissemination in order to accelerate growth.

But human capital theory also presented a dilemma to those concerned with the financing of higher education. While hundreds of studies all over the world have yielded ample empirical evidence that higher education is a good investment for individuals – graduates on average earned considerably more than non-graduates, even when allowances were made for differences in inherent ability (Psacharopoulos,

1973; 1985) – were there benefits to society over and above such higher incomes? The answer is not so clear-cut. Medical doctors clearly bring considerable benefits to other people. But doctors are also very well paid. Moreover, as some economists and sociologists have claimed (Arrow, 1973; Taubman and Wales, 1973; Wiles 1974), it may be that graduates earn more because their degrees are assumed to signal higher ability; they replace non-graduates in jobs that could be done just as well without a degree. If all the benefits of higher education go to the graduates who have received it, there are no sound ethical reasons why taxpayers in general should pay for it. Furthermore, if the individual beneficiaries pay for it, the operation of the market means it is likely, in practice, to lead to an efficient use of resources since, as Adam Smith pointed out, people who pay seek to ensure that they get value for their money. On the other hand, however, if there are benefits to others, over and above those received by the direct beneficiaries, a case can be made for some subsidy from public funds. The existence and extent of such external benefits has been the subject of more than half a century's debate amongst economists.

There are also issues of equity. If students have to meet the full cost of higher education, only those from relatively affluent families will be able to do so and they will obtain the financial benefits in later life. It was in 1968 that Howard Glennerster of the LSE Unit published *A Graduate Tax* (Glennerster, 1968). Exploring the implications of such preoccupations, Glennerster concluded that the fairest and most efficient way of paying for higher education was through a surcharge on the income tax paid by graduates.

At the beginning of the twenty-first century the issue of people contributing to the costs of their own higher education can be seen as part of a much wider debate about the distribution of personal incomes throughout an individual's lifetime. We all begin our lives in a state of dependency where others must provide resources for our upkeep. This is followed by a period in which most of us are able to meet our own needs and usually generate a surplus. Finally, in the sixth and seventh of Shakespeare's seven ages most of us again become dependent on the surplus generated by other people. It is now generally accepted that individuals must save some of their personal surplus during their good years to finance pensions later on. The argument for personal loans to finance at least the higher stages of an individual's education can usefully be seen as mirroring the debate about personal pensions. There are also issues about equity between individuals – some people are more able, or are born with other socio-economic advantages – but at least as important is the need to help people enjoy a satisfactory standard of living throughout their life cycle.

Such questions preoccupied economists for several decades but the message heard by most politicians, until mass higher education became a reality in the 1990s, was that more higher education was a wise way of spending public money and would bring ongoing long-term economic benefits and lead to a more equitable society. However, by 1980 there was a growing consensus in many countries that the collective provision of a very wide range of public services was failing and the virtues of the competitive market – on grounds of both efficiency and equity – became the dominant ideology. The ideological change was sharpest in the socialist economies of eastern Europe, but moves in this direction have taken place in most countries in the past quarter century.

A historical overview

Higher education is susceptible to economic analysis in that it requires resources. As in all resource-using activities, there are two basic ways in which it can be organized: as a collectively provided service: free at the point of delivery with its profile determined by political and managerial processes, or as a facility provided by Adam Smith's invisible hand in which thousands of individual decisions in markets decide how much is provided and who reaps the benefits. In practice, all higher education systems are a combination of the two extremes but the balance between them has changed over time.

Since the emergence of universities in the Middle Ages the dominant mode of higher education provision has been collective, firstly by religious organizations and subsequently by nation states. The basic reason was straightforward: both wanted to form the thinking of well-educated people and both wanted to train suitable people to run their organizations. Both controlled substantial resources and both wanted to recruit into their service the most able young people, whatever their social background. Such control of the thinking of each new generation and the upward mobility of the brightest individuals makes an important contribution to social stability: in societies where change was slow it worked rather well on the whole.

In the United Kingdom, the Industrial Revolution of the nineteenth century saw leaders of industry join the church and the government as sponsors of higher education in the great industrial cities for similar reasons. They wanted upcoming generations to embrace their commercial ideology and their share of the most able young people. Similar developments occurred in the United States, but in most other European countries church and government remained dominant, possibly because governments played a more leading role in the development of industry. However, the public service model prevailed everywhere until the late 1980s. Even in the United States, where there were many private universities, the ideal of public service was a major driving force for university boards of trustees. Higher education was a public service to which everyone was entitled if they could demonstrate that they had the intellectual capacity to undertake it.

The model fell apart in the 1990s, partly as a result of pressures brought about by massive expansion but also because of radical ideological changes in ideas about how public services are best provided. In higher education, as in many other publicly provided services, the Achilles heel was self-indulgence, not necessarily explicit bribery and corruption but because the management of universities was largely for the benefit of its providers. The most blatant example of this in many of the United Kingdom's universities was the decision to grant secure lifetime tenure to individuals shortly after they obtained a first degree. Tenure is certainly justifiable in terms of giving academic staff freedom from political interference after they have demonstrated that they have useful knowledge and intellectual skills to offer others, but as a standard form of employment of very highly specialized people it introduced rigidities that eventually came near to breaking the system. The clearest example came in 1981–3 when it proved impossible to reduce expenditure in some universities, in accordance with public policy decisions, because of legal commitments to excessive numbers of staff with lifetime tenure. Less dramatic were several cases where staff had to be retained despite having very few students to teach and little research output. The Soviet Union exhibited similar rigidities in an extreme form in its entire economic system – and that system did collapse.

The political reaction to the inefficiencies and inequities brought about by 'producer capture' was extreme, amounting – in many ways – to an anti-collectivist revolution, though for the most part a peaceful one. The past 20 years have seen a marked shift towards market hegemony, most dramatically in former communist countries. But in the past quarter century, market-based provision of public services has become increasingly global. In the former communist countries of eastern Europe, universities began almost immediately to admit full fee-paying students to supplement the regular students subsidized from state funds – and private higher education institutions burgeoned. In UK higher education the change was clearly marked by the 1988 Education Reform Act, which decreed that universities and colleges were no longer to be state-subsidized service providers but treated rather as economic organizations selling education and research services to the state and others who were willing to purchase them. Over the following quarter century there has been, in many countries, a further steady shift from quasi-market provision – in which the state is a pseudo-purchaser – to something approaching a real market in which larger shares of income for higher education institutions now comes from private purchasers. There are few countries now in which most students do not meet some of the costs of their higher education. OECD figures for 2010 show that only seven out of 37 OECD countries did not charge first-degree students some fees (OECD, 2011). In England all universities now receive less than half of their income directly from central government. The rest is paid by customers of various kinds.

However, even in England, a country that has moved a long way in this direction, it is important not to overstate the free market analogy. Higher education institutions have remained charitable organizations. As such they trade an inability to take profits out of the educational enterprise and various commitments to provide services on a public service basis for favourable tax treatment. They are subject to a good deal of government regulation and the government remains committed to repaying the debts of graduates on low incomes or working in countries out of reach of Her Majesty's Revenue and Customs, which may end up being a very large sum (HEPI, 2012).

However, the 2011 White Paper (BIS, 2011) marks a major shift towards a fully marketized higher education system in England. Similar developments are also occurring in several other countries in the form of an expansion of higher education provision by commercial profit-seeking enterprises (Kinser and Levey, 2006). While the shift has the potential to bring some benefits – especially in reducing costs to students by weakening the monopolizing power of providers – what has been described as the commodification of higher education (Lyotard, 1984; Naidoo, 2003) also brings dangers that are likely to be accentuated when profit seeking appears to be the primary driver.

Recent research into alternative providers of higher education has identified 698 institutions that offer privately funded Higher Education in the United Kingdom (HMRC, 2012: 14). HESA (2011) shows that over 56,000 students, of whom 45,000 were on business and related courses and 14,000 on postgraduate courses, enrolled on higher education courses in private institutions in 2010. At 2.2 per cent, this is a small proportion of the total number of students in that year, although it has been growing rapidly. The College of Law, part of a private commercial enterprise, was the first authorized to use the title 'university' and award its own degrees. At present the others award qualifications that are validated in some way by conventional universities, which clearly indicates the absence of a sharp boundary between non-profit-seeking and profit-seeking higher education. The purpose of the HMRC (2012) publication cited above is to canvas opinion on whether for-profit private providers should have similar tax advantages as traditional not-for-profit higher education institutions. It seems likely that their number will increase, particularly in the areas of business studies and law, which are cheap subjects to teach and potentially very profitable.

Such developments are occurring at a time when signs outside higher education suggest that the era of market hegemony may be evolving into something that recognizes the important role collective regulation has to play. Obviously the ideological landscape changed following the financial crash of 2008 and the subsequent worldwide depression. It was no longer possible to believe that a light-touch regulation of global financial transactions would result in sustainable long-term economic growth. The crash also revealed a huge amount of large-scale fraud and corruption. At a theoretical level the longstanding economic debate between the Keynesians and the Hayekians is gradually turning in favour of the former. Governments must intervene to return economies to health. But it is not just the economic crisis that is increasing doubts about market solutions to all social issues. For several years there has been evidence that societies with wide disparities in income score less highly on various measures of well-being than those with less overall wealth but more concern about the welfare of whole communities (for a useful literature review see Easterlin *et al.*, 2010).

Limits of marketization in higher education

As I've already indicated, throughout its history higher education has been predominantly provided collectively, partly through an inherent belief that young people should not be born to blush unseen, whatever their social backgrounds, and partly to co-opt able individuals into the existing social structure rather than risk their unmet aspirations turning into some sort of rebellion. Nearly half a century ago this longstanding foundation of provision was explicitly hardened into the assertion by the Robbins Committee that:

> it is a proper function of higher education, as of education in schools, to provide in partnership with the family that background of culture and social habit upon which a healthy society depends. This function, important at all times, is perhaps especially important in an age that has set for itself the ideal of equality of opportunity. It is not merely by providing places for students from all classes that this ideal will be achieved, but also by providing, in the atmosphere of the institutions in which the students live and work, influences that in some measure compensate for any inequalities of home background. These influences are not limited to the student population. Universities and colleges have an important role to play in the general cultural life of the communities in which they are situated.
>
> (CHE, 1963: para 28)

Robbins clearly had a firm belief that universities and colleges have a role in honing and transmitting social and cultural values as well as skills and knowledge, a belief at odds with the recent idea that the student as customer knows what is best for them and that the pursuit by each of their own interests is in the best interest of society as a whole. This is at the heart of most controversies about the aims of higher education. Is it an activity in which the customer knows best or is the student a neophyte who comes to university to be guided by those who are more knowledgeable or wiser? As always in the social sciences the answer is not straightforward. The question for political economists is how the economic losses and benefits compare as the system becomes increasingly marketized.

An argument in favour of a market approach is that higher education has become a very differentiated set of activities in which the best way forward to achieve one aim is not inevitably compatible with another. For example, it is not hard to recognize tensions between those who believe the top priority is for the most able young people in a range of intellectual endeavours to have the opportunity to stretch their talents in an environment conducive to the highest levels of scholarship, and those for whom the top priority is ensuring some equivalent provision for people whose abilities are more modest. In 2012 – the year of the London Olympics – it is hard not to see an analogy with sport. Are public funds better spent in enabling a few individuals to win gold medals or is it preferable to concentrate on promoting sporting endeavours amongst the non-elite mass of the population? Obviously the two are not entirely incompatible, but neither are they completely harmonious. In a market there is, in principle, a niche for everything, whereas in politically determined systems it is very difficult to make such choices since favouring one activity appears to be at the disadvantage of others and democratic governments that take unpopular decisions do not get elected. (For an academic analysis of these issues see Buchanan and Tullock, 1958.)

But the ethical benefits of the invisible hand are based on not-always-met assumptions. In higher education the market is far from perfect, the implications of which have been recently well analysed by Roger Brown (Brown and Carasso, 2013). There are considerable costs of entry in most STEM (science, technology, engineering, medicine) courses, for example, and the commercial returns from creating the facilities necessary for research and teaching in such areas are extremely uncertain. Private commercial universities are unlikely to teach or do research in such subjects. Within multi-faculty universities there are many opportunities for sharing facilities and cross-subsidization instead of profit taking. There are many services that can be jointly provided within institutions – an expensive computer system needed to meet the needs of engineers can provide services at marginal cost for historians, for example. Furthermore, many of the economic returns to higher education and for research, both for individuals and for society, are long term. Expenditure on higher education is a long-term investment and competitive markets are not usually enthusiastic about investments that bring uncertain returns only in the distant future.

The main restraint on a fully marketized provision of higher education is equity. It is not difficult to find private funding, from both employers and students' families, for low cost but well-rewarded areas such as law and accountancy. Many employers are also willing to finance students who have the potential to be high flyers in their future careers. In England several legal and accountancy firms have been reported in the media as providing scholarships and bursaries and subsidizing courses for the most promising individuals in these areas. The transformation of the private College of Law into an academically autonomous university and the concentration of commercial providers in various aspects of business studies have already been mentioned. In liberal arts subjects it was apparently not too difficult for the New College of the Humanities to obtain private backing provided it restricted entry to students who had performed particularly well in secondary education and might have just missed a place at Oxford or Cambridge. Even for staunch advocates of markets it is hard to see what the trickle-down effect of teaching safe subjects to safe students would be without government interference.

Markets involve competition on the basis of price and perceived quality, which invariably means that differentiation becomes stratification. It was over a century ago that Thorstein Veblen invented the phrase 'conspicuous consumption' to indicate the purchase of goods or services not to satisfy needs or wants in the most economical way but rather to identify oneself to others as having superior wealth and social standing (Veblen, 1994). Bourdieu (1986) used the term 'symbolic capital' to designate a similar idea. It is not difficult to see how institutional diversity within mass higher education lends itself to conspicuous consumption. In an article a few years ago I suggested that the concept of mass higher education has become somewhat misleading. The more marketized a higher education system, the more it consists not of a network of complementary institutions but rather of a series of concentric circles, with the most sought after traditional elite formation at the centre surrounded by a belt of high-level professional formation – which in turn is surrounded by a loose collection of more or less open access activities with rather blurred boundaries (Williams and Filippakou, 2010).

This view is exacerbated by the complementary function of research. There is a close, though not identical, link between the formation of an elite, and leading-edge, internationally recognized research universities – probably because the ablest students prefer to be taught by the most distinguished scholars (see Wiles, 1974). The professional formation belt of institutions is associated with applied research that often depends on original discoveries made elsewhere. The diffuse penumbra, meanwhile, is more often concerned with consultancy-type activities that apply research to practical problems in wider society. These are all absolutely necessary functions in a modern higher education system but it is unclear whether market solutions will organize them in an optimal way, especially if they result in the banding of institutions I have suggested.

All markets are subject to some measure of regulation, though this may range from individual integrity and self-discipline, through collective self-regulation, to statutory regulation by governments. Historically, British universities have always been legally autonomous institutions and their Royal Charters enabled them to do anything not expressly forbidden by them or the law of the land. However, as the previous quotation by Robbins suggested, they also submitted to an implied code of conduct in which it was considered inappropriate for a university or its members to move outside a limited range of traditional activities. While very honourable, this formed a fundamentally conservative attitude which made it difficult for new subjects to become established or for new ideas about teaching and learning to be accepted. The University Grants Committee system, which channelled public funds into universities until 1989, underwrote this conservatism in being composed of senior academics and by making unhypothecated grants to universities. Compared with the enormous contributions made by members of British and American universities in winning the Second World War, meanwhile, the constraints of German universities in the period leading to and during it demonstrated the value of relatively affluent academic freedom underpinned by ethically driven individual self-regulation.

However, such a system could not survive massive expansion and the huge increases in public funding it implied. It depended in large part on the existence of ample resources, on all the universities involved having similar interests, and on an implied compact between the universities and the governments that provided resources. Expansion meant diversification and increasing concern by governments to ensure that resources were used efficiently and in accordance with their priorities. The period from the 1960s to the 1990s saw increasing government monitoring and regulation of university activities (for detailed accounts see Shattock, 2012 and Brown and Carasso, 2013) and the creation of a powerful sector of higher education under more direct public control. The end of a system based ultimately on mutual trust came with the 1988 Education Reform Act. In the 1990s growing tensions between financially autonomous higher education institutions mounted and vastly increased monitoring and regulation by central government.

A bridge too far?

The final sections of this chapter consider whether, from an economic perspective, there are – or should be – limits to the marketization of higher education, and I suggest specifically that the idea of profit-making by universities is a step too far.

The two central weaknesses of markets as mechanisms for the strategic allocation of resources are their tendency to prioritize short-term decision-making and their lack of concern with how the outcome of the large number of individual decisions that make up a market distributes costs and benefits. The result are periods of unsustainable optimism and others of irredeemable pessimism – booms and busts – that we might liken to Keynes' 'animal spirits' exhibiting symptoms of bi-polar disorder. Second-order problems are venality – as the boundaries of legality and commercial acceptability are tested to the limit – and of extreme complexity, as authorities try to regulate and correct market failures.

The outcomes of both research and teaching can be appreciated only in the long term. For students, higher education is a set of experiences, most of which bring returns – such as higher average earnings for graduates and the wider benefits of improved citizenship, healthier lifestyles, and a lower propensity to commit crimes (Schuller *et al.*, 2004) – over a long period of time. It is important that universities match students' abilities and interests to courses that are most appropriate for them. However, when universities are totally dependent on the number of students they recruit, pressures mount to cut corners and recruit as many students as possible, without too much concern for whether students and courses are matched as well as possible. Such fevered recruitment has been apparent in the past two decades in the scramble for students from outside the United Kingdom (Forland, 2006).

In markets where repeat purchases are normal, consumers learn from experience and can avoid suppliers who fail to deliver satisfactory goods and services. Such avoidance is rarely possible in higher education: when making their choices of course and university or college, students rely largely on the experiences of their predecessors and the claims made by institutions seeking their custom. Much course advertising stresses the short-term benefits of a university: the immediate learning experiences, the social life, the speed of tutorial feedback on assignments, and the student societies, for example. In England the now compulsory Key Information Sets (KIS), which all universities are required to provide, concentrate mainly on short-term measures. While there is emphasis on the first employment experiences of recent graduates, no mention is made of longer-term prospects. In reality, many of the students from the most well-informed families choose to attend old, established, research intensive universities with well-established records of alumni in leading positions in society. Their doing so strongly contributes to the stratification of universities, one characteristic feature of a marketized system. Longevity is one of the main indicators of distinction.

'Whosoever hath, to him shall be given, and he shall have more abundance: but whosoever hath not, from him shall be taken away even that he hath' (Matthew, 13.12). It is not completely clear whether Jesus Christ was endorsing such an outcome, or merely describing one of the features of the Roman Empire. But two millennia later we can recognize it as an attribute of current global economic arrangements, one widely accepted as an inevitable and acceptable consequence of rapid economic growth through market competition.

Market competition also exalts inequities in individual sectors of the economy. In any industry some products and some enterprises succeed while others fail, as much the case in higher education as it is in more obviously commercial sectors. In the United Kingdom, so far university failures have been cushioned by mergers and takeovers and occasionally by support from public funds. But inequality in some service activities risks having particularly damaging and long-term consequences. Health and policing come to mind but the long-term effects of educational inequalities are also especially detrimental. Despite efforts to promote lifelong learning opportunities, it is inevitable both for psychological and economic reasons that the bulk of most individuals' education will be obtained early in life and will be a largely once for all experience. Ill-judged decisions taken in an environment of fierce competition for the custom of often immature minds affect people's life chances throughout their course. The inequitable consequences of inequalities in education, including higher education, are long lasting impediments to a harmonious society.

In any economic or social organization there is always a risk of corruption, as some people in positions of influence use their power for their own advantage rather than for that of the organization or society to which they owe allegiance. The principal–agent problem is intrinsic to any large-scale, complex organization or system. In a competitive market system those in positions of authority are particularly susceptible to temptation, especially if they promote entrepreneurial behaviour where success is measured largely in terms of effective innovations, which often means bending the rules, sometimes to breaking point. Traditional higher education systems have been tempted into adopting rules and procedures that operate more to advance the careers of academics providing the education and research than those of the students they were supposed to be serving. However, the adoption of market values and financial incentives greatly increases the temptation. Several cases have come to light showing student numbers being misreported or that advertising to attract overseas students is misleading, as have cases highlighting research plagiarism, allegations of manipulating students' grades, and, in a few instances, public funding being misappropriated and job applicants providing misleadingly embellished curricula vitae.

None of the problems outlined is insurmountable. They are all, in one way or another, examples of the principal–agent problem that is well known in economics. The more decision-making is devolved and organizations are encouraged to compete with one another, the harder it is to ensure that agents act in the common interest rather than for their own individual advantage. Some libertarians claim that this is a public benefit, even if it does lead to wide inequalities. But regulation and audit are common features of markets and even where states do not regulate, trade associations often set rules and standards for their members.

Short-termism can, in principle, at least be ameliorated by providing university funds on a long-term basis. For the UK's University Grants Committee, this was an underlying rationale of its quinquennial grant system from 1919 to the late 1970s, when it became one of the casualties of expansion and diversification. An alternative in a market-oriented system is endowments, which give universities some long-term control over their own resources. Well-endowed universities remain susceptible to certain of the vagaries of financial markets – as was shown in the United States in 2008–10 – but they are relieved to a large extent of the necessity to respond to every whim of consumer opinion. The danger, as Adam Smith observed, is excessive conservatism and an extreme toleration of self-interest. However, annual budgeting, which much of the quasi-contractual funding of new public management involves, exacerbates short-termism rather than alleviating it.

Inequities can be ameliorated through new public management techniques. For higher education, this involves making public funds available on a contractual basis so universities are not subject to direct control by the government. However, it does involve detailed monitoring of how the funds are used. British higher education institutions have, since 1989, received almost all their funding on contractual terms, either through public funding of clearly defined teaching and research activities or through private contracts to perform specific tasks. In English universities currently, targets are set for enrolments of categories of students deemed to be under-represented and there are threats to withdraw funds if these targets are not met. Alternatively, extra funding can be made available for students who are deemed by public authorities to merit such positive discrimination.

Inevitable questions that might be raised in response are: Who is entitled to positive discrimination? Are those who are able to take advantage of it really capable of benefitting from challenging courses? And does it result in unfairness towards those not considered to be entitled to the special treatment? Such matters have played out in the courts of the United States and on the whole were found to be unconstitutional. However, in 2003, a Supreme Court decision regarding affirmative action in higher education permitted educational institutions to consider race as a factor – a small plus factor – when admitting students, but ruled that strict point systems, like the one previously used by the University of Michigan Law School, are unconstitutional (Perry, 2007). Some states such as California have passed constitutional amendments banning affirmative action within their respective states (Myers, 2007).

Payment of fees by students subsidized by loans or grants is how the UK higher education systems are attempting to safeguard equity while shifting towards a fully marketized system. However, this begs the question – and creates the problem – of how to define both eligibility for grants or subsidized loans and the criteria for the latter's repayment out of subsequent and higher graduate incomes. HEPI (2012) has shown that likely repayments may leave substantial public sector deficits in relation to original estimates because of slight differences in prospective graduate earnings. It may also prove difficult to ensure that loans are repaid by European Union students who are legally required to receive the same subsidy as UK students but whose subsequent earnings cannot be checked by the British revenue authorities.

Improper management or dishonesty can be dealt with by intensive monitoring and audit accompanied by appropriate penalties for infringements. Certain British universities have been fined considerable sums for over-recruiting on student target numbers and occasionally for submitting misleading statistical returns about numbers of students and course completions.

It is my contention in this chapter that all the risks associated with market behaviour are likely to become more apparent the nearer higher education comes to being a service provided on an entirely financially transactional basis. As the examples in the previous paragraphs show, most of the weaknesses of marketized higher education can be overcome, but the 'steering from a distance' – that is, getting agents to act in ways the principals believe they should – involves extremely considerable transaction costs. As well as the costs of the regulatory procedures, these also include the advertising and marketing costs necessary for universities to compete with each other for students' custom. Such costs increase as institutions are given more financial autonomy: the widespread introduction of a profit-seeking motivation may be the straw that breaks the camel's back.

Conclusion

In the 1980s there was some justification for imposing a certain amount of market discipline on higher education institutions. There are reasons to believe that, at that time, producer capture of the system meant that some students at least were not receiving the learning experiences they had a right to expect. For individual members of staff, as well as their departments, success in research was usually more rewarding than success in teaching. The government's response was the Act of 1988 which made it clear that universities received public funds for the teaching and research services they provided. However, this was necessarily accompanied by a substantial increase in the statistical reports universities were required to make and more external scrutiny of their teaching and research. It also led to massive increases in the majority's marketing activities.

Such changes have hugely increased institutions' transaction costs – that is, the proportion of their total income spent on management and administration rather than directly on teaching and research. I have shown in earlier works that there initially was evidence that both teaching and research improved in a more competitive environment (Williams, 2004). The question facing those who make higher education policy in 2013 and beyond is whether these trends have gone too far. A major shift towards higher education provision by profit-making organizations, for which the financial bottom line is the key performance indicator, is likely to lead to even greater transaction costs than those currently facing a system presently largely marketized but which is nonetheless charitable at root.

Of course it may be that the whole ethos of higher education provision will change and Robbins's aspirations will become simply outdated. In an article some thirty years ago (Williams and Gordon, 1981) I showed that parents of most secondary school students wanted their daughters and sons to go on to higher education because it would likely lead to subsequently higher incomes, and that only teachers and academics thought personal development and cultural improvement were the main reasons for going to university. It may be that the commodification of higher education is acceptable to the majority of the population. That is an ethical and political issue, not an economic one.

Adam Smith's scribbling on the subject of financing higher education over two centuries ago has certainly found its way into the hearts and minds of men in authority, but I doubt whether the author of *The Theory of Moral Sentiments*, who accepted that social morality was largely a matter of convention but believed in the last analysis that wrong was recognizable by any reasonable person, ever imagined universities being driven mainly by the search for financial profit.

References

Arrow, K. (1973) 'Higher education as a filter'. *Journal of Public Economics*, 2 (3), 193–216.

Berg, I. (1971) *Education and Jobs: The great training robbery*. Boston: Beacon.

BIS (Department for Business, Innovation and Skills) (2011) *Higher Education: Students at the heart of the system*. London: BIS.

Blaug, M. (1970) *An Introduction to the Economics of Education*. London: Allen Lane.

Bourdieu, P. (1986). 'The forms of capital'. In Richardson, J.G. (ed.) *Handbook for Theory and Research for the Sociology of Education*. Westport, CT: Greenwood Press.

Bourdieu, P., and Passeron, J.C. (1977) *Reproduction in Education, Society, and Culture*. London: Sage.

Bowles, S. and Gintis, H. (1976) *Schooling in Capitalist America: Educational reform and the contradictions of economic life*. New York: Basic Books.

Brown, R. and Carasso, H. (2013) *Everything for Sale? The Marketization of UK higher education (Research into Higher Education)*. London: Routledge and SRHE.

Buchanan, J.M. and Tullock, G. (1958) *The Calculus of Consent: Logical foundations of constitutional democracy*. Indianapolis: Library of Economics and Liberty.

Collins, R. (1979) *The Credential Society*. New York: Academic Press.

CHE (Committee on Higher Education) (1963) *Higher Education: A report by the committee appointed by the Prime Minister under the chairmanship of Lord Robbins, 1961–63 (The Robbins Report)*. London: HMSO.

Denison, E. (1962) *The Sources of Economic Growth in the United States and the Alternatives Before Us*. New York: Committee for Economic Development New York.

—(1968) *Why Growth Rates Differ; Post-war experience in nine western countries*. Washington, DC: Brookings Institution.

Easterlin, R.A., McVey, L.A., Switek, M., Sawangfa, O., and Smith Zweig, J. (2010) 'The Happiness–Income Paradox Revisited'. *Proceedings of the National Academy of Sciences of the USA*, 107 (52). Online. www.pnas.org/content/early/2010/12/08/1015962107.full.pdf

Forland H. (2006) 'The international student learning experience: bridging the gap between rhetoric and reality'. Paper presented at Going Global 2, the UK's international education conference held in Edinburgh, 6–8 December.

Glennerster, H. (1968) *A Graduate Tax*. London: Allen Lane.

HEPI (Higher Education Policy Institute) (2012) *The Cost of the Government's Reforms of the Financing of Higher Education*. Oxford: HEPI.

HESA (Higher Education Statistics Agency) (2011) Press Release 159 – Survey of private and for-profit providers of higher education in the UK 2009/10. Cheltenham: HESA.

HMRC (Her Majesty's Revenue and Customs) (2012) *VAT: Consideration of the case to extend the education exemption to for-profit providers of higher education*. Consultation document. London: HMRC.

Keynes, J.M. (1936) *General Theory of Employment, Interest and Money*. London: Macmillan.

Kinser, K. and Levey, D.C. (2006) 'For-profit higher education: US tendencies, international echoes'. In Forest, J.F. and Altbach, P.G. (eds) *International Handbook of Higher Education: Springer International Handbooks of Education*. Vol. 18. New York: Springer.

Lyotard, J-F. (1984) *The Postmodern Condition: A report on knowledge*. Trans. Bennington, G. and Massumi, B. Minneapolis: University of Minnesota Press.

Myers, C. (2007) 'A cure for discrimination? Affirmative action and the case of California's proposition 209'. *Industrial & Labor Relations Review*, 60, 379.

Naidoo, R. (2003) 'Repositioning higher education as a global commodity: opportunities and challenges for future sociology of education work'. *British Journal of Sociology of Education*, 24 (2).

Neave, G. and Van Vught, F.A. (1991) 'Conclusion'. In Neave, G. and Van Vught, F.A. (eds) *Prometheus Bound: The changing relationship between government and higher education in Western Europe.* Oxford: Pergamon Press.

OECD (Organisation for Economic Co-operation and Development) (1995) *Governance in Transition: Public management reforms in OECD countries.* Paris: OECD.

—(2011) *Education at a Glance.* Paris: OECD.

Perry, B. (2007) *The Michigan Affirmative Action Cases.* Lawrence: University Press of Kansas.

Psacharopoulos, G. (1973) *Returns to Education: An international comparison.* Amsterdam: Elsevier.

—(1985) 'Returns to education: a further international update and implications'. *Journal of Human Resources*, 20 (4), 583–604.

Schuller, T., Preston, J., Hammond, C., Brasset-Grundy, A., and Bynner, J. (2004) *The Benefits of Learning: The impact of educational on health, family life and social capital.* London: Routledge.

Shattock, M. (2012) *Making Policy in British Higher Education: 1945–2011.* London: Routledge/SRHE.

Smith, A. (2010) *The Theory of Moral Sentiments.* Originally 1759. New York: Penguin Group USA.

—(1904) *An Inquiry into the Nature and Causes of the Wealth of Nations* (ed. Cannon, E.) 5th ed. London: Methuen.

Taubman, P.J. and Wales, T.J. (1973) 'Higher education, mental ability, and screening'. *Journal of Public Economics*, 81, 28–55.

Turner, R.H. (1961) 'Modes of social ascent through education: sponsored and contest mobility'. In Halsey, A.L., Floud, J., and Anderson, J. (eds) *Education, Economy and Society.* New York: Free Press.

Universities UK (2010) *The growth of private and for-profit higher education providers in the UK.* London: Universities UK.

Veblen, T. (1994) *Theory of the Leisure Class: An economic study in the evolution of institutions.* Originally 1988. London: Penguin Classics.

Wiles, P. (1974) 'The correlation between education and earnings: the external-test-not-content hypothesis (ETNC)'. *Higher Education*, 3 (1).

Williams, G. (2004) 'The higher education market in the United Kingdom'. In Teixera, P., Joengbloed, B., Dill, D., and Amaral, A. (eds) *Markets in Higher Education: Rhetoric or reality.* Norwell, MA: Kluwer Academic Publishers.

Williams, G. and Filippakou, O. (2010) 'Higher education and UK elite formation in the twentieth century'. *Higher Education*, 59 (1).

Williams, G. and Gordon, A. (1981) 'Perceived earnings functions and ex ante rates of return to post-compulsory education in England'. *Higher Education*, 10 (2).

Chapter 5

The end of mystery and the perils of explicitness
Ronald Barnett

Introduction

My argument in this chapter takes the following form. Within the White Paper *Higher Education: Students at the Heart of the System* lies a tacit idea of 'student'. A student (both before and following admission), according to the White Paper, is clear about her wants in relation to her higher education, makes rational choices about her course of study, is able to capture cogently her experience (in 'student satisfaction' surveys), is 'engaged' with her programme of study, is concerned about the number of class contact hours, and is developing her skills for the workplace. In turn, a course can be explicitly captured in a 'key information set', and its providers will work with employers in identifying the necessary skills to be taught. Among the assumptions in this set of ideas is the belief that a course can be explicitly set out in documents and data such that a student can form in advance a detailed sense of the experience awaiting her. Subsequently, when enrolled, a student can come to a total understanding of her course. All the features of a course, it seems, can be made transparent. All can be set out.

However, a genuinely higher education cannot be completely and explicitly described in advance of it happening or even when a student is enrolled on it – and this for three interrelated reasons. Firstly, a genuinely higher education is an unfolding process. It is a set of flows, unpredictable to a significant extent. Secondly, a genuinely higher education calls upon the student to give of herself. It is an encounter with strangeness that invites the student to venture forward in her own way. In the process, the student will acquire certain dispositions and qualities. The educational processes that a student experiences are significant in their own right, therefore, but that experience is partly a matter of the student's own efforts. A course is not separate from the student enrolled on it: the course and the student inhabit overlapping spaces. Thirdly, a sense of mystery inheres in the process of a genuinely higher education, in the sense that it is resistant to being made fully explicit. It lies in the minutiae of the spontaneous gesture and inflexion, in the spaces being opened, in the opportunities for nomadic venturing, and in the imaginative perceptions of the moment. Calling for explicitness in and of a course offering is like calling for explicitness in the meaning of a poem.

In its search for transparency, therefore, the White Paper is a pernicious ideology at work (Barnett, 2003). Its latent function is to produce a process devoid of spontaneity and unpredictability and likely to produce a student who might be 'satisfied' but whose experiences fall short of higher education's transforming potential. It heralds an anodyne process, with an absence of difficulty, challenge, and wonder. The White Paper would work to draw in horizons of thought and human unfolding, limiting the students' potential development.

While my argument here draws its impulse from the recent UK White Paper, it can and should be read as an argument about the marketization of higher education. As such it can apply to any system that has or is acquiring such a character.

Driving teaching excellence

Chapter 2 of the White Paper is entitled 'Well-informed students driving teaching excellence'. Both phrases – 'well-informed students' and 'driving teaching excellence' – are problematic. The idea of a well-informed student begs a number of questions: about what is it that a student is supposed to be informed? Should the student be well-informed, for instance, about the total number of hours her tutors and lecturers are working each week or the range of demands on their time and how this might limit their accessibility or ability to offer the student the support she needs? Can a student *ever* be well-informed about crucial aspects of her experience, such as the micro dimensions of her likely pedagogical situation? To what extent, for example, might a department of French realise that its pedagogical signature – as we may term it – is markedly different from that of the Italian department in the same building of the same university?

The phrase 'a well-informed student' further, and more significantly, begs questions as to the concept of student that lies within it, for it may tacitly work to pose a sense of the student separate from her pedagogical situation instead of being immersed in it. The very notion of students being well-informed about the situation in which they find themselves could reasonably imply students who are passive spectators of the situation about which they are trying to be informed. The student here is not part of the pedagogical situation and so has a limited responsibility towards the character of the pedagogical situation. Her course experience is conveyed all too easily here as a set of activities, processes, and materials presented to her, about which she has a right to be well-informed.

'Driving teaching excellence' also begs questions. 'Teaching excellence' is the object here, not 'learning excellence'. Here, again, the student's presence in the pedagogical situation is diminished. At stake is the quality of teaching the student receives, not her learning as such and nor, in turn, her part in (driving towards) her own learning excellence. Again, the student is set apart from her pedagogical situation, posited as an individual who deserves an experience that is excellent in its own right. That teaching excellence might have some relationship to learning excellence, and that learning excellence is in part dependent on the student, is hardly on the cards here in this policy framework.

The idea, too, implicit in this formulation, that excellence might be a general attribute of students' (plural) experiences across a system, is problematic since the concept of 'excellence' is necessarily a relational concept: if all entities or instances in a set are judged to be 'excellent', then the concept of excellence is largely shorn of its meaning. Further, the use of such a generalized application of 'excellence' can only serve to impose undue demands on an already stressed system since every instance is expected to be 'excellent'.

Perhaps, though, the most problematic term in the title of the chapter is that of 'driving', with its implication that well-informed students will and should be able to drive teaching excellence. 'Driving', of course, is a metaphor. It conjures, variously, a sense of a machine being driven (parallel to a student driving a car), or a sense of control in an otherwise disorderly situation (a cattle-owner driving his herd to a market), or a sense of a transmission of energy (as in one part of an engine driving another part). In each interpretation, the metaphor implies that the student is in a position of power, not just directly able to realise a pedagogical situation of increasing quality but *legitimately* able to do so. The implied powers of the tutors are, accordingly, diminished. Such a reading points to a de-professionalization of tutors: the power in the pedagogical situation is to be assumed by the students. It is they who are to drive towards teaching excellence.

Explicitness

The idea that students-as-customers can 'drive' excellence is linked in the White Paper, as intimated, to the idea of students being well-informed – and the latter idea is linked to the idea of explicitness. If students are to become well-informed through the provision of large quantities of data about their course experience and the opportunities it makes available, assumptions are being made here about the possibilities and power of explicitness: by making the relevant data explicit, students will be better informed, which will thus make higher education 'more responsive' as a market (BIS, 2011: para 2.8). Explicitness (in data provision) becomes a pivot, therefore, on which the policy framework turns. Indeed, the theme of explicitness is pervasive in the White Paper.

The White Paper looks to each university to make available on its website certain kinds of information and 'on an easily comparable basis' (BIS, 2011: para 2.10). 'These items, together with information about course charges, are [to be] called the Key Information Set (KIS) and will be available on a course by course basis' (*ibid*). That 'information set' contains 20 different kinds of information – listed in full in an appendix to this chapter – and is to be set out under the following four headings: course information (a key section here is that of 'student satisfaction', itself opening to eight sub-sections), costs, employment, and the students' union.

This apparent panoply of information institutions are being asked to provide turns out to be far from exhaustive. The White Paper goes on to express the hope that institutions will want to go on expanding the information they provide to students, mentioning, for instance, that 'it would be good practice for institutions to provide the sort of material that local councils offer to their residents, demonstrating what their council tax is being invested in' (BIS, 2011: para 2.12). The Paper also points to the government's intention to develop 'a national source of clear and comparable information', which it intends over time to build up from various national data sources 'so that prospective students can make more useful comparisons between subjects at different institutions' (BIS, 2011: para 2.15). It further exhorts a range of national agencies in higher education to develop their own websites so that, institution by institution and course by course, 'students can compare likely earnings' (BIS, 2011: para 2.18).

In itself, there can hardly be much objection to the idea that students should be able to have prior access to information on courses, in advance of deciding at which institution they might aspire to study. As a key part of a developing policy framework, however, two questions are prompted by such an idea: Is there a limit to the range and amount of information it is proper to seek from institutions and to provide to students *and* what might be the latent effects of providing such information?

On the first matter it can reasonably be judged that, of the range and amount of information being sought, there shall be no end. After all, no limit exists to the degree to which a student might become better informed about potential courses. It is difficult to see, therefore, why any limit might be imposed once the government starts asking institutions to generate such information. Certainly, no considerations are offered that might lead to a dispassionate reckoning of the value of providing such information – such as the possible overload of information on would-be students or the challenges they might have in making sense of information from disparate institutions, or the opportunity costs to institutions, for example.

On the second matter, potential latent effects could be very serious. The most serious might encourage the student to come to see herself precisely as a customer, purchasing a product. It could, in other words, orient the student towards adopting a passive stance, tacitly holding a sense that in return for the payment of her fee her student experience will be determined for her in a way that displaces any sense she might have of being significantly responsible for shaping that experience.

This pedagogical effect could go even further. As the sense of higher education as a market grows, and institutions come evermore to compete with each other for students, institutions may well be encouraged in their marketing ploys to emphasize the more enjoyable aspects of university life (especially on a particular campus) and also to devote more resources to student support services. Here, there opens – unwittingly – a path to, as it has been termed, the infantilization of students (Ecclestone and Hayes, 2009): a possible tendency to treat students as children, declining to treat them as adults with responsibilities towards themselves, and a subsequent disinclination to be explicit about the challenging nature of a genuinely higher education.

A pernicious transparency

One further possible latent effect of giving emphasis – 'driving', as it might be termed – to the provision of information lies again in the matter of explicitness. Within the drive towards the provision of public information could lie a presupposition that any valuable feature of the student experience can be made explicit. Such a view reflects the assumptive world (Sabri, 2010) within policy framing that holds that all can be made transparent. Ultimately, the would-be student need leave nothing to chance: her course can be fully described in advance of her enrolment and the subject contents of the course in question, its mode of delivery, its curricula hours, its forms of assessment, and its likely labour market prospects can all be set out.

In such a mindset and in its policy framing lies a pernicious transparency. It is not merely the point that a department, however self-aware and self-critical, is unlikely to fully understand the character of the student experience it opens – there is bound to be a degree of pedagogical blindness in any department towards its own courses. It is not even the point that students differ – that one may take a casual remark on an essay in her stride, while another might be traumatized by the same single phrase. And, if so, what is transparency to mean under such circumstances? It is not even the point that crucial matters of the student experience are observed and felt in the micro pedagogical processes at work and are only caught with the most sensitive of reflective instruments. It is the more penetrating point that much that is valuable in higher education is *always* beyond a full description. Much never *can* be made explicit.

There are two reasons here. Firstly, no matter how much lecturers, universities, and other agencies, such as professional bodies, attempt to set programmes of study within tight boundaries, still there will be elements of unpredictability in the pedagogical situation. Students might pose unexpected questions and surprising evidence or ideas might be uncovered – either by lecturer or by students – in the relevant research literature. More significantly, the pedagogical situation within a genuinely higher education is an open space – a space of reason indeed (Bakhurst, 2011) – in which the pedagogical dialogue is relatively unconstrained (except by rules of fair reasoning and critical dialogue). Consequently, the pedagogical situation is a situation of openness, always liable to yield an insight, idea, or utterance of some originality. It is a situation of some spontaneity and potential creativity.

Secondly, there are, in higher education, elements of mystery, as it may be reasonably termed (Cooper, 2002). That a higher education experience can transform a person's life, that a person can be inspired during the course of her studies as a result of her encounters with her field of study, lecturers, and others, that her studies can lead her to be genuinely creative and even original, that pedagogical experiences can be at once sources of delight, provocation, intrigue, anxiety, and exhilaration: we have no serious understanding as to how the transformatory potential of higher education effects its magic – even after 50 years of cross-national research into higher education on student learning, not to mention two thousand years of reflection since the Greeks on the 'epistemic virtues' (Brady and Pritchard, 2003) a liberal education might wrought.

There is, in other words, a gap between our descriptions of higher education and what actually happens on a daily basis. In part the situation is an indication of the impoverishment of concepts and methods used in the 'scholarship of teaching and learning'. But it is also, surely, an indication too of the intractability of higher education's pedagogical processes, of there always being a 'beyond' that is not susceptible to conventional research techniques. There is a necessary elusiveness about higher education that evades explanation and even description. We can never give a full account of what is happening in such transformatory pedagogical situations.

Accordingly then, genuine encounters and transactions in higher education contain an element of mystery. Talk of the complexity of interactions between lecturer, student (singular), students (plural), and the discipline or professional field, with its own corpus of knowledge, understandings, and ways of going on ('skills') only testifies to the limitations of our understandings. Some have even spoken of a holy ground here, and others of sacredness, where conversations take place and effort is made to enter and inhabit a space with its own infinities, evanescences, and subtleties. It is a space in which individuals may take off and ascend into a space of their own. (John Henry Newman was keen on the metaphor of 'ascent' in his depiction of liberal education.) As Richard Peters used to say, much of this can only be caught rather than taught.

If any of this carries weight, we can sense something of the ideology of transparency so evident in the White Paper. The text exemplifies, as noted, the belief that all that is significant about higher education can be made explicit. Two further points must be made here. Firstly, the undue belief in the powers of explicitness focuses attention on just those aspects of higher education that can be made explicit and expressed in simple (and characteristically numerical) terms: the number of curriculum hours, the proportions of students attaining employment in different professions, and the proportions gaining 'good' degrees. In the process, the more elusive aspects of higher education are not merely overlooked: they become invisible. No attempt is made to give an account of the pedagogical ethos, its tone, and its spaciousness, for example.

Secondly, and in turn, higher education – as a matter of public discourse – becomes reduced to its superficial characteristics and its transformatory potential is lost from view. As a result, the public understanding of the possibilities it may offer is severely and unduly limited. More perniciously still, institutions (including students' teachers) may come to sense that their responsibility lies in controlling and tightly bounding the space of the students' educational experience. Rather than encouraging a pedagogy of risk, in which a space is opened up for students' serendipitous and nomadic explorations, a risk-free pedagogy, devoid of metamorphosing potential, is liable to emerge.

Student engagement

Chapter 3 of the White Paper is entitled 'A better student experience and better-qualified graduates'. Its opening sentence reads as follows: 'A good student is not simply a consumer of other people's knowledge, but will actively draw on all the resources that a good university or college can offer to learn as much as they can' (BIS, 2011: para 3.1). In a section on 'student charters' it goes on to endorse the recommendation of the UK's Student Charter Group that 'each individual should have a student charter … to set out the mutual expectations of universities and students' (BIS, 2011: para 3.3). In the first sentence of the following paragraph, the White Paper emphasizes that the student's experience 'will be most enriching when it is based on a partnership between staff and students' (BIS, 2011: para 3.4). Such statements *prima facie* – in their implications of mutuality, partnership, and an active stance on the student's part, they seem to undercut many of the suggestions I posed earlier and suggest that the White Paper harbours an unduly passive sense of what it is to be a student. However, paragraph 3.4, which is a long paragraph, goes on to describe student charters more fully. Nothing in the following three sentences of that paragraph says anything about students' contribution to their own experience. On the contrary, the whole orientation of the paragraph is about institutions' provision to students and the contribution that charters can make in that way. For example, student charters: 'will help provide consistency of practice across different subject areas, such as about *what students can expect* in terms of assessment and feedback on their work' [my emphasis] (BIS, 2011: para 3.4). Nothing in this extract suggests what institutions might expect from their students. Nor does the extract justify why there should be 'consistency of practice across different subject areas'.

It might be expected that ways in which students might be actively involved in framing their own experience might be developed in the section that follows on 'student engagement'. What 'engagement' amounts to in this section, however, is students offering feedback on their modules (BIS, 2011: paras 3.5–3.9). Nothing is offered here as to the manifold ways in which students might engage of their own volition in enhancing their experience of their course of study – for example, in orchestrating their private study, in developing a schedule of work for themselves, in establishing intermediate goals for themselves, in constructing a reading programme, in engaging on course matters with the other students in the cohort, and so on and so forth. The section offers us a trivial account of 'student engagement', an account that, in turn, is likely to impoverish the student experience rather than enhance it.

How can it be that, far from leading to a 'better student experience', the White Paper's account of student engagement could actually result in its diminution? A genuinely higher education requires a student to give of herself. A higher education is an encounter with strangeness that invites the student to venture forward in her own way. It calls for the student to launch herself into a void that she makes her own. In the process, the student acquires and develops certain dispositions and qualities (Barnett, 2007):

- A will to learn
- A will to engage
- A preparedness to listen
- A preparedness to explore
- A willingness to hold oneself open to experiences
- A determination to keep going forward.

Among the qualities that students on a particular course might be expected to develop are:

- Integrity
- Carefulness
- Courage
- Resilience
- Self-discipline
- Restraint
- Respect for others
- Criticality
- Openness.

Such dispositions and qualities overlap in speaking to the 'affective grip' (Thrift, 2008: 39) that – at their best – institutions such as universities can have. However, dispositions and qualities – as I am advancing them here – differ in a number of crucial respects. The dispositions are *necessary* features of what it is to be a student, or, at least, a graduate. They are the *sine qua non* of a student having the fortitude, painstakingly, to acquire new knowledge or skills and the persistence to keep going when matters become difficult. The six dispositions have, accordingly, a universal aspect: they are *necessarily* present, and are nurtured, in any process worthy of being called higher education. The qualities, on the other hand, are much more optional, and in two respects. Qualities will be developed in different measure by different students – each student will come to form their own profile of qualities. Qualities are the kinds of attribute that lecturers recall when they come to provide references for individual students, perhaps some years after graduation. Whereas dispositions are enjoyed in common by students, qualities *differentiate* students. But qualities will also characteristically differ across disciplines and professional fields and even, perhaps, institutions – although such empirical work is, to my knowledge, yet to be conducted. Although they will overlap, disciplines and professional fields will also – we may surmise – characteristically orient their students to develop in certain kinds of ways.

Another way of describing these differences is to observe that the dispositions are – as it might be termed – *ontologically foundational.* Unless the student is forming the six dispositions listed above, they are liable to fall by the wayside, become unengaged with their studies, and ultimately withdraw. The dispositions, in other words, offer a possible line of enquiry for the considerable volume of empirical investigation into (rising) student attrition rates across the world. The hypothesis here is that rising levels of attrition are in part attributable to a dissolution of students' dispositions for learning – of their will to learn. The qualities, on other hand, are much more *ontologically optional:* though also necessary – they supply authenticity, enabling each student to feel personally involved with their studies, with going out on a path partly of their own making – their precise pattern has an openness attached to it. So students can and will differ, possibly quite profoundly, in the ways in which and the extent to which qualities unfold in them during their student journey.

It will have been noted that the term 'engagement' has appeared in the lists above and actually in the list of six dispositions, so questions arise as to how the sense of 'student engagement' posited there correlates – or doesn't – to the sense posited in the White Paper (we noticed above that the phrase is used as a significant marker in the latter, as a sub-heading for the one and a half pages, paragraphs 3.5–3.9). The two senses differ significantly, hinging, essentially, the relationship the student has to her experiences as a student. In the White Paper, the desired engagement is of an *outwardly* oriented kind: the student is being encouraged to be critical of the experiences being extended to her by the institution in question. She is expected to participate in institutions' student surveys and to offer her feedback in all manner of ways, both 'formal and informal' (BIS, 2011: para 3). Here, however, the idea of student engagement is of a much more *inner* kind: the student has an inner identity as a student, which enables her to keep going and pressing forward in engaging with her feelings and experiences.

In making this distinction between inner and outer forms of engagement, I am not suggesting that the inner engagement is entirely the student's responsibility. On the contrary: it is a major responsibility on the part of educators to nourish the student's dispositions – which are necessary to develop the student's inner engagement. The dispositions are fragile, they cannot be taken for granted. Indeed, unwittingly, they can be easily damaged, by a single careless word in a classroom situation or when commenting – giving 'feedback' – on a student's essay. But the will to learn ultimately belongs to the student. The teacher might want the student to acquire the will to learn (and the other associated learning dispositions) – indeed, it is fair to say that encouraging the dispositions is the teacher's primary responsibility, and that they can – and should – strive as much as possible to help nurture and sustain them – but ultimately it has to be the student who drives herself forward, wanting to learn, to explore, and to engage with her educational experiences. It follows that, in large part, her educational experiences will be opened by the student herself.

Another way of putting such points is to observe that the kind of engagement being advocated by the White Paper is *bureaucratic*. The student is being enjoined to take up opportunities to: engage in giving feedback on her educational experiences to the institution concerned on 'what to do if expected standards are not met' (BIS, 2011: para 3.4), engage in 'student surveys' (*ibid*: para 3.5), and engage in 'student evaluations of teaching surveys' (*ibid*: para 3.7). Again, none of this is, in itself, to be criticized. What is missing is any account of the student being *pedagogically* engaged, and the responsibilities that idea places on the student – as well as on her institution.

Students at the heart of the system

There is, then, a large void in the White Paper. While its subtitle is 'students at the heart of the system', how it frames what it means to place students at the heart of the system is unbalanced, focusing on the student's bureaucratic engagement and largely silent on her pedagogical engagement. Such asymmetry is surely connected with the government's drive to develop the higher education 'system' as a market. At the centre of a market lies a relationship – and an economic relationship at that – between a supplier and a customer. In turn, therefore, institutions and students are given the roles of supplier and customer, with the former supplying a 'high quality' experience to the student, and the student as customer being invited to form her views on that service's character, and to voice her complaints if the service falls short of her expectations – in other words if she is left 'unsatisfied'.

Viewing the higher education 'system' as a kind of market – and attempting to drive its development thus – downplays the student's role as a significant player in her development. In turn, learning is largely neglected in the White Paper. In its Foreword, the government ministers state that:

> We want there to be a renewed focus on high-quality teaching in universities
> so that it has the same prestige as research. So we will empower prospective
> students … We will deliver a new focus on student charters, student feedback
> and graduate outcomes. We will oversee a new regulatory framework with
> the Higher Education Funding Council for England (HEFCE) taking on a
> major role as a consumer champion.
>
> (BIS, 2011: Foreword)

There is nothing here about learning. There is not even any mention of institutions' learning and teaching strategies, which we might have expected to have been brought into play, even in helping to secure the goals of the White Paper. Nor is there any suggestion of continuing the HEFCE's role as a champion of institutions' learning and teaching strategies, both of which it has done much to promote over the past decade and more. We ought to be concerned, therefore, that this White Paper heralds a reversal in pedagogical thinking, for over the past 20 years or so the idea of teaching has been surpassed by that of learning in policy framing. Here, though, in this White Paper, learning has fallen out of view, and with it the student's responsibilities towards her own achievements. Far from heralding a development in policy, as far as the student's experience is concerned, it represents a retreat.

I have just touched on learning as a silence in this White Paper, and with it, too, the idea of student development. The latter silence is particularly astonishing: in a document subtitled 'students at the heart of the system' there is no reference, so far as I can see, to the idea that a process of higher education is one in which students actually develop, and in all manner of ways. On the contrary, what the Paper portrays, perhaps unwittingly, are students who are largely fixed, whose educational and pedagogical interests are well informed even before they enter higher education, and whose institutions function as a mere supplier of those wants. No possibility exists, therefore, that a student's wants and interests might be redefined in the course of her educational journey and through her pedagogical relationship with her institution – and perhaps radically so.

The matter is one that ought to be taken seriously since the conception of this relationship as a customer–supplier transaction serves not only to limit the student's pedagogical possibilities but to point to their (and the student's) regression. Some might take this to be an exaggeration – surely it's unlikely for students to regress, educationally – but there is long-standing evidence that students do sometimes regress, in their comprehension of key (or 'threshold') concepts, for example, which are taken on board at a surface level, without any personal insight or ownership. I noted earlier how it is possible for teachers to unwittingly – and even unknowingly – undermine students' pedagogical dispositions towards their learning. Unless students are pedagogically engaged (in the terminology adopted here), energised in favour of their learning, and investing of themselves as persons in their learning, they are liable to become disenchanted and disengaged. Under such circumstances, ultimately, their withdrawal from their course is a highly possible course of action.

To put it more formally, their *pedagogical ontology* – their being as a student – may dwindle. Far from their higher education representing, as it should, a process of their becoming (Deleuze and Guattari, 2007), the kind of market relationship the White Paper portrays could orient the system and its students towards a process of their *un*becoming. In a process of higher education, there is no pedagogical steady state available. The student is always pedagogically in motion. Either they are going forward, energized and enthused by their studies, or they are disengaged from their work, not investing their energies and commitment in it. Insofar as there might be more neutral states available, these are surely highly fragile, always liable to turn into states of disenchantment at the slightest provocation.

As I've said before, to make these observations is not to downplay the responsibilities of an institution and its teachers towards this state of affairs. On the contrary, it is to open out the way not just towards a more dynamic conception of the relationship between institution and student than is on offer in the White Paper, but also towards a much more educationally nuanced conception. Simply placing 'students at the heart of the system' is not sufficient, for it is an open matter as to what that means. When the student's educational experience is understood merely as a system in which being a student is a reactive moment, where she responds to the workings of the institution in which she finds herself, the idea of 'student' is so severely narrowed as to vanquish the possibilities that a process of higher education can open.

The ministers' defence

Were either (or both) of the ministers responsible for the White Paper to see this critique, a response might take the following line. 'We understand what you are saying and we agree with it. Of course, a good higher education experience is one in which there is a mutuality between the student and institution. That, after all, is precisely why we want to see each institution develop a student charter, so as to spell out "the mutual expectations of universities and students". Of course a good higher education experience also requires a student to be involved ("engaged") in their own studies so that they will develop in all the ways – and others (for example, in their "lifelong learning") – envisaged in this chapter. However (so the response may run on), it is no part of government to dictate such matters to institutions. These are matters of professional judgement that are properly left to lecturers and their institutions. They are not matters for national policy framing.'

Such a likely response needs to be addressed here. It seems to be a measured and fair response. It recognizes the limits of national policymaking and it explicitly recognizes a significant area of professional activity and decision-making in its own right – in which it would not be proper for the state to intervene. It seems to be setting up a dual set – and a proper apportionment – of responsibilities, with the state taking care of the financing and orchestration of the 'system' (the word used in the title of the White Paper), leaving the more educational matters to the jurisdiction of universities and other institutions of higher education. The problem, however, is that the higher education sector does not permit such a neat division of its territory.

Two points need to be made here. The first and more significant is that national policymaking, ultimately (and sometimes very quickly), has an effect on the micro character of higher education, including the student experience and the student's pedagogical relationship. Indeed, that is often precisely its point. The introduction of considerably higher fees, which will render students indebted to the state for much of their working lives, is not only a technical matter, concerning an adjustment of the income flows to institutions – much as some in the Treasury and the ministries and among vice-chancellors and some economists of higher education might want to suggest. It is a change that will have highly significant implications for the pedagogical relationship, likely to lead students to think of themselves as customers of their experience and to see their institutions as the providers of that experience.

Whether one views such a change with favour or disapproval is a separate matter: the value judgement to be made here is beside the point (at this precise point in the argument). What cannot be disputed, I think, is that though this set of major changes to the pedagogical relationship is not only likely to occur, that, precisely, is its very point. It is *intended* to introduce this market relationship into higher education and, indeed, into the student experience itself. The defence, therefore, on the part of ministers and others – that the introduction of a more market-oriented system is pedagogically neutral – would be disingenuous.

The other point to be made here, and especially in relation to this White Paper, is that the government wants not simply to make policy at the stratospherical level, leaving it to institutions to fill in the educational gaps, so to speak. On the contrary, the government wants to see instituted, and requires, the establishment of several instruments that are intra-institutional in character. Changes are being sought here to the ways in which institutions manage their own affairs – consider the establishment of student charters, a greater use of online student feedback systems (that is, feedback from students), institutions publishing summary reports of their student evaluation surveys, and the public provision of a 'key information set' with its prescribed contents. All this amounts to a complex panoply of institutional changes that some or even many institutions would otherwise have shrunk from making. The imagined response (on the state's part) to the critique I have presented – that it leaves the balance of responsibilities between the state and institutions untouched – once again seems disingenuous. Indeed, in seeking significant changes *within* institutions, the White Paper is implicitly raising matters of institutional autonomy that fall outside the scope of this chapter but deserve further attention.

It follows that there is no opening for a Pontius Pilate situation here. The government cannot wash its hands of the effects its current policy framing is having and is likely to have on institutions, the pedagogical relationship, and a student's pedagogical experience. Indeed it would be strikingly disingenuous if the government were to claim that its policies leave the student experience unchanged and, further, that that remains the province of institutions and students' teachers.

As stated, it is precisely part of the policy intentions at play here that the pedagogical relationship *is* changed, with the student exerting more influence in it as a customer. In turn, it is hardly surprising if some severe educational repercussions are also felt. And nor is the option available to the government to 'have its cake and eat it': in the presence of a *pedagogical logic* it cannot say that it only intends certain pedagogical changes (set out in this chapter) and not others to close the pedagogical space. The one option that *is* available to the government is for it to recognize its failure to consider the impact its policies, including those set out in this White Paper, are likely to have.

Conclusions

Much of the educational force of the White Paper lies in its assumptions that there is value in making explicit much of what has hitherto been somewhat hidden from view, so far as prospective and enrolled students are concerned. This set of assumptions is connected with the view that a market situation requires well-informed customers who can make rational choices about the goods they purchase and comment on and even criticise their experience from an informed position. Since, too, it is the government's intention to further orient the higher education system in the direction of a market, it follows that as much as possible should be made explicit.

Connected with this policy framing are the assumptions that students *wish* to be understood as customers, and that higher education is a kind of product that could be made transparent in advance of it being experienced, independently of the student's own efforts. Every one of these assumptions, and related others, is questionable, not only as a kind of academic exercise – academics will question anything, after all – but because the policies to which they are leading in the White Paper are *self-undermining*. Far from heralding an improvement in the student experience, the policies being proposed here are liable to lead to an *impairment* of the student experience.

Appendix: Students at the heart of the system

Key information set
(from para 2.10: 28–9)

Course information

- student satisfaction:

    a. Overall satisfaction with quality of course
    b. Staff are good at explaining things
    c. Staff have made the subject interesting
    d. Sufficient advice and support with studies
    e. Feedback on work has been prompt

    f. Feedback on work has clarified things

    g. The library resources are good enough to meet needs

    h. Access general IT resources when needed

- Proportion of time spent in different learning and teaching activities – by year of study
- Different assessment methods used – by year of study
- Professional bodies that recognize the course

Costs

- Accommodation costs
- Tuition charges
- Bursaries, scholarships and other financial support

Employment

- Destinations of students six months after completing their course (e.g. employment or further study)
- Proportion of students employed in a full-time 'graduate' job six months after completing course
- Salary for course six months after graduating
- Salary for that subject across all institutions six months after graduating
- Salary for that subject across all institutions forty months after graduating

The students' union

- Impact students' union has had on time as a student

References

Bakhurst, D. (2011) *The Formation of Reason*. Chichester: Wiley-Blackwell.

Barnett, R. (2003) *Beyond All Reason: Living with ideology in the university*. Buckingham: Open University Press and SRHE.

—(2007) *A Will to Learn: Being a student in an age of uncertainty*. Maidenhead: McGraw-Hill/ Open University Press.

BIS (Department for Business, Innovation and Skills) (2011) *Higher Education: Students at the heart of the system*. London: BIS. Online. www.gov.uk/government/uploads/system/ uploads/attachment_data/file/31384/11-944-higher-education-students-at-heart-of- system.pdf

Brady, M. and Pritchard, D. (eds) (2003) *Moral and Epistemic Virtues*. Malden, MA, and Oxford: Blackwell.

Cooper, D. (2002) *The Measure of Things: Humanism, humility, and mystery*. Oxford: Clarendon.

Deleuze, G. and Guattari, F. (2007) *A Thousand Plateaus: Capitalism and schizophrenia*. Originally 1980. London and New York: Continuum.

Ronald Barnett

Ecclestone, K. and Hayes, D. (2009) *The Dangerous Rise of Therapeutic Education*. Abingdon: Routledge.

Sabri, D. (2010) 'Absence of the academic from higher education policy'. *Journal of Education Policy*, 2, 191–205.

Thrift, N. (2008) *Non-Representational Theory: Space, politics, affect*. Abingdon and New York: Routledge.

Chapter 6

As easy as AAB: The impact of the quasi-market on institutions, student numbers and the higher education sector

Gill Wyness

Introduction

The English higher education system is still firmly rooted in the public sector. Even with the dramatic cuts to university teaching grants laid out in the White Paper (BIS, 2011), so high is the bill for student support – in the form of maintenance grants and the proportion of student loans that remains unpaid – that the government has to maintain control of student numbers, effectively restricting institutions to only enrolling a limited number of full-time students. This quota has been in place for many years and, in conjunction with constant increases in the demand for a university education, has resulted in a sector characterized by limited supply and excess demand.

An important side effect of the unequal supply and demand relationship is the little competition between institutions: some are more in demand than others but the majority are able to fill their annual quota eventually. With little subsequent competition, institutions have little incentive to improve quality, productivity, or efficiency, or to charge lower than the (government mandated) maximum tuition fee.

The White Paper aimed to overturn these restrictions on competition and supply, and move towards a more market-based system.

Removing the cap on full-time student numbers altogether would be highly expensive, so instead the Coalition has created a quasi-market. At the centre of this is the key reform outlined in the White Paper to remove the cap on student numbers – albeit on a very limited basis. From September 2012, the government abolished all quotas for students with A-level (or equivalent) grades of AAB or better. By removing controls and effecting a nearly three-fold increase in the tuition fee cap to £9,000 per year, the Coalition intended to drive some price variation amongst institutions. This would see students gravitate towards the most popular, well-run courses – which could now expand to accommodate them – and force less popular courses to either improve quality, reduce their prices, or simply shut. As an additional measure to encourage price competition (which did not immediately materialize after the increase in the tuition fee cap was announced in the months leading up to the White Paper's publication), an additional 20,000 student places within the quota system were made available to universities charging tuition fees of less than £7,500 per year.

In this chapter I explore the consequences for the higher education sector as a whole of these changes to the long-established student numbers quota, in conjunction with the increase in tuition fees. I begin by describing the impact changes to the quota system have had on different types of higher education institution, which in the short-term depends largely on what proportion of each institution's student intake achieved A-level grades of AAB or higher and whether they chose to charge fees of less than £7,500 per year. However, the impact on institutions, and to the quota system as a whole, will also depend heavily on how students respond to tuition fee increases. UCAS final estimates for 2012 outline a large decrease in applications. Compared to 2011, 46,500 fewer students applied in 2012 (UCAS, 2012c).[1] I therefore go on to examine which types of applicant appear to be most affected by the tuition fee increase – and where this, in conjunction with the quota changes, leaves the sector. But, 2012 is a transition year. Student numbers might be down, but this is typical in the first year of a fee increase and numbers tend to recover in future years, as indeed they have for younger students. Furthermore, the government has also announced that the removal of controls on AAB+ is just the beginning: further quota changes are planned for 2013. In this chapter I also therefore consider the shape of the sector in the future as controls on the supply of places for students are further relaxed.

The pre-2012 system and how the White Paper changed it

The user cost of higher education has been on the rise for the past two decades, beginning in 1992 with the introduction of maintenance loans and the phasing out of maintenance grants and continuing with the reintroduction of tuition fees in 1998. Despite these increases in costs, student numbers have risen dramatically. Figure 6.1 shows the extent of the increases in numbers from the 1960s to 2011. As is clear, over the entire period between the introduction of maintenance loans in 1992, through the tuition fee increases in 1998 and 2006, participation in higher education has risen almost unabated. Whilst the rise in participation has occurred intermittently and for various reasons – the introduction of the GCSE, for instance, dramatically increased staying-on rates and hence university attendance, and the conversion of 42 polytechnics into universities increased degree enrolments overnight (Blanden and Machin, 2004) – it is nonetheless true that past increases in tuition fees have not resulted in any obvious decline in participation. The percentage of the population enrolled in tertiary education at age 19 (the age group at which school-leavers are first eligible for education) in the UK reached 36 per cent in 2010 – above the OECD average of 31 per cent, though lower than the participation rate for the US (55 per cent) and France (41 per cent) on the same measure (OECD, 2012: Indicator C1).

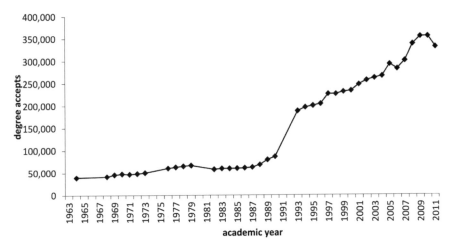

Notes: All UK-domiciled HE students to English institutions. Full-time equivalent data represent the institution's assessment of the full-time equivalence of the student instance during the reported academic year

Figure 6.1: Degree acceptances (volume) by academic year, 1963–2011

Source: Higher Education Statistics Agency (HESA)

These numbers hide the important fact that England's higher education sector has long suffered from a supply constraint, with around 1.4 applicants to every acceptance in 2011.[2] As Figure 6.2 – which shows the volume of applications and acceptances between 1996 and 2011 – illustrates, the issue is a long-term one.

One important reason why demand has so dramatically outstripped supply was the strict quota system in place in England's higher education sector before 2012. Since almost all English higher education institutions are, in effect, publicly owned, the running costs to the government are high. The two main ways the government subsidizes higher education are first, through block grants paid directly to universities to teach their students – known as the Higher Education Funding Council (HEFCE) teaching grant, which totalled £4.7 billion for English higher and further education institutions in 2010 (HEFCE, 2010), and secondly, through heavy subsidies to students via maintenance grants and tuition fee and maintenance loans. These subsidies arose because student tuition fee and maintenance loans were offered on quite favourable terms under the pre-2012 system – loans were not repaid until the borrower had left university and was earning at least £15,000 per year. At that point the loans were paid off at 9 per cent of earnings above this threshold. Thus a significant proportion of tuition fee and maintenance loans – issued by the government via the Student Loans Company – remained (and still remain) unpaid. The government estimate that around 15 per cent of students will not fully repay their loans under the pre-2012 system (Bolton, 2012), which translates into a sizeable cost. The public sector subsidy on student support – the part of tuition fee and maintenance loans that remain unpaid, and which the government has to write off – was estimated at 23 per cent in 2010. In other words, for every £1 loaned to students for tuition fee and maintenance loans under the pre-2012 system, the taxpayer had to pay out 23p (Dearden *et al.*, 2010).

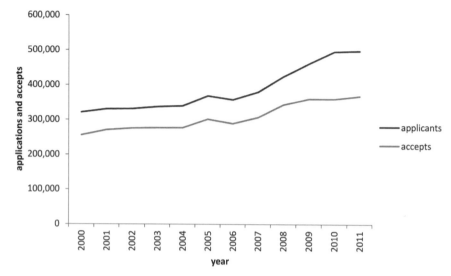

Notes: Figures include degree, HND, and other HE qualifications. Data relates to home (UK) applicants only.

Figure 6.2: Higher education applications and acceptances to English institutions, 1996–2011
Source: UCAS. www.ucas.ac.uk/about_us/stat_services/stats_online

It is here that the quota system comes into play. To ensure the higher education bill does not become unmanageable, the government imposes a cap on numbers of undergraduate students that may attend higher education institutions in England. Supply is strictly limited and no institution may expand its numbers beyond a small percentage of students per year.[3] The cap has been in place since 1994, and whilst the sector has been allowed to expand since then – for example, when Tony Blair announced the 50 per cent higher education participation target – the extent to which it can grow has been firmly under the government's control. Any university attempting to expand beyond its government quota will face a heavy fine.

An important side effect of the restricted supply and high demand for university education is the little competition between institutions. Some institutions are more in demand than others but the majority are able to fill their annual quota of places eventually, as Figure 6.3 (p. 94) illustrates by showing the ratio of degree applications to acceptances at Russell Group and non-Russell Group institutions.[4,5]

As Figure 6.3 demonstrates, demand for a place at the prestigious Russell Group universities significantly outstrips supply. The average number of applications for every acceptance at Russell Group universities was around 7.5 to 1 in 2011 – with some universities in extremely high demand. In the same year, the London School of Economics received 13.9 applications, for example, the University of Bristol 10.6, and University College London 9.5.[6]

Whilst the overall ratio of applications to acceptances is clearly higher at Russell Group universities, it is important to note that many non-Russell-Group universities have greater application: acceptance ratios than those found in the Russell Group. Non-Russell-Group universities in particularly high demand include the University of Bath, City University, and the University of Reading. In any case, there is clearly also a significant excess demand at non-Russell-Group institutions. For example, the University of Lancaster received 6.2 applications for every acceptance in 2011 and the University of Middlesex received 6.7.

It is also interesting that the ratio has decreased at both types of institution in the last 20 years. However, as Figure 6.2 shows, the decline is due to sustained increases in applications combined with little movement in acceptances, rather than a decrease in both.

Excess demand yields little incentive for institutions of any type to improve quality, productivity, or efficiency, or to charge lower than the (government mandated) maximum tuition fee. In response, the Browne Review of Higher Education, which led up to the White Paper, advised against quotas, pointing out that they meant that 'less successful institutions are insulated from competition' (IRHEFSF, 2010).

The government significantly cut the taxpayer cost of funding universities by increasing tuition fees to £9,000 per year. Since tuition fees are transferred directly to institutions the government was able to cut the HEFCE teaching grant by 80 per cent (Chowdry *et al.*, 2011) without making universities any worse off – the increased tuition fee revenue would make up the difference. This did not allow the government to remove the quota on full-time student numbers, however, because students are still able to access maintenance grants and tuition fee and maintenance loans. As the latter are still offered on extremely favourable terms, and are almost three times as large as they were previously, an even larger amount of money will remain unpaid – still a major cost to the taxpayer. Indeed, the maintenance and fee loan subsidy is estimated to rise to around 30 per cent following the 2012 tuition fee increase (Chowdry *et al.*, 2011). Thus the government is still in no position to remove the quota on student numbers and create a free market in higher education.

Instead the government has created a quasi-market, at the centre of which lies one of the key reforms of the White Paper that will, for the first time in almost twenty years, remove the cap on student numbers on a partial basis. From 2012 the government abolished all quotas for students with A-level (or equivalent) grades of AAB or better. They sought to create more competition in the sector both to increase university quality and, with a tuition fee cap set at a new level of £9,000 per year, generate some price variation among institutions. The measures were intended to encourage students to gravitate to the most popular, well-run courses and force less popular courses to improve their quality, reduce their prices, or simply shut.

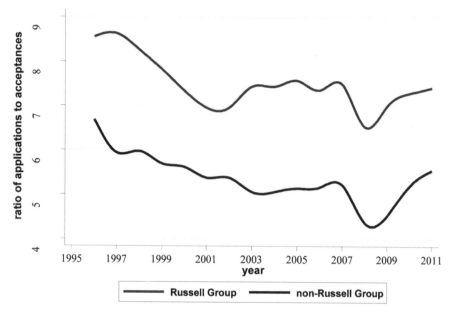

Notes: Data relates to home (UK) students only

Figure 6.3: Ratio of degree applications to acceptances, 1996–2011

Source: UCAS. www.ucas.ac.uk/about_us/stat/_services/stas_online

Between the announcement of the tuition fee cap increase in December 2010 and the publication of the White Paper in June 2011, the majority of universities set their fees at or very close to £9,000 per year. The price variation the government hoped to see simply failed to materialize. Given that demand continues to outstrip supply, this should not seem surprising. With so many students in the market for a university place, universities can charge the maximum tuition fee more or less without concern. To encourage institutions to reduce their prices, the government decided to take 20,000 student places within the quota and re-assign them to universities charging less than £7,500 per year. The 'core–margin' policy had some effect. Twenty-four universities – including the University of Chester, the University of Hertfordshire, the University of Gloucester, and Nottingham Trent University – and three further education colleges dropped their prices in response to this announcement, though critics pointed out that many simply increased their tuition fee waivers in order to reduce their net fee – thereby limiting the effect (Martin, 2011). Nevertheless, 2012 saw the most dramatic changes in the quota system since it was introduced in 1994.

The impact of the changes in full-time student number controls on institutions

Table 6.1 illustrates the impact on student numbers of these changes in the quota system on the university sector in England. For simplicity, the table is divided into institution types – Russell Group, non-Russell Group and further education colleges.

Table 6.1: Full-time student number control limits for 2012–13

		1	2	3	4
		Total	**Russell Group**	**non-Russell Group**	**FE colleges**
A	2012 controlled total	268,027	24,857	217,570	25,600
B	of which, places at <£7,500 p.a	19,997	0	9,643	10,354
C	AAB students assumed	85,388	51,057	33,365	966
D	2012 implied total (A+C)	353,415	75,914	250,935	26,566
E	2011 controlled total	364,325	77,210	269,116	17,999
F	change (2011–12)	-10,910	-1,296	-18,181	8,567
G	% change	-3.0%	-1.7%	-6.8%	47.6%
Note: English HE and FE colleges only					

Source: HEFCE (2012a)

Column 1 shows the data for all types of institution. Row A shows the *controlled total* number of students for 2012, or the number of students in the quota for 2012. The number represents the maximum of non-AAB students universities are allowed to recruit for a HEFCE-funded place at a university or college, including the 20,000 funded places for students at courses costing £7,500 per year or less. To derive the 2012 controlled total, the HEFCE estimated the number of students predicted to achieve AAB or higher at A-level or equivalent – 85,388 students – and removed them from the overall quota of students. The government also allowed itself some leeway – presumably in case there was a significant and unexpected increase in students getting AAB or higher in 2012 – so that *the implied total for 2012* (which represents the total number of students, including those with AAB or higher, the government expected to be enrolled in 2012) is 353,415. Compared to the figure recorded for 2011 (364,325) this figure is down by 10,910. In other words, the HEFCE budgeted for 10,910 *fewer* students in 2012, representing a fall of 3 per cent since 2011.

Columns 2 and 3 show how the government's new system impacts different types of university, including Russell Group universities, non-Russell-Group universities, and further education colleges. Because 85,388 students have been removed from the quota (in addition to the overall cut of 10,910), every university has effectively lost some students. Only those who can attract as many AAB+ students as have been removed from their quota will break even in terms of students and funding. In fact, the government assumed that some universities – those who traditionally attract high numbers of AAB+ students – will, at the expense of other institutions, gain more such students than they did previously and hence have more students than they did in 2011. However, it is worth pointing out that few universities announced expansion plans in 2012 as a result of the new AAB+ policy, suggesting that few could or were willing to accommodate more students. The University of Bristol announced plans to expand by 600 places in 2012, and other elite institutions, such as University College London, also expected to grow but only marginally (Morgan and Grove, 2012). Given the short time frame in which universities were aware that they could expand their funded places for AAB+ students, this is perhaps unsurprising. However, the expansion of such major universities will certainly impact others, particularly those lower down in the pecking order.

The new rules surrounding courses charging less than £7,500 per year also had a greater impact on certain universities than on others. Twenty thousand students were effectively removed from the quota of any university charging more than that amount, and re-assigned to the institutions charging less.

In general, then, any university with the ability to attract high proportions of AAB+ students is unlikely to have been affected by the new quota system – they might have even gained from it. It was assumed that the London School of Economics, for example, would attract 748 AAB+ students – 82 per cent of its total student number – as well as 162 students without AAB. Thus LSE's implied total for 2012 – or the number of students the government assumed it would enrol – is 910 students, an increase of 75 students, or 9 per cent, on 2011.

Any university charging less than £7,500 per year may also gain. For example, University College Birmingham was awarded 204 places through the margin – i.e. it won 204 of the 20,000 places (17 per cent of its total number) allocated for courses costing less than £7,500 per year. University College Birmingham is only assumed to attract 68 AAB+ students (or 6 per cent of its total number of places), but the 204 student places awarded through the margin far outweighs that number. University College Birmingham, then, will (so the government assumes) end up with a near 6 per cent increase on 2011.

On the other hand, universities that charge over £7,500 per year for all or the majority of their courses, and who do not traditionally attract many AAB+ students, might have lost out. Middlesex University, for example, was awarded none of the 20,000 places through the core–margin policy since it charges over £7,500 for all of its courses. Middlesex University was also assumed to attract only 362 AAB+ students (or 8 per cent of its total student numbers) out of its implied total of 4,306. It was therefore expected to be down 599 students (or 12 per cent) compared to its numbers for 2011. Since Middlesex has had its quota for students without AAB decreased, and cannot win any students through the core–margin policy, the only way it could make such numbers up is by attracting more AAB+ students than it has done previously. Given its general failure in the past to do so, such a scenario seems unlikely.

Columns 2, 3 and 4 summarize the respective positions for Russell Group, non-Russell- Group, and further education colleges in 2012. For example, Column 2 shows the total impact for Russell Group universities, indicating that despite gaining no places through the core–margin policy – they all charge over £7,500 per year – they have a very high proportion (67 per cent) of AAB+ students. If the government's new assumptions are to be confirmed, there is likely to be little change between 2011 and 2012 in Russell Group universities' overall position – though numbers are predicted to be down by 1.7 per cent. This group is therefore relatively protected from the reforms and have little incentive to compete against each other.

Non-Russell-Group universities, on the other hand, appear to fare far worse. AAB+ students are assumed to make up only 13 per cent of their student body which, if confirmed, will cause them to struggle to make up for the cuts in their quota. Furthermore, only 4 per cent of their student body was constituted by places awarded through the core–margin policy, which again resulted in a loss of students to cheaper universities. The net result is damaging for such institutions – the implied total for 2012 is down by 18,181 students (or 6.8 per cent) on 2011 – and could drive a degree of competition between them. Since they tend not to have a strong tradition of attracting AAB+ students, however – which they would need to reverse if they were to make up their shortfalls – such an outcome seems improbable.

Further education colleges, meanwhile, fare rather well, by and large because of benefits resulting from the core–margin policy. Whilst these colleges attract very few AAB+ students (only 4 per cent of the total in 2011), they were awarded over 10,000 students through the aforementioned policy. At 40 per cent of their total intake, further education colleges are assumed to be the only net gainers, up on 2011 by 8,567 students (or 47 per cent) in 2012.

As Table 6.1 makes evident, the potential impact of the government reforms on student number controls is highly positive for low-cost further education colleges, whilst in high prestige universities such as those in the Russell Group numbers will be largely unchanged. However, those mid-tier universities – which the majority of the student population attend – were the net losers. Their quotas have been cut, they have lost students to cheaper universities, and their only way of making up the numbers is by attracting large numbers of AAB+ students, or competing with other mid-tier universities. Such institutions are now commonly referred to as the 'squeezed middle' (Morgan, 2010).

As universities with a traditionally low proportion of AAB+ students are unlikely to be able to compete with the more prestigious Russell Group institutions, the most likely scenario is that institutions in the squeezed middle begin to compete with each other for students. However, this competition will be weak compared to the sort that would be generated by a completely free market; if these universities are already squeezed for cash due to excess capacity caused by falling demand, this will affect the amount of teaching and tuition fee revenue they receive and limit their ability to compete in any meaningful way, such as by improving their facilities.

Table 6.2 shows the ten universities with the largest percentage fall in student places following the changes to the government quotas. These institutions might be hit worst of all by the 2012 reforms. The most severely squeezed of the 'squeezed middle', include the University of East London, Middlesex University, the University of Northampton and the University of Central Lancashire. For these institutions, and others like them, 2012 might be a difficult year, given the reduction in their quotas. If they also suffer falls in demand due to tuition fee increases, the increase in capacity might result in real funding drops. They might also lose additional students in 2012 if they failed to maintain expected numbers of AAB students.

Table 6.2: Full-time student number control limits for 2012–13 by institution

	2011 controlled total	2012 implied total	% change 2011–2012
University of East London	4,940	4,318	-12.6
University of Bedfordshire	3,351	2,936	-12.4
Middlesex University	4,905	4,306	-12.2
University of Northampton	2,848	2,502	-12.1
Liverpool Hope University	1,490	1,311	-12.0
Edge Hill University	2,687	2,367	-11.9
University of Central Lancashire	6,711	5,926	-11.7
University of Lincoln	3,315	2,930	-11.6
University of Sunderland	2,852	2,522	-11.6
Leeds Metropolitan University	6,264	5,543	-11.5

Note: Farnborough College of Technology has the largest percentage change between 2011 and 2012 but is excluded from this table due to the small number of students studying there.

Source: HEFCE (2012a)

In general, then, the reforms to the quota system do not seem sufficient to engender the sort of competition between universities the government would like to see. They have also caused additional uncertainty in the sector, particularly amongst universities in the 'squeezed middle'.

However, two other important factors could affect the position of universities in 2012 and might possibly threaten the government's reforms. Firstly, the number of AAB students anticipated by the government – which impacted on how many students were cut from the quota – turned out to be somewhat lower than expected. The HEFCE predicted the number of students likely to get AAB by looking at historical trends and changes in the population. Most notably, they considered that the number of 18-year-olds was lower in 2012 than it was in 2011 (see Vasager, 2012) and hence came up their estimated 85,388 students. In reality, however, the number of students gaining AAB or higher came to 79,186 – some 6,200 less than the HEFCE's predictions (UCAS, 2012b).

For the first time in two decades, the number of students gaining the top grades at A-level did not rise in 2012. This is one possible explanation for the miscalculation. As Figure 6.4 illustrates, a total of 26.6 per cent exam entries were graded A or A*, a fall of 0.4 per cent on 2011's 27 per cent. A grades seem to have been affected in particular, as the Figure also indicates.

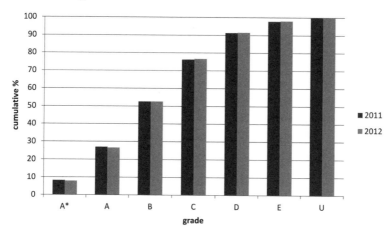

Figure 6.4: A-level grades, 2011 and 2012

Source: Joint Council for Qualifications, 2012, all UK candidates

Several explanations have been offered to explain why the predictions were wrong. Exam boards have attributed the fall in A level grades to the fact that more young people – with a broader range of abilities – took A-levels in 2012 than they did in 2011 (Coughlan, 2012). Others have speculated that teachers, having learned about the new benefits of getting AAB, inflated some students' predicted grades knowing that it would improve their chances of receiving an offer from a top institution (Fazackerley, 2012), since university offers are made to students based on such predictions.

By way of a summary consider the following: the proportion of 18-year-olds who were accepted into higher education with qualifications in the AAB+ group increased significantly between 2006 and 2011. In 2012, however, it had reduced by around 3 per cent proportionally (UCAS, 2012c: 60).

The decrease caused further problems for the new quota system – particularly for Russell Group universities, who would normally recruit such types of students. The students themselves might have also lost out on the place they were offered when their predicted grades failed to materialize. Some might have even deferred university for a year to re-sit exams or in the hope of gaining a place at their preferred university in the future. Indeed by October 2012 – by which point the first university terms were underway – six Russell Group universities reported having unfilled places on their courses (BBC News, 2012).

In addition to the unexpected dip in AAB students, 2012 saw further pressure on student numbers due to an additional fall in the overall number of applications. Final UCAS figures (UCAS, 2012c) show that full-time applications at UK higher education institutions were down by some 46,500 on 2011,[7] with those from UK domiciled students down 44,600. The rise in tuition fees was, unsurprisingly, widely cited as the reason for the decline.

Very little research has looked at the impact of tuition fees on participation in the UK. Work by Dearden *et al.* (2010) shows a negative impact, but positive impacts of maintenance grants and loans. Dearden *et al.*'s analysis indicates that the tuition fee increases of 2006 may have had little impact on participation because, although there were large increases in tuition fees, similarly large increases in upfront student support – in the form of grants and loans – outweighed any negative effect. It is difficult to apply their results regarding 2006 to the fee increases of 2012, however, since the latter are of a much larger magnitude. The same problem applies to work from the US, which provide evidence that higher education finance does affect participation (Dynarski, 2003; Seftor and Turner, 2002). It is nonetheless important to understand the impact of fees on participation, since the true impact of the 2012 reforms on individual institutions and the sector as a whole depend significantly on why applications declined in 2012.

The next section considers why that particular change occurred and looks at the types of students – and therefore the types of institutions – that have been most impacted.

In 2006, tuition fees increased from a maximum of £1,300 per year to £3,300 per year.[8] In 2005, the year immediately before, anxious to avoid paying the higher fee students applied in increased numbers. A year later applications were down by 5.6 per cent but seemed to recover in the following few years. The tuition fee hike in 2006 does not appear, therefore, to have caused a permanent drop in participation. However, it is worth noting that this occurred when the higher education sector was expanding – in many OECD countries as well as the UK (see, for example, BBC News, 2008) – and there was a demographic rise in the cohort.

The impact of changes in applications on institutions and the sector

Figure 6.5 shows the volume of applications made by English/home full-time students (i.e. those predominantly affected by the tuition fee reforms) to higher education institutions from 2004–12. As the Figure illustrates, it is common to see a large rise in applications in the year, or years, preceding a tuition fee increase, followed by a fall in the first year of the new fee regime. It may therefore be possible that the decline in 2012 is nothing more than a temporary dip.

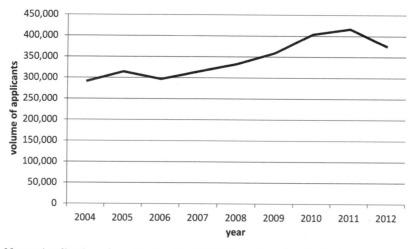

Notes: Applications from England to UK higher education institutions

Figure 6.5: Volume of English applicants to UK HEIs 2004–12

Source: UCAS (2012a) and ONS population data

A slightly different pattern has emerged in the past few years, however. While there is clearly a significant drop off in applications between 2011 and 2012, applications did not noticeably spike the year before the tuition fee increase. Instead the increase is somewhat more spread out over the period 2009–11. After a considerable increase in 2010 and a subsequent increase a year later, the volume of applications reached an all-time high in 2011. Prior to that, of course, was the Browne Review – set up in December 2009 to discuss the issue of tuition fees amidst a great deal of hype surrounding their possible increase. It might be the case, therefore, that certain types of student – older individuals who have already left school and are in a position to enrol in university immediately, for example – anticipated the tuition fee increase and decided to enrol as soon as possible. The proportion of students aged 18 taking a gap year or deferring university for a year might have also decreased, especially because students applying in 2011 for a deferral in 2012 (in order to take a gap year) would be liable to pay the higher 2012 tuition fees, unlike previous occasions when tuition fees were increased. There was thus a significant disincentive to defer entry in 2011 for 2012 (Clark, 2010).

The large increases in participation from 2009 to 2011 might have also stemmed from the UK's deep recession during this period. Many have speculated that rises in university participation were driven by a lack of employment opportunities for young people (Curtis, 2009).

Figures 6.6 and 6.7 drill deeper into the overall numbers, examining applications by age group. Since application and participation rates are dramatically lower for older individuals, Figure 6.6 shows application rates for 18–20-year-olds and Figure 6.7 for those over 21. It is clear from both figures that application rates were down for all age categories in 2012. Compared to 2011, the proportion of 18-year-olds was down by 1 percentage point (from 33.6 per cent to 32.3 per cent), while the proportion of 19-year-olds was down by 2 percentage points (from 12.9 per cent to 10.7 per cent). There were also decreases amongst older age groups, though as the numbers of students in these categories are significantly smaller, so too are the percentage point differences.

However, since individuals of all ages applied in significantly higher numbers from 2009 to 2011, as the charts make evident, it may be that the pool of potential students was greatly reduced in 2012. This could account for a large proportion of the decrease in applications, which would again imply that the drop in 2012 is temporary.

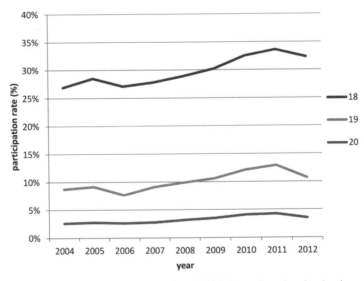

Notes: Applications from England to UK higher education institutions

Figure 6.6: Application rate, English 18-, 19-, and 20-year-olds

Source: UCAS (2012a) and ONS population data

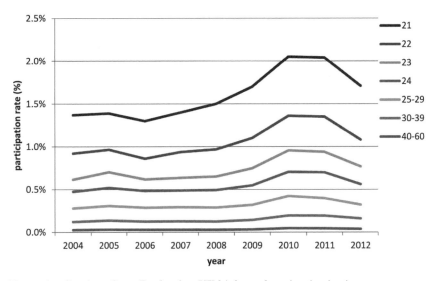

Notes: Applications from England to UK higher education institutions

Figure 6.7: Application rate, English students age 21+

Source: UCAS (2012a) and ONS population data

To give a better illustration of this, Table 6.3 shows the annual percentage change in application volumes by age group over time.[9]

Table 6.3: Year-on-year change in English applications, by age

Age	2005	2006	2007	2008	2009	2010	2011	2012	% change 2011–12
18	13840	-4472	3090	8842	12247	11985	6414	-8732	-3.9
19	2986	-9301	11564	4607	5661	11373	5669	-15358	-17.1
20	1797	-968	1193	3382	1831	4513	1819	-5183	-17.1
21	585	-185	708	777	1589	2429	105	-2356	-16.2
22	505	-409	809	200	937	2152	-281	-1930	-20.0
23	514	-410	319	279	642	1606	-116	-1242	-18.1
24	378	-286	143	162	504	1191	-190	-997	-19.9
25-29	1095	-421	462	86	1234	3982	-629	-2816	-19.3
30-39	978	-1005	-72	-375	1129	3500	213	-2327	-17.1
40-60	605	-210	-19	-39	508	1997	-137	-994	-15.6

Note: Applications from England to UK higher education institutions

Source: UCAS (2012a) and ONS population data

As Table 6.3 makes evident, severe declines in applications occurred between 2011 and 2012. The greatest decreases in volume are amongst 18- and 19-year-olds: around 24,000 fewer students aged 18 and 19 were at university in 2012. This drop will have severe consequences across the board and for Russell Group universities in particular, since they tend to attract the youngest students.

However, large declines in the student population also occurred amongst older age groups, for whom application volumes are smaller. Most severely, there is a 20 per cent drop in applications amongst 22-year-olds, with volumes down by nearly 2,000 compared with 2011. Consequences of this drop will affect mid- to low-tier universities and further education colleges since they are more likely to attract older students.

Are these drops in application rates really cause for alarm, or do they simply reflect the fact that there were very large increases in applications in previous years? For instance, although the number of applications by 19-year-olds declined by 15,300 (or 17 per cent) in 2012, this followed an *increase* of 6,400 applications by 18-year-olds in 2011. In other words, the pool of potential 19-year-olds that could go to university in 2012 was reduced by 6,400 – so the increase in 18-year-olds applying in 2011 could account for almost half the decrease amongst 19-year-olds in 2012. UCAS analysis bears this conclusion out, showing, interestingly, the significant drop in deferrals by 18-year-olds in 2011 – i.e. those enrolling but then taking gap years – which resulted in a large decline amongst 19-year-olds enrolling in university in 2012. UCAS report that:

> a greater proportion of those acceptances were … to the 2011–12 academic year at age 18 rather than deferring to start in the following year. Together these effects gave a substantially above-trend proportion of the 18-year-old population who were accepted and started courses in 2011.
>
> (UCAS, 2012c: 32)

In other words, a higher than usual proportion of 18-year-olds chose not to defer their university entry in 2011 until they were aged 19, but instead decided to participate immediately. Strikingly, deferrals amongst 18-year-olds fell from 9.1 per cent in 2010 to a mere 3 per cent in 2011. In 2012 the figure had all but recovered to 7.8 per cent (UCAS, 2012c: 32).

Similar patterns emerge amongst the younger student groups: large increases in applications in previous years preceded large decreases amongst applicants in the same cohort. A record increase in applications by 18-year-olds occurred in 2010 – showing an increase of nearly 12,000 applicants year on year – suggested to have been driven by the recession. Since this particular increase would have affected the pool of potential 20-year-olds going to university in 2012, it could account for why 5,100 fewer students in this age group decided against going to university in that year.

Looking at those in slightly older age categories, however, there could be some cause for alarm. Amongst 24-year-olds, for example, there was a drop of 19.9 per cent in 2012. The number of 23-year-olds applying in 2011 had also fallen, however, and increases in 2009 and 2010 were not major. It may be the case, therefore, that amongst students in older categories there are signs of a genuine and more permanent decrease in application rates as a result of tuition fees. Indeed as Figure 6.7 shows, following the tuition fee increases in 2006, applications among older students took longer to recover. Should this conclusion be confirmed, it is particularly likely to affect further education colleges and mid-tier universities – the squeezed middle – in future years, as they become more reliant on older applicants.

In contrast, Russell Group universities typically have very low rates of mature students. For example, less than 1 per cent of undergraduate degree students at the London School of Economics were aged 23 or over, while the corresponding figure at the University of Bristol was not much higher at 4 per cent (UCAS, 2012d). Further education colleges, on the other hand, attract very large proportions of mature students at degree level. Indeed as figures for 2011 show, of the top 50 institutions whose degree acceptances came from people aged 23 and over, 46 were further education colleges. In the next 50 institutions ranked in the same terms, however, almost half are non-Russell-Group universities. The proportion of students at these institutions aged 23 and over is high. For example, at London South Bank University, 35 per cent of the University's degree intake in 2011 were 23 and over; at London Metropolitan 27 per cent; and at the University of Wolverhampton 21 per cent. A fall in the number of applicants outside the traditional age range could therefore affect the squeezed middle – who are not protected by increases in their intake from the core–margin policy – even further in future years.

New UCAS figures also allow us to examine changes in application rates by students from different backgrounds in 2012. Indeed a key concern amongst several critics of the government's policy on tuition fees was that students from deprived backgrounds might be more likely to be put off attending university as a result of higher fees. Should this happen it would have severe consequences for institutions that traditionally accept students from poorer backgrounds.

Figure 6.8 shows application rates for English 18-year-olds by IDACI quintile over time, where individuals in Q1 are from the richest areas and individuals from Q5 from the poorest.[10] Unsurprisingly, those from the poorest backgrounds are significantly less likely to go to university than are those from more affluent backgrounds are.

Interestingly, though, the largest falls in application rates between 2011 and 2012 are amongst those from the richest quintile. It is important to note, however, that application rates amongst students from poorer backgrounds have been increasing more rapidly than for those whose from richer backgrounds. Had these trends continued, one would have expected a larger increase amongst those from poorer backgrounds compared with their richer counterparts in 2012. Taking this into account, decreases in applications amongst all IDACI groups seem to be of a similar magnitude – suggesting that the increase in tuition fees in 2012 did not especially impact individuals by their family background.[11]

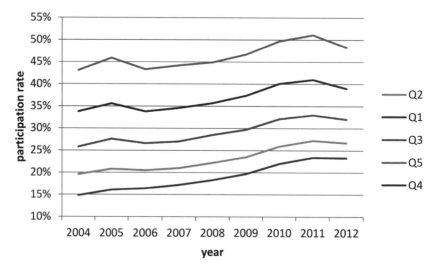

Notes: English 18-year-old application rates for areas grouped by proportion of children living in lower income households (IDACI Quintile 5 (Q5) = lowest proportion of lower income)

Figure 6.8: Participation rate among 18-year-olds by IDACI quintile

Source: UCAS (2012a)

The UCAS data also enables analysis of students' cost preferences. UCAS analysis shows little evidence that those students enrolling in 2012 gravitated towards cheaper courses – 'there has been no substantial move towards or away from higher fee courses compared to choices made by young applicants in previous cycles' (UCAS, 2012a: 10) – which suggests that tuition fees have not changed student behaviour regarding the types of courses they choose.[12]

To summarize, as a result of the 2012 reforms there were very few changes in student enrolment by background or regarding the courses students applied for. However, there were differential decreases in application rates and volumes by age group, with a substantial decrease in the volume of 19-year-olds applying in 2012 in particular. The decrease is likely to have a greater impact on Russell Group universities – which tend to take on larger proportions of younger students – and might have contributed specifically to the fall in numbers in 2012 at six of their institutions. However, applications amongst older students were also down in 2012, which will affect further education colleges and mid- to low-tier universities that are more likely to enrol such students. Whilst applications amongst older students might recover in future years, a permanent fall in mature students – and a fall in student numbers in general – could have serious consequences for certain institutions and be a major threat to the government's reforms.

As discussed, many non-Russell-Group universities were affected by the HEFCE's cuts to the student quotas and would have experienced a decline in their numbers in 2012 as a result. Such institutions in the 'squeezed middle' might also be the hardest hit by he overall decline in applications in 2012.

What about the fate of these universities in future years? In 2013/14 the controlled allocation of places will be subjected to another reduction of 5,000, with these places reallocated by the HEFCE. No further places will be awarded to institutions offering courses priced below £7,500 and, more crucially, ABB, not just AAB, students will be removed from the quota in 2013.

What will happen in 2013 and beyond?

Upon creating the quasi-market, now in operation in the higher education sector, the Coalition Government also announced that the removal of controls on AAB+ 'will represent a starting point' (BIS, 2011: 50). To create a truly marketized system, however, the government would have to remove the quota of students – and the cap on fees – altogether and allow universities to expand and to recruit as many students as they wanted to, regardless of their grades. As discussed above, some 130,000 applicants did not gain a place in 2011 and the figure for 2012 – though down – remained high. UCAS statistics (UCAS, 2012c: Table 10a) report 455,414 applications and 343,902 acceptances in England in 2012 – i.e. 115,512 unplaced students (*ibid*: Table 1a). In other words, there is still a great deal of spare capacity in the system. If the government were to remove the cap on students completely, and if some more prestigious universities expanded their numbers, the most likely result would be a gradual 'trading up' of students. The Russell Group universities would attract high-quality students away from the mid-tier or 'squeezed middle' institutions, who in turn could make up the difference by attracting students away from lower ranking universities – and so on. Assuming institutions were more willing than previously to accept students with lower grades, this would likely continue for a while – until all spare capacity was used up. However, it may eventually lead to competition between institutions, particularly if some announce expansion plans.

Since the Coalition is highly unlikely to remove the cap altogether – even if universities were willing to recruit the remaining students, the policy would still be very expensive – the scenario is also an unlikely one. Even if the HEFCE refused to fund universities for these students, there would still be a significant extra cost in terms of student support.

The most likely scenario will see the Coalition's somewhat awkward quasi-market prevail. Indeed, the government have already announced plans to remove the cap on ABB students as well as on those with AAB. The move is likely to have a similar effect to the reforms of 2012, with Russell Group and other prestigious universities protected by their long-standing tradition of attracting such high quality students. Indeed, UCAS data for 2012 (UCAS, 2012c: 21) confirm that high-tariff institutions such as those in the Russell Group were less impacted by participation falls than were medium and low-tariff institutions.

Meanwhile, further education colleges and universities near the bottom of the pecking order – those who tend not to recruit ABB+ students – will be largely unaffected by the policy change (though they are likely to lose some students once a further 5,000 places are cut from the student number control limit). Again, it is likely that the 'squeezed middle' higher education institutions will suffer in 2013 and beyond, particularly if more of the elite institutions announce expansion plans. Indeed, the planned changes for 2013 might be having an impact already. ABB students who narrowly missed a place at their preferred university in 2012 might have deferred for a year, knowing they have a good chance of gaining a place at a top university in 2013 when these universities can expand.

But while we can be sure of the government's plans for 2013, what is by no means certain is whether student numbers will recover, or if the 2012 slump in participation will continue for years to come, for all or some particular student groups. Coupled with the changes to the quota system for 2013, such questions could spell trouble for the squeezed middle, who may have some tough decisions to make in the coming years.

Conclusions

By increasing the tuition fee cap to a level almost three times as high as it was previously, freeing up 85,000 students from the strict quota system and auctioning 20,000 student places to institutions willing to charge less than £7,500 per year, the government has further oriented the higher education system in the direction of a market.

Combined with a 46,500 decrease in university applications and an unexpected shortfall in top-grade A-level students, far from generating the competition between universities it so desired, the government's somewhat awkward 'quasi-market' has only increased uncertainty in the sector and created a 'squeezed middle' of institutions. Such mid-tier universities have had their quotas cut and lost students through the core–margin policy. With little history of attracting AAB students, they are unlikely to be able to make up the numbers.

If the government were to completely remove the cap on students, and if some more prestigious universities expanded their intakes, the most likely result would be a gradual 'trading up' of students until all spare capacity is used up. This would eventually result in competition at all levels., However, given the cost of removing all controls altogether, the scenario is highly unlikely.

Instead the quasi-market is likely to prevail in the future, which might generate some competition amongst 'the squeezed middle' universities if Russell Group institutions expand capacity and attract high-grade students away from less prestigious institutions. However, such competition is weaker than the sort that would be generated by a completely free market, and hence unlikely to lead to vast improvements in the quality of courses. And with student numbers down in 2012, and fears of further declines in the coming years, the future of higher education in England – and the success of the government's reforms – is highly uncertain.

Notes

[1] Applicants for full-time undergraduate courses at UK higher education institutions (all student types); UCAS, 2012c: Table 4a.

[2] UCAS statistics (UCAS, 2012c: Table 10a) report 498,119 unique applicants, and 368,316 UK domiciled accepts for England in 2011.

[3] The UK higher education system is devolved, but quotas are in place in all four constituent countries, and operate in a similar way.

[4] The Russell Group represents 24 UK institutions, which are considered to be particularly prestigious because of their focus on research. In 2010, Russell Group members received 72 per cent of all university research grant and contract income in the UK. The Russell Group was formed in 1994 by 17 British research universities: Birmingham, Bristol, Cambridge, Edinburgh, Glasgow, Imperial College London, Leeds, Liverpool, London School of Economics, Manchester, Newcastle, Nottingham, Oxford, Sheffield, Southampton, University College London and Warwick. In 1998 Cardiff University and King's College London joined the group. In 2012, a further five institutions (Durham, Exeter, Queen Mary, University of London, and York) joined the group, though these are not included in Figure 6.3 (source: The Russell Group website: www.russellgroup.ac.uk/research).

[5] Note that unlike Figure 6.2, these figures depict the ratio of applications to acceptances, rather than unique applicants since applicants can make applications to as many as five universities simultaneously through the UCAS system.

[6] Application: acceptances ratios are for UK students applying to individual institutions, derived from UCAS statistical services, available at www.ucas.ac.uk/about_us/stat_services/stats_online/

[7] See footnote 1; End of Cycle figures for English institutions not available at time of writing.

[8] At 2012 prices. In nominal prices, fees were set at £1,000 per year in 1998 and £3,000 per year in 2006.

[9] Note that these figures are derived from application rates and population data so are approximate.

[10] The IDACI measure shows the percentage of children in each area that live in families that are income deprived (i.e. in receipt of Income Support, income based Jobseeker's Allowance, Working Families' Tax Credit or Disabled Person's Tax Credit below a given threshold). A rank of 1 is assigned to the most deprived area and a rank of 32,482 is assigned to the least deprived area.

[11] For more details on this, see UCAS (2012a), 28–31.

[12] See UCAS (2012a) 48–9.

References

Bawden, A. and Mansell, W. (2010) 'University applications reach record levels for fourth year in a row'. *The Guardian*, 9 September.

BBC News (2008) 'Student growth risks widening gap'. BBC News, 9 September.

—(2012) 'Russell Group universities have student places'. BBC News, 14 September.

BIS (Department for Business, Innovation and Skills) (2011) *Higher Education: Students at the heart of the system.* London: BIS. Online. www.gov.uk/government/uploads/system/uploads/attachment_data/file/31384/11-944-higher-education-students-at-heart-of-system.pdf (Accessed June 2011).

Blanden, J. and Machin, S. (2004) 'Educational inequality and the expansion of higher education'. *Scottish Journal of Political Economy,* 51 (2).

Bolton, P. (2012) *Changes to Higher Education Funding and Student Support in England from 2012/13.* SN/SG/5753. London: House of Commons Library.

Chowdry, H., Dearden, L., and Wyness, G. (2011) *Higher Education Reforms: Progressive but complicated with an unwelcome incentive.* IFS briefing note no. 113. London: Institute of Fiscal Studies.

Clark, L. (2010) 'Increase in university fees will kill off 2011 gap year as students fail to avoid charges hike'. *Daily Mail,* 23 November.

Coughlan, S. (2012) 'A-level results: three-quarters of degree places filled'. BBC News Online, August 2012. Online. www.bbc.co.uk/news/education-19290596

Curtis, P. (2009) 'Universities warn of stiff competition as recession prompts big rise in applications'. *The Guardian,* 16 February 2009.

Dearden, L., Goodman, A., Wyness, G., and Kaplan, G. (2010) *Future Arrangements for Funding Higher Education.* IFS commentary C115. London: Institute of Fiscal Studies.

Dynarski, S. (2003) 'Does aid matter? Measuring the effect of student aid on college attendance and completion'. *American Economic Review,* 93, 279–88.

Fazackerley, A. (2012) 'University chiefs fear for the future after admissions chaos'. *The Guardian,* 10 September.

HEFCE (Higher Education Funding Council for England) (2010) *Table 3: Recurrent Grants for 2010–11.* London: HEFCE.

—(2012a) *Annex B, Table 4: Recurrent Grants and Student Number Controls for 2012–13.* London: HEFCE.

—(2012b) *Student Number Controls for 2013–14.* London: HEFCE.

HESA (Higher Education Statistics Agency) (2010) *Table E: Statistics – finances of UK HE institutions.* London: HEFCE.

IRHEFSF (Independent Review of Higher Education Funding and Student Finance) (2010) *Securing a Sustainable Future for Higher Education (The Browne Report).* London: Department for Business, Innovation, and Skills. Online. www.bis.gov.uk/assets/biscore/corporate/docs/s/10-1208-securing-sustainable-higher-education-browne-report.pdf.

JCQ (Joint Council for Qualifications) (2012) *A, AS and AEA Results Summer 2012.* London: JCQ.

Martin, D. (2011) 'Universities to cut fees to £7,500 to get extra students following dramatic fall in applications'. *Daily Mail,* 3 December 2011.

Morgan, J. (2010) '"Squeezed middle" feels pinch as grant and numbers decline'. *Times Higher Education,* 29 March 2010.

Morgan, J. and Grove, J. (2012) 'Elite feel pinch of AAB shortfall'. *Times Higher Education,* 13 September 2012.

OECD (Organisation for Economic Co-operation and Development) (2012) *Education at a Glance 2012.* Paris: OECD.

Seftor, N. and Turner, S. (2002) 'Back to school: federal student aid policy and adult college enrolment'. *Journal of Human Resources,* 37, 336–52.

UCAS (2012a) *How Have Applications Changed in 2012?* Cheltenham: UCAS. Online. www. ucas.com/about_us/media_enquiries/2012/2012applicationsanalysis

—(2012b) '*Interim Assessment of UCAS Acceptances by Intended Entry Year, Country of Institution and Qualifications Held.* Cheltenham: UCAS.

—(2012c) *End of Cycle Report 2012.* Cheltenham: UCAS.

—(2012d) UCAS Statistical Services. Online. www.ucas.ac.uk/about_us/stat_services

Vasager, J. (2012) 'University applications drop amid higher tuition fees'. *The Guardian,* 9 July 2012.

Chapter 7

Widening participation and social mobility

Anna Vignoles

Introduction

In the last fifty years higher education has expanded substantially in England. While only around one in twenty young people attended a university in the 1960s (CHE, 1963), now more than 40 per cent of each generation goes to university. Such a transformation of higher education was supposed to bring about major improvements in social mobility by providing a route to better jobs and higher income for young people previously unable to access it. Yet in practice the expansion has not allayed concerns about the under-representation of certain types of students in higher education. In particular, it remains the case that young people from poorer backgrounds are very much under-represented, relative to their share of the population as a whole. The need to further widen participation for these poorer students, and indeed for other groups currently under-represented in higher education, therefore remains a pressing policy issue.

Given the extensive evidence that higher education is an important route by which individuals might achieve social mobility, the case for widening participation in higher education is a compelling one. Indeed the 2011 White Paper dedicated an entire chapter to make the argument that higher education is an important driver of social mobility. Particularly striking about that chapter was how it firmly reaffirmed the government's commitment to making improvements in *relative* social mobility – it explicitly states that the policy aim is not just to increase the chances of someone from a lower socio-economic background going to university but to increase their chances *relative* to their more socio-economically advantaged peers. This is a bold statement: it necessarily implies a decline in the relative chances of a young person from a middle or higher socio-economic status family going to university – a policy unlikely to be popular with their parents. The White Paper is therefore not lacking in ambition. The Paper does acknowledge, however, that there is a long way to go in terms of improving social mobility and indeed in ensuring that higher education plays a key role in our efforts to improve the economic success of those from poorer backgrounds. There is reason to be cautious on this point. Some research has suggested that the chances of a student from a disadvantaged background going to university actually fell in relative terms during the 1980s and early 1990s, and hence during the period of higher education's rapid expansion the socio-economic gap in higher education participation worsened (Blanden and Gregg, 2004; Galindo-Rueda *et al.*, 2004; Glennerster, 2001; Machin and Vignoles, 2004). More recent research is more optimistic about whether the socio-economic gap in university enrolment has actually widened (Raffe *et al.*, 2006) but most commentators, including the government, are in agreement that there remains a need for further policy action to widen participation in higher education to students from lower socio-economic groups. Also increasingly clear is that simply expanding the size of higher education does not necessarily lead to major improvements in relative social mobility.

Of course widening participation and the role of higher education in improving social mobility have become more topical issues in light of fears, following the introduction of – and continued increases to – university tuition fees, that we may be pricing poorer students out of higher education. Certainly, the cultural shift from the 'free at point of use' system that we had 20 years ago to a system where universities are charging substantial sums, has led many to question whether this will make it even harder to encourage poorer students into higher education. The tuition fee reforms introduced in 2012 have ensured that poorer students continue to receive means-tested financial support for their studies and, even more importantly, that all students do not need to find the means to pay their tuition fees upfront. Despite this, however, the reforms have not assuaged fears that the psychological impact of introducing higher tuition fees will tend to put off poorer students. Going forward, the level of fees and arrangements for their means testing and repayment are also likely to be important factors. When fees were introduced in 1998 the amount charged was low (£1,000) and means tested, though students did need to find the fees upfront. Even at that time there were signs that the *fear* of fees might create a barrier to participation for poorer students (Callender, 2003) and indeed that poorer students were more debt averse (Pennell and West, 2005). In fact, the higher education participation rate of poorer students did not decline after the introduction of fees in the late 1990s, nor did the socio-economic gap in higher education participation widen (Ramsden and Brown, 2007; Wyness, 2009). However, as we enter an era of much higher fees of £7,000 to £8,000 plus, we may not remain so sanguine about their impact (Chowdry *et al.*, 2010).

In this chapter I describe how poorer students remain under-represented in higher education despite the substantial expansion in the proportion of young people going to university. I then explain the significance of this for social mobility and the life chances of young people. I conclude by considering the various policy issues that arise in our attempt to widen participation and discuss the specifics of the proposed policies in the White Paper.

Trends in higher education participation

As Figure 7.1 makes apparent, the higher education participation rate in the UK has increased significantly over the last decade.

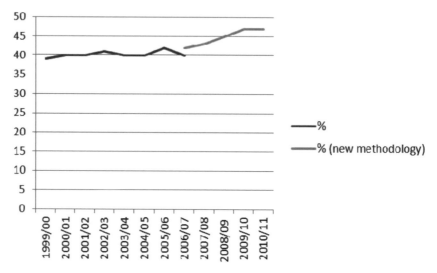

Figure 7.1 Higher Education Initial Participation Rate (HEIPR) for English-domiciled first-time participants in higher education courses at UK higher education institutions and English, Welsh, and Scottish Further Education Colleges (males and females)

Source: Statistical First Release (2011)

During the mid-2000s, the previously sharp upward trend in higher education participation somewhat stagnated, despite the target set by the previous Labour Government that 50 per cent of the population should attend higher education. The government has since recalculated the way it measures participation rates, which has led to a discontinuity in the official figures for 2006. Despite this, both figures from the Department of Business, Innovation and Skills and from the University and College Application System (UCAS) – the body responsible for the UK centralized higher education admissions process – indicate that since 2006 the upward trend in full-time higher education applications and participation continued before plateauing from 2009/10.[1] A decline in the cohort size is also expected over the next few years, which is also likely to impact both on applications and higher education participation, independently of any impact from increased tuition fees (McNay, 2012).

Of course an overall rising higher education participation rate might still disguise a different trend for lower income students. However, as UCAS data[2] indicates – see Figure 6.8 in chapter 6 – application rates from pupils in poor areas (with a high proportion of children living in low income households) and from pupils living in richer areas displayed a similarly upward trend during this period. In other words, there is evidence to suggest that even after the introduction of tuition fees in the late 1990s, not only did the higher education participation rate continue to rise, the increase occurred in poorer areas as well as in those where individuals are wealthier. Certainly, there is very little to suggest that participation amongst the poorest students fell during this period. So why do we need to remain concerned about widening participation in the face of what appears to be a steady increase in participation or at least no major decline amongst poorer students? Somewhat at odds with the tone of regular newspaper reports of declining applications to higher education from poorer students, UCAS calculate[3] that the general higher education entry rate for young people was on trend in 2012. More specifically, in the same year the entry rate for *disadvantaged* young entrants (18-year-olds) rose, even in the face of impending financial reforms. However, despite no overall decline in higher education participation after the introduction of higher fees (see Figure 6.8 in chapter 6), and no decline amongst disadvantaged young people in particular, we cannot ignore the fact that there remains a very large socio-economic gap in higher education participation rates.

The size of the socio-economic gap in participation really is substantial. Ermisch *et al.* (2012) report that students with graduate parents are approximately 2.8 times more likely to go to university than students whose parents have a low level of education. Looking at the issue in a slightly different way, Chowdry *et al.* (2012) show that students from the bottom fifth of the socio-economic status distribution are 40 percentage points less likely to go to university than a student from the top fifth. However one measures the socio-economic gap in higher education participation, all the evidence clearly suggests that family background significantly determines the likelihood of going to university. There is much more to be done before we can claim to have widened participation to the poorest students and hence to have provided them with equal access to the better jobs and higher pay associated with many degrees. However, to determine what policy action is needed to widen participation further, we need to be clear about the reasons for the low participation rate of poorer students.

The drivers of university participation

I have made the point that even if higher education participation has increased for all students, irrespective of family income, there is no doubt that a young person's chances of going to university are heavily influenced by their family background and that the problem of socially disadvantaged students' underachievement is historically entrenched (Ball, 2003; Field, 2010). Research from the UK, the US, and indeed other OECD countries has conclusively found that parental characteristics – and parents' education levels and socio-economic status especially – are key determiners of whether their children will participate in higher education (Blanden and Gregg,

2004; Blanden and Machin, 2004; Carneiro and Heckman, 2002; 2003; Gayle *et al.*, 2002; Meghir and Palme, 2005; Haveman and Wolfe, 1995). More controversial, however, are the causal mechanisms by which a child's family background influences their chances of going to university.

It is agreed that socio-economic gaps in children's educational achievement emerge very early on (Feinstein, 2003). In the pre-school period we can already see poorer children falling behind their more advantaged counterparts. The trend is not just unique to the UK but is also evident in numerous other countries – the US in particular (Cunha and Heckman, 2007; Demack *et al.*, 2000) – and has important implications for how we think about widening participation in higher education. There are two possible stories one could tell here. The first is of poorer students being unable to access university because they cannot afford to go, either because they need to start contributing to the family finances or, alternatively, because they are put off by high tuition fees – this is especially relevant to the US, where fees can be very high indeed. Should this view be borne out, then clearly we ought to be very concerned about the introduction of and continued increases in higher education tuition fees in the UK. An alternative view, more compatible with the evidence that socio-economic gaps in education achievement emerge early, is that a child's family background has such a major influence on their early development that by the time the student reaches university age they do not have the necessary educational achievement to access higher education, regardless of the tuition fees being charged. Should *this* view be borne out it would suggest that our primary policy response ought to be targeted at improving poorer children's prior achievement whilst they are in the compulsory phase of their schooling.

The evidence on whether barriers at the point of entry into higher education prevent young people from going on to higher education varies by context. Firstly, the evidence from the US has indicated that tuition fees and the problems arising from poorer parents having low income and a lack of access to funds have *not*, historically, played a major role in determining whether or not a young person from a poorer background goes to university (Cunha and Heckman, 2007; Carneiro and Heckman, 2002). The situation might be changing, however, as tuition fees continue to rise and parents' economic situations deteriorate. Even before the US's recent recession, a paper by Belley and Lochner (2007) suggested that financial considerations were indeed starting to play a more important role in determining higher education participation.

In the UK, early evidence from Gayle *et al.* (2002) and Dearden *et al.* (2004) suggested that financial considerations, specifically credit constraints, did play a role in ensuring that poorer students were less likely to enrol in university, even allowing for differences in their educational achievement in secondary school. However, more recent evidence from Chowdry *et al.*, (2012), Ermisch and Del Bono (2012) and Bekhradnia (2003) shows that if one compares students with similar levels of academic achievement in secondary school (i.e. similar GCSE and A-level grades), socio-economically disadvantaged students have quite similar higher education participation rates, though a modest socio-economic gap remains. In other words, it is primarily because poorer children have lower levels of prior achievement in school that they are less likely to go on to university. Anders (2012) has also confirmed that whilst poorer students are less likely to apply to go to university, for a given level of prior achievement poorer students are almost as likely to be accepted into university as those from wealthier backgrounds.

If we factor such evidence into our consideration about the fact that socio-economic gaps in children's educational achievement emerge early in the UK – and indeed are large by international standards – it suggests that policy action needs to be targeted at an earlier stage of schooling (Goodman and Gregg, 2010; Jerrim *et al.*, 2012; Vignoles and Crawford, 2010). A successful policy is therefore likely to focus on pre-school and school-aged children, rather than just on students applying for university – a key point realized by the UK's AimHigher programme,[4] which switched its focus to younger school children in light of the aforementioned evidence. We must also acknowledge how difficult is the task of narrowing socio-economic gaps in educational achievement, and that despite being the focus of much government effort in the last 30 to 40 years, progress has been slow. We know it is not easy for schools to overcome pupils' social disadvantage (Mortimore and Whitty, 1997). Furthermore, while schools might be the main policy lever we can use to try and improve poorer children's educational achievement, we also know they are not the most important determiners of achievement: family characteristics matter far more than which school a child attends. The challenge of improving poorer children's educational achievement almost certainly requires policy action not purely focused on improving school quality, necessary though that may also be, but on other factors such as the home and community environment, and, of course, parenting.

While low achievement at school is the main reason why poorer students do not go to university, we do know that students face a range of other barriers when they are considering applying (see comprehensive reviews from the National Committee of Inquiry into Higher Education (NCIHE) (1997) and, more recently, by Gorard *et al.* 2006). Thus the university sector also has a role to play, firstly in encouraging as many students from disadvantaged backgrounds as possible to go into higher education, and secondly in ensuring that these students complete their studies and go on to access better quality and higher paid jobs when they do. We cannot of course allow universities to avoid taking up their role simply because socio-economic gaps in achievement emerge early on in a child's life.

Higher education and social mobility

Clearly, widening participation in higher education is a goal in its own right, ensuring that individuals, regardless of their family background, can get the wide range of benefits that come from it. However, widening participation in higher education is also crucial because a degree is likely to have a substantial impact on an individual's economic prosperity and hence on their social mobility. Higher education is undoubtedly a potential pathway by which individuals from poor and modest backgrounds can acquire higher quality jobs and better earnings. Here I discuss why this is so.

The evidence on higher education's economic benefits for the individual is convincing. Having a degree has a significant impact on future earnings: on average graduates earn considerably more than non-graduates (Blundell *et al.*, 2004; Bratti *et al.*, 2005; O'Leary and Sloane, 2005; Walker and Zhu, 2011). Latest estimates from Walker and Zhu (2011) suggest that male graduates can make anywhere from 5 to 30 per cent return on their degree, women from 15 to 20 per cent return. The estimates are so varied because the wage benefit or economic return having a degree confers contrasts quite substantially according to several factors: whether the graduate is male or female, which institution they attend, and which degree subject they take (Hussain *et al.*, 2009; Walker and Zhu, 2011). For women, for example, regardless of their degree subject, the impact of higher education on their wages is substantial (Walker and Zhu, 2011). For men, by contrast, the subjects students study cause the value to vary quite significantly: some, such as economics, have a much higher value than others like English, for example. In general, however, the impact of a degree on a student's subsequent wages is likely to be significant.

In sum, if poorer students are less likely to access higher education, they will be subsequently less likely to secure a professional level job and, in turn, to achieve higher levels of income (Ermisch *et al.*, 2012). The strength of the relationship between a parent's socio-economic background and their child's achievement in the educational system appears to strongly account for the very marked relationship in some countries between parental income and a child's eventual income – i.e. low social mobility. The extent of the UK's social mobility is an extremely controversial issue amongst researchers. Some studies have suggested the UK has a particularly low level of social mobility, with a very strong link between a parent's income and their child's (Blanden, 2011; Jantti *et al.*, 2006). Others have been more sceptical about whether the UK is an outlier in this regard, arguing that the UK's level of social mobility is not particularly low, nor has it worsened over time (Gorard, 2008; Goldthorpe, 2012; Saunders, 2012). The difference in view partly derives from how one measures social mobility – specifically, whether one emphasizes occupation or income as denoting the more important measure of economic success.

Whilst I do not here attempt to resolve the complex issues of how best to measure social mobility, what is very evident from a broad range of research studies using different data and different methods is the strong link in the UK between family background and educational achievement. In particular, there appears to be a large gap in educational achievement between the most advantaged pupils – those from, say, the income distribution's top quintile – and the rest of the student body (Jerrim *et al.*, 2012). The gap is not entirely driven by the private school sector – only around 7 per cent of students attend private schools – though its role in British society undoubtedly explains part of it. What it does imply, however, is that policies to increase the higher education participation of the poorest students – e.g. individuals in the bottom quintile, such as those eligible for Free School Meals – will not address an evidently large gap in the likelihood of going to university between the very rich and the rest. In turn, this implies that occupations carrying the highest status will continue to be dominated by students from the richest fifth of families. Again, this reinforces the point that higher education is an important route to occupational and economic success and hence to social mobility.

Policy developments and widening participation

The aforementioned evidence implies that any attempt to make substantial improvements to social mobility in the UK is likely also to need to widen participation in higher education. Indeed it is for this reason that widening participation in higher education has been an important goal of education policy for a long time (CHE, 1963; NCIHE, 1997). However, running alongside this clear policy imperative is a parallel policy development: namely, the push to increase students' contribution towards the costs of their higher education. On the face of it, these two policy goals appear to be contradictory: how can we reconcile our desire to encourage poorer students to enrol in higher education whilst reducing the subsidies paid to students for the costs of their higher education?

Certainly, the public seems to view these two policy aims as contradictory. The introduction of tuition fees by the Labour Government in 1998 was met with widespread opposition from students and parents while recent reforms resulting in much higher fees – averaging £8,389 in 2012[5] – have been even more vehemently opposed – even by politicians. Much of the opposition has been expressed as a fear that fees will prevent young people from poor or middle income families accessing university. But it has also illustrated a clear desire that our system should be designed in such a way that students should *not* need to have high levels of income in order for that to happen.

However, policies aimed at widening participation and at reducing the subsidies paid to some students for their higher education are not necessarily entirely incompatible. On the tuition fee front, the design of the finance system is important.

Means-tested tuition fees and fees that only need to be paid back after graduation are one way to protect poorer (and indeed richer) students from the impact of the proposed financial changes. England currently has an income-contingent loan system for tuition fees, designed to ensure that students do not need to find the resources to pay their fees upfront. Poorer students, in theory, then, should not be deterred from attending university if they know that their degree is a good investment, one that will lead to a better job and higher earnings in the long run. Whether poorer students really are reassured by the income contingent loan system is a moot point, however – and debt averseness a serious issue (Callender, 2003). Furthermore, as the White Paper has recognized, many students lack good information about the value of different degrees in the labour market. Both problems – and their potential impact on the higher education participation rate of poorer students – have been acknowledged by the government so means testing to reduce their tuition fee burden consequently remains in place.

However, equally importantly, tuition fees are not the only form of subsidy received by full-time students. Previously, students were paid a living expenses grant to assist them with the costs of studying and it has long been recognized that the costs they incur whilst doing so are an important factor in making higher education accessible to students whose parents do not have the resources to support them. In policy terms, what we have seen alongside increases in tuition fees is a decline in the level of support for students in the form of grants. The trend has not been linear, however. In fact there have been a number of changes to successive governments' policies on the issue of student support. For example, the real value of grants was reduced systematically throughout the 1990s before grants were abolished completely, leaving poorer students with little in the way of financial support whilst they were at university. Current policy has actually reversed this position with a number of reforms to the system designed to increase the funds available to poorer students during their studies. Hence when fees were increased to £3,000 in 2006, grants were simultaneously increased – an important and insufficiently discussed policy development.

Work by Dearden *et al.* (2011) has shown that whilst the introduction of higher tuition fees is likely to have a negative impact on higher education participation, it can be offset by the countervailing effect of improving the level of support available to students while they study. For instance, Dearden *et al.* calculated that a £1,000 increase in fees (at 2006 prices) would have reduced participation rates by 4 per cent. However, they also calculated that £1,000 worth of non-repayable support in the form of maintenance grants resulted in a 2.6 percentage point increase in participation. The White Paper has partially recognized this point and I discuss the proposed means to help poorer students with their living costs – and their limitations – in the next section of this chapter.

Before I discuss the White Paper's specific proposals and how well evidenced they might be, I first consider some important policies that have previously aimed to widen participation and discuss whether or not they have been successful. Calculating the impact particular policies have had on higher education participation is, of course, problematic. Many policy developments occur simultaneously and it is therefore difficult to untangle the impact of tuition fees from other policy changes. For instance, the recent abolition of the Education Maintenance Allowance (EMA) scheme, in addition to the abolition of AimHigher, is likely to impact on attempts to widen participation. Such policy changes will then interact with any impact the increase in tuition fees in 2012 might have.

Certainly, since the Education Maintenance Allowance scheme was found to have increased staying-on rates amongst 16-year-olds from poorer backgrounds, it is distinctly likely that removing it will have a negative impact on the participation of such students in post-16 education. Whether this subsequently reduces the number of lower income students participating in higher education is unclear, although McNay (2012) has highlighted the small fall in the proportion of 16–18-year-olds staying on in full-time education beyond 16 in 2012. Any downward trend in post-16 participation amongst lower SES pupils might of course be countered by another recent policy: raising the education participation age to 18. While the policy will require students to undertake some education to age 18, its effectiveness will depend on whether it has any 'bite' – in other words, if it does indeed increase how much education or training young people participate in and how long they do so for.

Evidence of how the AimHigher scheme impacted disadvantaged students' higher education participation is rather more mixed. It is therefore far from clear that abolishing it will have a negative impact. Harrison (2012) suggests though that whilst AimHigher was not found to have had a major impact on the higher education participation of young people from poorer backgrounds, this might have been partly because it attempted to influence the aspirations of younger children not yet at an age where they could have progressed into higher education (Harrison, 2012). If the policy was successful in this regard, in the longer term its abolition may yet have a negative impact on higher education participation rates amongst the target group of more disadvantaged young people.

In any case, we need also to be mindful that one aim of introducing higher and variable tuition fees was to influence pupils' choices. As I discussed previously, the economic benefits of a degree vary substantially both by institution attended and by degree subject. In other words, whilst higher education is potentially a route to improved social mobility, the choices students make when enrolling significantly determine the benefits they will reap from their degree. Widening participation will only improve graduates' earnings and social mobility if poorer students enrol in high-quality institutions and on courses in economically valuable subjects. Following the introduction of higher tuition fees in 2012, then, students might think harder about which institutions they intend to study at and the subject they plan to take. Theoretically, therefore, the introduction of higher fees might encourage students to make more economically rational subject choices, which could lead in turn to actual improvements in social mobility. Work by Walker and Zhu (2011) suggests this is only a theoretical benefit of the reforms, however. As their evidence indicates, even a large rise in tuition fees – such as what occurred in 2012 – is unlikely, in practice, to make a significant difference to the value of particular degrees since the economic gain for high-value subjects far outweighs the marginal increase in costs implied by the rise in tuition fees. Students, consequently, are unlikely to change their choice of institution or subject just because there are relatively small differences in tuition fees for different degree courses.

We also need to think further about the experience higher education affords poorer students – and particularly about the types of institutions such students tend to access. Poorer students are not only less likely to apply to and enrol in Russell Group institutions (or institutions with a similar research quality) compared to their equally qualified but more advantaged counterparts, they are also more likely to drop out of university (Chowdry *et al.*, 2012; Vignoles and Powdthavee, 2009). It is therefore key for universities to help disadvantaged students make aspirational choices in terms of institution and indeed to help them remain in higher education until they have completed their degree. In the next section I consider how the specific policy proposals in the White Paper relate to the evidence I have just outlined and the argument I have put forward.

The White Paper

What has the White Paper promised in terms of policy development on widening participation and how effectively are the policy proposals likely to address the underlying causes of social immobility?

First and foremost, although the onus to widen participation remains with universities and colleges, the government has recognized the central role of schools. If we are to expect higher education to serve as an engine for social mobility, this will only be achieved by improving poorer children's educational achievement in school. We should therefore welcome the acknowledgement of this in the White Paper.

The government has also recognized the tension school performance measures have created in the system. Schools have, not surprisingly, focused on improving their performance on the metric by which they are judged, which up to now has largely been the total of GCSE points per pupil or, indeed, the proportion of pupils who achieve five A*–C grades. Encouraging pupils to get more GCSE points does not necessarily improve their chances of getting into university, however, if certain of their qualifications are not widely respected or accepted by universities. Another performance measure has been introduced in response to this problem: namely, the proportion of students achieving a particular GCSE curriculum described as the English Baccalaureate, which includes a set of subjects universities are more likely to favour. It remains to be seen whether the English Baccalaureate will usurp the focus on the GCSE and become the main metric by which schools are judged. However, it is possible that schools will shift their focus towards a curriculum more likely to be favoured by many universities.

A more significant shift, however, is the potential publication of school-level information on students' progression rates into higher education. Undoubtedly, parents will be very interested to know what proportion of students is going on to university. More importantly, compared with other performance markers – such as total GCSE point scores – the measure is much more difficult to 'game'. Publishing such data will also likely increase the emphasis in schools on university bound students. Such effects raise the question, however, as to what schools will be able to do to get their poorer students into higher education. Encouraging them to apply and helping them with the application process are two possibilities, as is providing better information and guidance. The last of these suggestions is one the government has also recognized: schools will have a legal duty to provide independent careers advice to students in years 9 to 11. The government has also proposed policies to improve the quality of the advice given and to up the number of skill career advisors. All this is to be welcomed, but the resources available within schools to provide advice and guidance are very limited and are likely to be scarcer going forward as limited budgets bite. Perhaps more importantly, all schools – and not just academies – need to have sufficient flexibility to find adequate space in the timetable to cover such issues thoroughly. Advice is also crucial for students not bound towards university and we need to ensure that support for them is not squeezed out.

The White Paper is not silent on the role of higher education institutions – indeed the biggest proposed change will enable universities to use contextual data when making decisions about student admissions. In other words, universities now have political insurance to use specific and transparent criteria to take social background into account when making offers to students. The move is likely to make a difference at the margin, providing universities with more flexibility in admitting students who are somewhat less well-qualified on paper but whose grades represent a greater level of achievement once their socio-economic background is taken into account. How this operates in practice, the extent to which parents will see it as fair, and, most crucially of all, how universities validate information provided by students about their socio-economic background remain important and unanswered questions.

The White Paper also ups the ante on access agreements, stating that greater priority and greater investment needs to be given by universities to widening participation issues. A strengthened and larger Office for Fair Access (OFFA) is likely to put still more pressure on universities to make real and measurable progress on widening participation in order to improve social mobility. What is less clear is how OFFA will judge universities' widening participation efforts and what will constitute success. The research evidence described above suggests that universities should be working with disadvantaged school children well before they make their GCSE and A-level choices, and that clearly the pay-off to that kind of outreach will be both a long time coming and might also result in students attending institutions different to the one doing the outreach. While such activity might be valuable, it is difficult to know how it would satisfy OFFA's need to measure success. There is a clear danger that universities will focus less on such long-term outreach work and more on getting students to apply to their particular institutions. The net result might increase competition between universities in their efforts to attract those poorer students who are university bound, but it will not necessarily increase the overall number of disadvantaged students applying to university. It is important that OFFA strikes a balance between recognizing the value of general outreach activity whilst ensuring that universities make measurable improvements in the proportion of poorer students who enrol. Trying to measure the former's effectiveness is another pressing issue for the sector as a whole.

The National Scholarship Programme (NSP) is obviously the White Paper's major initiative, requiring, as it does, all institutions charging fees over £6,000 to offer scholarships to undergraduate students. However, here the government has granted universities autonomy to decide how they operate the programme – a move that has a major drawback: students cannot possibly understand the daunting array of university schemes currently on offer. Furthermore, in many institutions the amount a student will receive depends on numerous personal characteristics and is conditional on the number of other poorer students who apply. Students are often only told how much support they will receive very late on in the day. If they cannot be clear about the figure before they make their application, it is unlikely to have a major influence on their decision. Moreover, if a student does make a decision about their degree choice on the basis of the scholarship, it is unlikely to be in their long-term interests since the benefits of a degree are likely to be greater than the amounts the scholarship scheme makes available. Decisions about degree subject or institution in response to small differences in financial support are therefore unlikely to be beneficial. In summary, the benefits of a national scheme that varies by student characteristics rather than by institution – and that is well publicized and transparent – would be substantial and the weaknesses of the NSP have been recognized. In addition, incentivizing universities to use their resources to undertake outreach work and other activities that have been shown to make a difference (e.g. summer schools) is likely to be more effective at widening participation (Chowdry *et al.*, 2012).

Finally, one set of students receives welcome attention in the White Paper. Part-time students will now have access to loans to cover their tuition fees, a step in the right direction and important for social mobility since many from more disadvantaged backgrounds often enter higher education as mature part timers. Issues facing part-time students are discussed in more detail by Claire Callender in chapter 8. Unfortunately, the White Paper is not forthcoming on how we can tackle another pressing issue: access to postgraduate study, as discussed by Whitty and Mullan in chapter 10. Whilst most policy attention has focused on ensuring that poorer students have access to university at undergraduate level, higher level occupations increasingly require applicants to possess postgraduate qualifications, which do not enable deferred payment and whose fees are high. Thus to make improvements in social mobility, access to postgraduate study also needs to be needs blind and at the moment it is far from that.

Conclusions

In this chapter I have affirmed and confirmed the importance of widening participation for improving levels of social mobility: access to higher education is certainly a major route by which poorer students can achieve labour market success. Thus far, however, progress in narrowing the socio-economic gap in access to higher education has been slow.

Widening participation in higher education therefore needs to be a long-term project. I have made the case that the causes underlying the socio-economic gap in higher education participation are largely rooted in lower levels of prior achievement amongst students from poorer backgrounds. A continued policy effort needs to be directed at improving the school achievement of our society's disadvantaged children – something that has indeed been recognized in the White Paper. In this context, the impact of the 2012 financial reforms on widening participation is unlikely to be substantial for two reasons. Firstly, poorer students have been protected from some of the reforms, not least by the continued access to means-tested support whilst studying for a degree. Secondly, the reason why poorer students are less likely to go to university is not so much because they are put off by tuition fees, but rather because they failed to reach the level of achievement necessary to go to university.

That said, we must be clear on one point. Even amongst students who achieve similar results at A-level there remains a modest socio-economic gap in who is more likely to go to university. Students with the necessary level of prior achievement but who are from poorer backgrounds are more likely to pursue non-degree options than similarly qualified students from higher income backgrounds (Sutton Trust, 2004). While tuition fees have not been solely responsible – the gap has persisted since the pre-fee era – it still requires policy action nonetheless. We need to encourage universities to do outreach work that connects with this group of students and find ways of getting them to apply to university (Tough *et al.*, 2008). I have argued, along with others, that the National Scholarship Programme is not necessarily the right way to achieve this. There is a huge amount of work to be done to reassure poorer students that tuition fees are not a barrier to them participating in university and that they will receive support whilst studying. As evidence of a continuing information deficit – not helped by the dismantling of the advice and guidance service in schools – many are not aware of this.

Notes

[1] Whilst a very small (0.1 per cent) decline in undergraduate student numbers was reported by the Higher Education Statistics Agency for 2010/11, this did not translate into a decline in the official initial higher education participation rate as calculated by the Department for Business, Innovation and Skills. See UCAS (2012).

[2] UCAS analysis (July, 2012: Figure 18) *How Have Applications for Full-time Undergraduate Higher Education in the UK Changed in 2012?*

[3] http://www.ucas.com/documents/End_of_Cycle_Report_12_12_2012.pdf

[4] AimHigher was a UK government programme introduced in 2004 to improve the chances of poorer children enrolling in university. It was recently abolished and is discussed in more detail later in the chapter.

[5] www.ucas.com/documents/End_of_Cycle_Report_12_12_2012.pdf

References

Anders, J. (2012) 'The link between household income, university applications and university attendance'. *Fiscal Studies*, 33 (2), 185–210.

Ball, S.J. (2003) *Class Strategies and the Education Market: The middle classes and social advantage.* London: Routledge.

Bekhradnia, B. (2003) *Widening Participation and Fair Access: An overview of the evidence.* Oxford: HEPI.

Belley, P. and Lochner, L. (2007) 'The changing role of family income and ability in determining educational achievement'. *Journal of Human Capital*, 1 (1), 37–89.

Blanden, J. (2011) 'Cross-national rankings of intergenerational mobility: a comparison of approaches from economics and sociology'. *Journal of Economic Surveys*, 27 (1), 38–73. Online. Doi: 10.1111/j.1467-6419.2011.00690.x

Blanden, J. and Gregg, P. (2004) 'Family income and educational achievement: a review of approaches and evidence for Britain'. *Oxford Review of Economic Policy*, 20, 245–63.

Blanden, J. and Machin, S. (2004) 'Educational inequality and the expansion of UK higher education'. *Scottish Journal of Political Economy*, Special issue on the economics of education, 51, 230–49.

Blundell, R., Dearden, L., and Sianesi, B. (2004) *Evaluating the Impact of Education on Earnings in the UK: Models, methods and results from the NCDS.* CEE discussion paper 47. London: Centre for the Economics of Education.

Bratti, M., Naylor, R., and Smith, J. (2005) *Variations in the Wage Returns to a First Degree: Evidence from the British Cohort Study 1970.* IZA discussion paper no. 1631. Germany: Institute for the Study of Labor.

Callender, C. (2003) 'Student financial support in higher education: access and exclusion'. In Tight, M. (ed.) *Access and Exclusion: International perspectives on higher education research.* London: Elsevier Science.

Carneiro, P. and Heckman, J. (2002) 'The evidence on credit constraints in post-secondary schooling'. *Economic Journal*, 112 (482) 705–34.

—(2003) 'Human capital policy'. In Heckman, J., Krueger, A. and Friedman, B. (eds) *Inequality in America: What role for human capital policies?* Cambridge, MA: MIT Press.

CHE (Committee of Higher Education) (1963) *Higher Education: A report by the committee appointed by the Prime Minister under the chairmanship of Lord Robbins, 1961–63 (The Robbins Report)*. London: HMSO.

Chowdry, H., Crawford, C., Dearden, L., Goodman, A., and Vignoles, A. (2012) 'Widening participation in higher education: analysis using linked administrative data'. *Journal of the Royal Statistical Society, Series A*. Online. Doi: 10.1111/j.1467-985X.2012.01043.x

Chowdry, H., Dearden, L., Goodman, A., and Jin, W. (2012) 'The distributional impact of the 2012–13 higher education funding reforms in England'. *Fiscal Studies*, 33, 211–36. Online. Doi: 10.1111/j.1475-5890.2012.00159.x

Chowdry, H., Dearden, L., and Wyness, G. (2010) *Higher Education Reforms: Progressive but complicated with an unwelcome incentive*. IFS briefing notes, BN113. London: Institute for Fiscal Studies. Online. www.ifs.org.uk/publications/5366

Cunha, F. and Heckman, J. (2007) 'The technology of skill formation'. *American Economic Review*, 92, 31–47.

Dearden, L., Fitzsimons, E., and Wyness, G. (2011) *The Impact of Tuition Fees and Support on University*. CEE discussion paper no. 126. London: Centre for the Economics of Education. Online. http://cee.lse.ac.uk/ceedps/ceedp126.pdf

Dearden, L., McGranahan, L., and Sianesi, S. (2004) *The Role of Credit Constraints in Educational Choices: Evidence from the NCDS and BCS70*. CEE discussion paper no. 48. London: Centre for the Economics of Education.

Demack, S., Drew, D., and Grimsley, M. (2000) 'Minding the gap: ethnic, gender and social class differences in achievement at 16, 1988–95'. *Race, Ethnicity and Education*, 3, 112–41.

Ermisch, J. and Del Bono, E. (2012) 'Inequality in achievements during adolescence'. In Ermisch, J., Jäntti, M., and Smeeding, T. (eds) (2012) *From Parents to Children: The intergenerational transmission of advantage*. New York: Russell Sage Foundation.

Ermisch, J., Jantti, M., and Smeeding, T. (eds) (2012) *From Parents to Children: The intergenerational transmission of advantage*. New York: Russell Sage Foundation.

Feinstein, L. (2003) Inequality in the early cognitive development of British children in the 1970 cohort. *Economica*, 70 (177), 73–97.

Field, F. (2010) *The Foundation Years: Preventing poor children becoming poor adults. Report of the Independent Review on Poverty and Life Chances*. London: Cabinet Office.

Galindo-Rueda, F., Marcenaro-Gutierrez, O., and Vignoles, A. (2004) 'The widening socio-economic gap in UK higher education'. *National Institute Economic Review*, 190, 70–82.

Gayle, V., Berridge, D., and Davies, R. (2002) 'Young people's entry into higher education: quantifying influential factors'. *Oxford Review of Education*, 28, 5–20.

Glennerster, H. (2001) *United Kingdom Education 1997–2001*. Working paper no. 50. London: Centre for the Analysis of Social Exclusion.

Goldthorpe, J. (2012) *Understanding – and Misunderstanding – Social Mobility in Britain: The entry of the economists, the confusion of politicians and the limits of educational policy*. Working paper 1/2012. University of Oxford: Department of Social Policy and Intervention. Online. www.spi.ox.ac.uk/fileadmin/documents/pdf/Goldthorpe_Social_Mob_paper.pdf

Goodman, A. and Gregg, P. (eds) (2010) *Poorer Children's Educational Attainment: How important are attitudes and behaviour?* London: Joseph Rowntree Foundation.

Gorard, S. (2008) 'A reconsideration of rates of social mobility in Britain'. *British Journal of Sociology of Education*, 29 (3), 317–24.

Gorard, S., Smith, E., May, H., Thomas, L., Adnett, N., and Slack, K. (2006) *Review of Widening Participation Research: Addressing the barriers to widening participation in higher education. Report to the HEFCE by the University of York, Higher Education Academy and Institute for Access Studies*. Bristol: HEFCE.

Harmon, C. and Walker, I. (1995) 'Estimates of the economic return to schooling for the United Kingdom'. *American Economic Review*, 85 (5) 1278–86.

Harrison, N. (2012) 'The mis-measure of participation: how choosing the 'wrong' statistic helped seal the fate of Aimhigher'. *Higher Education Review*, 45 (1).

Haveman, R. and Wolfe, B. (1995) 'The determinants of children's attainments: a review of methods and findings'. *Journal of Economic Literature*, 33 (4), 1829–78.

HM Government (2010) *Opening Doors, Breaking Barriers: A strategy for social mobility*. London: Cabinet Office. Online. www.dpm.cabinetoffice.gov.uk/sites/default/files_dpm/resources/opening-doors-breaking-barriers.pdf_

Hussain, I., McNally, S., and Telhaj, S. (2009) *University Quality and Graduate Wages in the UK*. IZA working paper 4043. Germany: Institute for the Study of Labor.

IRHEFSF (Independent Review of Higher Education Funding and Student Finance) (2010) *Securing a Sustainable Future for Higher Education (The Browne Report)*. London: Department for Business, Innovation, and Skills. Online. www.bis.gov.uk/assets/biscore/corporate/docs/s/10-1208-securing-sustainable-higher-education-browne-report.pdf

Jantti, M., Bratsberg, B., Roed, K., Raaum, O., Naylor, R., Osterbacka, E., Bjorklund, A., and Erikson, T. (2006) *American Exceptionalism in a New Light: A comparison of intergenerational earnings mobility in the Nordic countries, the United Kingdom and the United States*. IZA discussion paper 1938. Germany: Institute for the Study of Labor.

Jerrim, J., Vignoles, A., and Finnie, R. (2012) *University Access for Disadvantaged Children: A comparison across English speaking countries*. Working paper. London: Institute of Education.

Machin, S. and Vignoles, A. (2004) 'Educational inequality: the widening socio-economic gap'. *Fiscal Studies*, 25, 107–28.

McNay, I. (2012) The new decade: a watershed in UK higher education? *Higher Education Review*, 45 (1).

Meghir, C. and Palme, M. (2005) 'Educational reform, ability, and family background'. *American Economic Review*, 95, 414–24.

Mortimore, P. and Whitty, G. (1997) *Can School Improvement Overcome the Effects of Disadvantage?* London: Institute of Education.

NCIHE (National Committee of Inquiry into Higher Education) (1997) *Higher Education in the Learning Society (The Dearing Report)*. London: HMSO.

O'Leary, N. and Sloane, P. (2005) 'The return to a university education in Great Britain'. *National Institute Economic Review*, 193 (3), 75–89.

Pennell, H. and West, A. (2005) 'The impact of increased fees on participation in higher education in England'. *Higher Education Quarterly*, 59, 127–37.

Raffe, D., Croxford, L., Iannelli, C., Shapira, M., and Howieson, C. (2006) *Social-Class Inequalities in Education in England and Scotland*. Special CES briefing no. 40. Edinburgh: Centre for Educational Sociology.

Ramsden, B. and Brown, N. (2007) *Variable Tuition Fees in England: Assessing their impact on students and HEIs – 2nd report*. London: Universities UK.

Saunders, P. (2012) *Social Mobility Delusions*. London: CIVITAS.

Statistical First Release (2011) *Participation Rates 2006/07 to 2010/11*. London: Department for Business, Innovation, and Skills. Online. www.bis.gov.uk/analysis/statistics/higher-education/national-statistics-releases/participation-rates-in-higher-education/HEIPR-2006-to-2011

Sutton Trust (2004) *The Missing 3000: State school students under-represented at leading universities*. London: Sutton Trust.

Tough, S., Sasia, A., and Whitty, G. (2008) *Productive Partnerships? An examination of schools' links with higher education*. London: Sutton Trust.

UCAS (2012) *How Have Applications for Full-time Undergraduate Higher Education in the UK Changed in 2012?* Cheltenham: UCAS. Online. http://ucas.com/documents/ucas_how_have_applications_changed_in_2012_executive_summary.pdf

Vignoles, A. and Crawford, C. (2010) 'Access, participation and diversity questions in relation to different forms of post-compulsory further and higher education (FHEs)'. In David, M. (ed.) *Improving Learning by Widening Participation in Higher Education*. London: Routledge.

Vignoles, A. and Powdthavee, N. (2009) 'The socioeconomic gap in university dropouts'. *The B.E. Journal of Economic Analysis and Policy*, 9 (1). Online. Doi: 10.2202/1935-1682.2051

Walker, I. and Y. Zhu (2011) 'Differences by degree: evidence of the net financial rates of return to undergraduate study for England and Wales'. *Economics of Education Review*, 30 (6), 1177–86.

Wyness, G. (2009) 'The impact of higher education finance in the UK'. PhD thesis, Institute of Education, University of London.

Chapter 8

Part-time undergraduate student funding and financial support
Claire Callender

Introduction

According to many observers, one of the most positive elements of the 2011 White Paper *Students at the Heart of the System* (BIS, 2011) is the enhanced support for part-time undergraduate students, with the introduction – for the first time – of loans for their tuition fees. The government, too, proudly points to this achievement, declaring in the White Paper that this change 'remedies a longstanding injustice in support for adult learners' (BIS, 2011: 61). This chapter provides a critique of the reforms of part-time student finances, and of the White Paper more generally. It argues that the new loans are more likely to re-enforce or perpetuate existing injustices rather than eradicate them. The loans' very restrictive eligibility criteria mean that the majority of part-time undergraduates do not qualify for them, and yet are faced with far higher tuition fees that they have to pay upfront, and out of their own pocket. These policies are designed for the 'typical student and graduate': a young school leaver who studies full-time and who, on graduation, enters the labour market for the first time. Such students are the focus of the White Paper, and the higher education sector's and media attention. The policies fail to acknowledge the distinctive characteristics of the part-time student population and consequently most miss out on the loans, while others shun them. This is depressing demand for, and the supply of part-time study, contrary to the government's intentions.

The chapter, therefore, focuses on the 'forgotten' third of all English undergraduate students who study part time. Arguably, part-time study is central to lifelong learning and national skills policies, promoted by the Organisation for Economic Co-operation and Development (OECD) (2012) and others (CBI, 2013) to transform lives, drive economies by providing high-level skills, and thus enhancing a country's competitiveness and economic strength. Part-time provision is significant for the higher education policy too. It can contribute to a more flexible, diverse higher education sector (Santiago *et al.*, 2008) and help broaden higher education access and social mobility, enhancing social justice (Eurydice, 2011). Older part-time students are also an alternative source of recruits in the face of the demographic downturn of traditional university-age students. Indeed, recent research confirms the considerable value of investing in part-time study and its private and public benefits (Callender and Wilkinson, 2012; 2013).

In this chapter I explore part-time undergraduate financial support in England, highlighting some of the funding challenges. By way of context, I start by defining what is meant by part-time study, and examine trends in part-time enrolments. I then outline the key socio-economic characteristics of part-time undergraduates and how they differ from their full-time peers. The regional distribution of part-time provision is also charted as this is likely to affect prospective students' access to higher education. Next, I explore the financial support available to part-time undergraduates before and after the 2012/13 reforms, and the limitations of the systems introduced. I question whether the student loans introduced for part-time students in 2012/13, designed specifically for full-time young students, are an appropriate student support tool for part-timers given their 'atypical' characteristics.

Defining part-time undergraduate higher education study

In England, there is no clear definition of part-time study or students. The most common definition, employed in research and in the statistical analysis below, is the one used by the Higher Education Statistical Agency (HESA), the official agency for the collection, analysis and dissemination of quantitative information about UK higher education. This definition of part-time undergraduate students is negative – it is those who do not fit the definition of full-time students.

> Full-time includes students recorded as studying full time, normally required to attend an institution for periods amounting to at least 24 weeks within the year of study, plus those enrolled on a sandwich course (thick or thin), irrespective of whether or not they are in attendance at the institution or engaged in industrial training, and those on a study-related year out of their institution. During that time students are normally expected to undertake periods of study, tuition, or work experience which amount to an average of at least 21 hours per week for a minimum of 24 weeks study/placement.
>
> Part-time includes students recorded as studying part time, or studying full-time on courses lasting less than 24 weeks, on block release, or studying during the evenings only.
>
> (HESA, n.d.)

This definition characterizes part-time study by attendance whereby all distance learning students, irrespective of their hours of study, are defined as part-time students, and by the length and intensity of study.

A review of UK research on part-time undergraduate students (Callender and Feldman, 2009) also identified an important conceptual and practical difficulty in this research. The research neglected the diversity of part-time students, who were, as a result, frequently subsumed under other headings. For instance, 'part-time' was often added to descriptions of students as diverse as, non-traditional, working-class, mature, or having low entry qualifications. Consequently, part-time students were classed as just another disadvantaged student group, and 'part time' ceased to be a mode of study, but a student attribute. Even where part-time students were included among these groups, the specific barriers they might face and their different needs were often neither specified nor explored.

Trends in part-time enrolments

Demand for part-time undergraduate study in the UK is far more volatile than demand for full-time study, with some years (until 2012/13) recording a fall in numbers in contrast to the steady rise amongst those studying full time. Overall, part-time UK student enrolments increased by around 13 per cent between 2000/01 and 2009/10 – a much slower rate than the 24 per cent recorded for full-time students. However, this expansion was driven exclusively by the Open University (OU), which dominates the part-time sector. Excluding the OU, over the same period part-time student numbers fell by just over 1 per cent while the OU's undergraduate numbers increased by 54 per cent. Furthermore, at an institutional level, enrolments also fluctuated. Between 2000/01 and 2009/10, half of all higher education institutions in England increased their part-time undergraduate numbers – in some cases more than doubling their provision. The other half saw their part-time provision decrease (Pollard *et al.*, 2012).

The socio-economic characteristics of UK part- and full-time undergraduates

The first defining characteristics of UK part-time undergraduates are that they are older and more likely to be female than their full-time peers (Table 8.1). In 2009/10, 80 per cent of part-time undergraduates were aged 25 and over compared with 14 per cent of full-timers, while 63 per cent were female compared with 56 per cent of full-timers. They were slightly less likely to come from an ethnic minority group (18 per cent compared with 22 per cent) (Pollard *et al.*, 2012). Survey data confirm that around two-thirds have family responsibilities and two in five have children (Callender *et al.*, 2010a) whereas the vast majority of full-time students are single (85 per cent) and childless (92 per cent) (Johnson *et al.*, 2009).

Part- and full-time students also have different educational backgrounds (Table 8.1). Part-timers are more likely than full-timers both to have had some prior experience of higher education and to enter their part-time course with higher entry qualifications, or to have low levels of prior educational attainment and to start their part-time course with lower qualifications or none at all. Such polarization of the part-time undergraduate population helps to distinguish between those with existing higher education qualifications who are mostly re-skilling, and those with low-level qualifications who are up-skilling, for whom part-time study offers a second chance at learning. In 2009/10, 54 per cent of part-time undergraduates started their studies with a bachelor's degree or higher, 37 per cent with A-levels or equivalent, and 8 per cent with other or no formal qualifications. The comparable figures for full-time students were 10 per cent, 85 per cent, and 5 per cent respectively (Pollard *et al.*, 2012).

Another distinguishing characteristic of part-time students, compared with their full-time peers, is where and what they study. The OU, which exclusively provides distance learning courses, is the main UK part-time provider, absorbing over a third (36 per cent) of all part-time undergraduates. Birkbeck College, University of London, is the only research-intensive university with nearly a 100 per cent part-time provision, and around 2 per cent of all part-time undergraduates study there. Outside of these two universities, part-time students are concentrated in less research-intensive higher education institutions and colleges, and are less likely than full-time students to attend the most prestigious research-intensive Russell Group universities (8 per cent compared with 22 per cent).

Associated with this concentration, in 2009/10 only 37 per cent of part-timers aimed for a bachelor's degree, with most (63 per cent) studying for other sub-degree undergraduate qualifications including professional qualifications, higher education certificates, and institutional undergraduate credits. By contrast, 90 per cent of full-time students studied for a bachelor's degree (Table 8.1). Part-time undergraduates also are more concentrated than full-time students in vocational subjects such as those allied to medicine, business and administrative studies, and education.

The final distinct characteristic of part-time undergraduates is that they combine paid work with their part-time studies. Around 81 per cent of part-time students are employed, mostly in full-time, public-sector jobs, while around half of full-timers also work at some point in the academic year (Johnson *et al.*, 2009). In most cases, both the nature and level of the work undertaken is very different, as is the role it plays in their identity. Part-time students tend to have full-time jobs in higher level occupations; they fit their studies around their jobs, and see themselves as workers who study (Callender and Wilkinson, 2012). In contrast, full-time students work part-time in lower level occupations (mostly retail and catering) that they fit around their studies, and see themselves as students who happen to work. In 2010/11, the median earnings of part-time students with full-time jobs of £25,000 were in line with the national average (Callender and Wilkinson, 2012). In 2007/08 the median earnings of part-time students amounted to £17,494 and of full-time students to £12,016 (Johnson *et al.*, 2009: 68).

Table 8.1: UK-domiciled undergraduate student characteristics by mode of study, 2009/10

Characteristic		Part-time	Full-time
		%	%
Age			
	Under 25 years	20	86
	25 years or over	80	14
Gender			
	Female	63	56
	Male	37	44
Ethnicity			
	White	82	78
	Not White	18	22
Highest qualification on entry			
	Postgraduate & PGCE	8	0.5
	First degree, other graduate, HE credits, other HE & professional	46	9
	GCE A Level	37	85
	Other and no formal qualifications	8	5
Qualification aim			
	Bachelor's degree	37	90
	Sub-degree and other HE qualifications	63	10
All		**100**	**100**

Source: HESA student records 2009/10. In Pollard *et al.* (2012)

Part-time undergraduate students, therefore, are a heterogeneous group. There is no 'typical' part-time student. Many, but not all, are at a disadvantage compared with their full-time peers. Some have low-level entry qualifications, come from low-income backgrounds, are concentrated in less prestigious universities and in sub-degree programmes, and have to work full-time and/or care for their families while studying. Given part-time students' work and family pressures and the need to juggle their studies around such commitments, perhaps unsurprisingly, they also have higher non-completion rates than their full-time colleagues. In 2008/09, a third of part-time bachelor degree students dropped out after two years of study compared with 12 per cent of similar full-time students aged 30 and over after one year of study (HESA, n.d.). However, some of these students may have 'stopped out' rather than 'dropped out', and may eventually return to study. Even so, 56 per cent of first degree part-time students commencing programmes at higher education institutions (other than the OU) had not completed that programme within seven academic years (HEFCE, 2009).

The geographical spread of undergraduate part-time provision

As discussed, most part-time students fit their studies around their work and domestic commitments. They are less mobile then their full-time peers and usually live at home while studying, and so opt for local higher education providers that are easy and convenient to reach. Indeed, around three-quarters of part-time undergraduates travel an hour or less to their place of study from their home or work (Callender *et al.*, 2006). Ultimately this limits their choices of where to study. Consequently, the geographical spread of part-time provision is vital in determining prospective part-timers' access to higher education, and their higher education choices.

Part-time provision, as mentioned, is dominated by the OU and all their students are recorded as studying at Milton Keynes in the South East. Excluding OU students, the regions with the largest proportions of non-OU part-time undergraduates are London (16 per cent), the North West (12 per cent), and the West Midlands (11 per cent). Those with the smallest are Northern Ireland (2 per cent), the East Midlands (5 per cent) and the South West (6 per cent). This pattern generally mirrors that of full-time students but when compared with full-time students, part-timers are over-represented in the North East, and under-represented in the East Midlands (Pollard *et al.*, 2012).

These data, while interesting, tell us nothing about whether the supply of part-time provision meets the potential demand while the regions are too large to judge whether part-time courses are available within prospective students' reasonable travelling distance. In a recent study (Callender *et al.*, 2010b), we used data on the proportion of people in the working population who lack qualifications at least to NVQ4 level as a proxy for demand for part-time study, along with smaller 'city regions'. By combining Labour Force Survey data with HESA data, we estimated – at city-region level – the ratio of part-time higher education student numbers in universities per 1,000 working-age persons without a NVQ Level 4 or equivalent.

Our exploratory study shows large disparities in part-time provision. For example, in some city-regions, such as Preston, Cambridge, Coventry, Brighton/Hove, and Plymouth, the ratio of part-time university-based undergraduates to persons without NVQ4 qualifications is two to four times the national average. At the other extreme some city-regions such as Peterborough and Ipswich have no part-time university-based undergraduate courses at all. Thus opportunities to study part time are very unequally distributed across the UK. However, there is no obvious overlap between employment rates and the distribution of part-time higher education provision and correlation analysis confirms that the two variables are not significantly related at city-region level (Callender *et al.*, 2010b).

Tuition fees and financial support for part-time undergraduate students prior to the 2012/13 reforms of higher education finances[1]

Student funding and financial support policies reflect the ideological, economic, and social functions of higher education and are shaped by a society's prevailing history, culture, ideology, or politics. This helps explain the enormous variation in policies globally regarding part-time study and students (Eurydice, 2011). At one extreme are countries where the legal status of a part-time higher education student does not exist, nor does any financial support. At the other extreme are countries like Australia which are 'mode of study blind' – there is no distinction in tuition fee and student aid policies between those studying part time and those studying full time. Between these extremes is a raft of other policy approaches. England had two separate systems of financial support, one for part-time students and another for full-time students, although developments in full-time provision influenced policies targeted at part-time students. The two systems were separate but unequal.

Prior to 1997 and the *Dearing Report*, part-time students did not qualify for any government-funded financial support. It was assumed that because part-time students are older and in paid employment, they did not need government financial help with fees or the costs of study, or that their employers would pay for their studies. Despite a variety of reforms since Dearing (Callender, 2011), these strongly held beliefs still inform financial support policies for part-time students today.

For historical reasons, part-time tuition fees were unregulated and providers were able to charge whatever fees they liked, unlike those for full-time courses. When full-time undergraduate fees were increased to £3,000 a year in 2006, some universities set their part-time fees at a pro rata rate of full time fees, some did not raise their fees, while others set them in line with the maximum level of public fee support available for low-income part-time students (discussed below) (Brown and Ramsden, 2009).

In part, these fee variations reflect the nature of the part-time undergraduate market, which is much more segmented than the full-time undergraduate market. As noted, the part-time student population is heterogeneous, while students' extrinsic and intrinsic motivations for studying and their study outcomes are also mixed (Feinstein *et al.*, 2007; Swain and Hammond, 2011; Callender and Wilkinson, 2012; 2013). In addition, their qualification aims and programmes of study are more varied and they are concentrated in vocational courses but also take non-vocational courses.

No national data are systematically collected on part-time tuition fees, unlike data on full-time fees since 2006. Part-time study initially lay outside the remit of the Office for Fair Access, set up by the 2004 Higher Education Act to safeguard access following the introduction of higher tuition fees in 2006. HEFCE data from 2007/08 suggests that the average undergraduate part-time equivalent fee was £1,805, significantly less than the undergraduate full-time fee of £3,070 (BIS, 2010b), while survey data suggest that in 2009/10 tuition fees averaged around £1,467[2] (Callender and Wilkinson, 2012).

Since 2004/05, the government has provided part-time undergraduates with two means-tested grants: a grant for tuition fees of between £820 and £1,230 (in 2011/12) with the amount varying depending on a student's intensity of study[3]; and a course grant to meet the costs of books, travel and other course expenditure of up to £265 (in 2011/12). Eligibility for these two grants was restricted to a narrow and arbitrary definition of part-time student and part-time study. The grants were limited first to students who did not already hold a bachelor's degree, secondly, to students studying 50 per cent or more of a full-time course, and finally, to students with very low household incomes (lower income thresholds compared with full-time students' means-tested grants).

Consequently, part-timers' access to financial support was not driven by financial need, but was determined initially by a student's existing qualifications and how many hours they studied. The rationale for excluding students already with a bachelor's degree was supposedly on the grounds of equity, but was also a device to leverage the greater involvement of employers in funding higher education. However, there was no obvious reason for the cut-off of 50 per cent of a full-time course. As the profile of part-time students discussed above highlights, together these eligibility criteria automatically disqualified the majority of part-timers from receiving government-funded support. Moreover, the amount of tuition fee and course grants received by part-time undergraduates was inadequate as they did not cover students' costs in full (Callender *et al.*, 2010a).

In 2009/10, 57,000 students received a fee grant of an average value of around £700 a year, while 59,000 benefited from a course grant worth an average of £260 a year (BIS, 2010b). Consequently, only a minority (15 per cent) of all part-time undergraduates and those studying for a bachelor's degree (35 per cent) received any government-funded financial assistance (BIS, 2010a). The majority paid their tuition fees upfront. For these students, higher education was not free at the point of access and they, rather than the state, were expected to meet their costs. Cost sharing was limited, the financial burden rested primarily on the shoulders of individual students.

By comparison, full-time students' financial support was, and continues to be, far more comprehensive and generous. First, all first-time full-time students, irrespective of their family's household income, are eligible for government-subsidized, income-contingent student loans to cover all their tuition fees. They repay these loans on graduation, so that no full-time student is required to pay tuition fees upfront. Second, all students qualify for government-subsidized, income-contingent maintenance loans to cover some of their living costs. Third, low-income students also receive means-tested, government-funded maintenance grants towards their living costs. Finally, some students, especially low-income students, can get institutional grants or bursaries. Full-time students continue to receive all these forms of financial support, even after the introduction of the 2012/13 student finance reforms.

The case for reform of financial support for part-time undergraduate students

To summarize, the main drawbacks with government funding support for part-time undergraduates in England until the 2012/13 reforms were as follows. First, the system clearly favoured full-time higher education at the expense of part-time higher education, and younger school leavers at the expense of mature students. In effect, the government guaranteed and underwrote the tuition fees of all full-time students via student loans but provided no such guarantees for all part-time students, not even among those receiving tuition fee grants since the grants did not always cover all of their fees. From a higher education institution's perspective, student loans for full-time students meant all full-time students were creditors and were a guaranteed income stream. Part-time students, by contrast, were potential debtors and an unpredictable income stream. Such an unequal playing field was considered inequitable by many.

Second, part-time financial support (or lack of it) was based on two flawed assumptions: that employers pay for their employees' higher education, and that those who are employed can afford higher education and meet their costs through their earnings. Survey data refute both assumptions. Surveys over time consistently show that only around a third of part-time undergraduates receive financial help from their employer with their tuition fees (Woodley, 2004; Callender *et al.*, 2006; Johnson *et al.*, 2009; Callender *et al.*, 2010a). Our most recent survey of nearly 4,000 part-time undergraduates shows how, understandably, employers are cautious and selective in whom they sponsor. They favour the most advantaged employees to the detriment of those most in need – those from low-income households with poorly paid, part-time jobs and low levels of educational attainment. Our multivariate analysis revealed that the part-time students most likely to benefit from financial help with their tuition fees, once a range of characteristics were controlled for, were white, full-time workers from the wealthiest households who already held a bachelor's degree and were taking a vocational qualification (Callender *et al.*, 2010a). Consequently, the most disadvantaged groups missed out. Moreover, employer support is an unreliable source of financial aid, especially in a recession, as education and training budgets are cut (Mason and Bishop, 2010), particularly in the public sector where most part-time students work. In addition, evidence suggests that liquidity constraints inhibit the participation of potential part-time students from low-income households who are unable to receive employer support, leading to unmet demand (Pollard *et al.*, 2008).

Third, most part-time students do not receive financial support and have to pay their own tuition fees upfront because of the restrictive eligibility criteria. For those who do receive government support, the level of help is inadequate. As research on full-time students, in the UK and elsewhere, demonstrates, university tuition fees may have a negative impact on participation, and fee increases tend to cause a decline in participation, particularly among students from lower socio-economic backgrounds, unless accompanied by equivalent increases in student support (London Economics, 2010; Long, 2008). For instance, Dearden *et al.*'s (2010) results imply that a £1,000 increase in fees results in a 4.4 ppt decrease in university participation, while a £1,000 increase in loans results in a 3.2 ppt increase in participation, and a £1,000 increase in grants results in a 2.1 ppt increase in participation. However, their results indicate 'that a £1,000 increase in loans or grants is not sufficient to counteract the impact of a £1,000 increase in fees' (Dearden *et al.*, 2010: 24).

They conclude:

> These results are highly relevant for policy makers, who ought to be aware of *the negative impact of upfront fees* – i.e. those not covered by a fee loan – and the positive impact of aid on participation. Maintenance grants can potentially be used to offset the negative influence of fee increases, given their opposing influences on participation. Policy makers should also be aware of particularly vulnerable groups when setting levels of fees and grants, and may need to target specific groups with more generous aid to counteract any increases in tuition fees.
>
> (Dearden *et al.*, 2010: 31; my italics)

The relevance of these findings for part-time students is unclear, however. Dearden *et al.*'s, (2010) research – like the vast majority of other research, both in England and elsewhere, that models the impact of tuition fees and financial support on higher education participation – is based on the university participation decisions of 18-year-olds and the financial assistance available to full-time students. This begs the question of the extent to which, first, the costs of part-time higher education are a barrier to participation, and second, the relative effectiveness of different types of financial aid in promoting part-time higher education study.

The 2012/13 reforms

Elsewhere in this volume the context and contents of Lord Browne's review of higher education – *Independent Review of Higher Education Funding and Student Finance* – and the Coalition Government's subsequent 2011 White Paper *Higher Education: Students at the Heart of the System* (BIS, 2011) are discussed at length (see chapters 1, 2 and 3) and will not be repeated here.

The Coalition Government's reforms of undergraduate funding, outlined in the 2011 White Paper (BIS, 2011) and introduced in 2012/13, aim to make higher education financially sustainable, to improve the student experience, and increase social mobility. The economic context within which these reforms occurred – the global recession and unprecedented cuts in public expenditure – are paramount in understanding them. The reforms seek to reduce both undergraduate student support costs and higher education public expenditure, in line with the Coalition's broader strategy to cut the fiscal deficit and stimulate economic growth. The Coalition's ideologically driven vision is of a higher education sector defined by the market, which they believe delivers high-quality services efficiently, equitably, and is responsive to consumer choice (BIS, 2011). For choice and competition to operate effectively, money must follow users' choice, there must be a variety of types of provision, with new providers entering the market and failing ones exiting, and users must be properly informed.

This political and ideological environment is not exceptional. As Johnstone and Marcucci in their global review of funding remind us, tuition fees are the 'political and ideological flashpoint for debates over the need for, and the propriety of, cost-sharing in all its forms' (2010: 102). They continue, 'tuition fees are almost everywhere contested' (p. 123), reflecting the cultural and historical acceptability of tuition fees as well as the prevailing political ideologies. Johnstone and Marcucci insist that 'cost-sharing for almost all countries is not only an imperative for the financial health of their colleges and universities, but it can also bring about enhanced efficiency, equity and responsiveness' (2010: 282).

Discussion in the White Paper focuses nearly exclusively on full-time students. However, it announced that 'We are committed to *ensuring that higher education in England is affordable* for students too … And one of the biggest changes we are making is that many part-time and distance-learning students will also be able to access loans to cover the full tuition costs for the first time' (BIS, 2011: 16) [emphasis added].

The one paragraph in the White Paper devoted exclusively to part-time students reads:

> For the first time, students starting part-time undergraduate courses in 2012/13, many of whom are from non-traditional backgrounds, will be entitled to an up-front loan to meet their tuition costs so long as they are studying at an intensity of at least 25 per cent, in each academic year, of a full-time course. *This is a major step in terms of opening up access to higher education,* and remedies a long-standing injustice in support for adult learners. Up to around 175,000 part-time students will benefit. Under the

new system, distance learning students studying full-time will also benefit from a loan to cover their tuition costs.

(BIS, 2011: 61, my italics)[4]

The rationale for this change is discussed in Lord Browne's 2010 report, *Independent Review of Higher Education Funding and Student Finance* (IRHEFSF, 2010). One of the principles informing the *Browne Report* was:

> Part-time students should be treated the same as full-time students for the costs of learning. The current system requires part-time students to pay upfront. This puts people off from studying part-time and it stops innovation in courses that combine work and study. In our proposal the *upfront costs for part-time students will be eliminated, so that a wider range of people can access higher education* in a way that is convenient for them.
>
> (IRHEFSF, 2010: 5, my italics)

Browne also observed:

> The lack of support for part-time study makes it much more difficult for this country to catch up with other countries on the skill levels of the existing workforce. Individuals who are already in work and do not have a higher education qualification are usually unlikely to give up their jobs and enter full-time study. Part-time study may be a realistic option for them, but *access to part-time study is hampered by the lack of Government support.* The potential exists to combine the experience of individuals already in work with the skills that higher education can provide; but it is not being exploited.
>
> (IRHEFSF, 2010: 22–3, my italics)

This policy change has to be located alongside the other finance reforms introduced in 2012/13; specifically, the withdrawal of universities' teaching grants for most undergraduate courses and its replacement with higher tuition fees; and the raising of the government-set cap on full-time undergraduate tuition fees from £3,290 to £9,000 a year including, for the first time, a cap of £6,750[5] on part-time tuition fees. This maximum part-time fee is independent of intensity of study, so in theory a university could charge this for a course which amounts to only 25 per cent of a full-time course. All full-time students as before, and now some part-time students for the first time, can repay their tuition fees through government-subsidized income-contingent loans.

Consequently, there is no, or limited, taxpayer support for part-time undergraduate teaching; these costs are met by students paying higher fees. Government support for some part-time undergraduates, therefore, has shifted from teaching grants to student loans – from a block grant to private contributions from individual students – informed by the idea of cost sharing. Ultimately, these changes valorize the private benefits of higher education at the expense of the public benefits, and in not questioning the private subsidy of public benefits, they position higher education as a private investment rather than as a public good (Reay, 2012).

To reduce the government's costs of extending loan provision, the interest rate on loans was increased so that both student loan repayments and the interest charged on them vary according to a graduate's earnings. Both graduates from part- and full-time study do not repay their loans until they are earning £21,000[6] a year (up from £15,000 for full-time students), while the interest on their loan is limited to the rate of inflation. Graduates earning between £21,000 and £41,000 per annum are charged interest on a sliding scale up to a maximum of inflation plus 3 per cent when earnings exceed £41,000 per year. Both graduates from part- and full-time study will pay 9 per cent of their income until they have repaid all their loans, with outstanding debt written off after 30 years (up from 25 years for full-time students).

A key difference in the treatment of part- and full-time students is when loan repayments commence. Part-time students are liable for repayments four years after their course begins, or in the April after their course ends, if their courses last for less time. Students on courses lasting more than four years, namely most bachelor degree programmes, therefore start repaying their loans while still studying and before graduating. This brings into question whether higher education is really free at the point of access for most part-time bachelor degree students. In contrast, graduates from full-time bachelor degrees start repaying their loans in the April after they graduate, irrespective of the duration of their course.

The overall structure of student financial assistance for full-time students remains unchanged by these reforms; although some of the terms and conditions attached to them have altered. In contrast, tuition fee grants and course grants for part-time students have been abolished, so that in future new part-time students, even the poorest, will receive no financial help with other study costs. And it is still presumed they do not need help with their living costs, even when not in paid employment, as these are paid through the social security system. Such benefits are worth less than maintenance loans and grants afforded to low-income full-time students, however.

Assessing the 2012/13 reforms

Loan eligibility, like part-time student grants before them, is restricted. Only part-time students who do not already hold an equivalent level or higher qualification qualify for the new loans. Again, those who already have had one bite of the higher education cherry are mostly barred from receiving financial aid for a second. This criterion excludes about 54 per cent of all part-time undergraduate students. In addition, entitlement is limited by students' intensity of study – only those studying at least 25 per cent of a full-time course can access the new student loans eliminating a further 15 per cent of students from qualifying (Pollard *et al.*, 2012). Consequently, as before, access to financial support is not driven by financial need, but is determined initially by a student's existing qualifications and how many hours they study.

According to the Department for Business, Innovation and Skills, twice as many part-time students could benefit from tuition fee loans compared with those receiving fee and course grants. Government calculations suggest 33 per cent of all part-time undergraduates will be entitled to student loans in 2012/13, and around 67 per cent of those will be aiming for a bachelor's degree (BIS, 2010a). Other estimates are not as optimistic. While a similar proportion (32 per cent) of all UK domicile part-time students studying at English higher education institutions will be eligible, only 45 per cent of those taking a bachelor's degree and 23 per cent of those taking other part-time undergraduate qualifications will qualify (Pollard *et al.*, 2012). Whichever estimate proves correct, the majority of part-time students cannot access the new loans and their upfront costs are not eliminated, as Browne suggests.

A central objective of these loans, reflecting Ziderman's classification (2013), is cost-sharing. The replacement of fee and course grants with loans both reduces public expenditure and shifts the costs of higher education away from government and taxpayers so that more of these costs are borne by students. The loans also facilitate the raising of part-time tuition fees, while their income-contingent nature makes fee increases more politically and socially acceptable. The disincentive effects of upfront tuition fee increases, raised by the *Browne Report*, are offset by the loans.

Moreover, in line with market principles, and the Coalition's desire to create a quasi-higher education market, the bulk of universities' money will follow students' choices, while student loans – which are like an educational voucher that students redeem at the institution of choice – will encourage both consumer choice and provider competition. Theoretically, consumer demand will determine what courses higher education institutions offer, while higher education institutions will compete on price.

The new system of financial support for part-time students replicates and exacerbates the previous system's limitations, except now more students will qualify for government help. It continues to favour full-time higher education and school leavers at the expense of older, part-time students. All full-time tuition fees are underwritten by student loans but the same cannot be said for all of part-time students. Higher education institutions will continue to recruit full-time students where there is an excess demand for such places, rather than fill their places with 'riskier' part-time students. And the reduction of the HEFCE's part-time premium, which sought to compensate institutions for the additional costs associated with part-time provision could make part-time courses even less appealing, unless institutions can charge higher pro-rata tuition fees.

It is still assumed that employers will pay tuition fees for their employees, especially those ineligible for loans. It is impossible, however, to gauge how the availability of loans might affect employers' willingness to sponsor those employees who are entitled to loans, or the level of deadweight. Similarly, it is presumed that part-time students do not need any help with their study or maintenance costs, apart from tuition fees. As the government has argued, 'part-time students are also most likely to be in employment, so there is the assumption that income derived from this should cover their maintenance costs' (BIS, 2010b: 21). In their response to the consultation on the White Paper, they claim:

> We understand the desire to make maintenance support available to part-time students, but government must also consider what is affordable within current spending limits. Students on part-time courses are able to combine study and work, and access other government benefits, which is generally not true for full-time students. This is why we are maintaining our decision not to extend maintenance support to part-time students. Our judgement is that access to loans for tuition costs represents a more significant benefit for these students.
>
> (BIS, 2012: 8)

Budgetary constraints were also the reason given for denying loan access to those students who already hold an equivalent level or higher qualification: 'it remains our policy to focus support on those entering higher education for the first time and to provide no further support to students once they have achieved an honours degree' (BIS, 2012: 8). This policy is likely to thwart those wishing to re-skill without employer support.

Part-time tuition fees in 2012/13

Predictably, undergraduate part-time tuition fees have risen as a result of the reforms. Despite part-time study now falling within its remit, the Office for Fair Access (OFFA) have yet to publish any detailed national data on part-time fees as it has done for full-time courses. However, OFFA estimates[7] that under the new system higher education institutions' fee income above the basic part-time fee[8] will amount to £31.2 million in 2013/14, and rise to £46.7 million in 2016–17 (OFFA, 2012a). No similar data are published by OFFA for 2012/13. Yet it is clear that part-time tuition fees for 2012/13 vary, and more so than full-timers', whose average annual fees are £8,527, and £8,363 after fee waivers[9] (OFFA, 2012b).

Table 8.2 shows the maximum tuition fees charged in 2012/13 for part-time bachelor degree courses for a full-time equivalent (FTE) course (120 credits) at those universities in England that had large numbers of part-time undergraduates in 2009/10.[10] Among the universities listed, their fees range from £3,000 to £9,000 a year for a full-time equivalent course.[11] As discussed, this wide variation reflects the fragmented and highly segmented nature of the part-time market, and in line with government aspirations, sharpens the price competition between part-time providers.

However, we might question the impact on the quality of provision arising from such competition and aggressive pricing.

Table 8.2: Maximum tuition fees charged in 2012/13 per year for a part-time bachelor degree for a full-time equivalent course at English universities with large numbers of part-time undergraduates

	Full-time equivalent tuition fee
Open University	£5,000
Teesside University	£6,480
Birkbeck College	£9,000
University of Central Lancashire	£3,000
London South Bank University	£8,450
University of Plymouth	£9,000
University of Hull	£9,000

Source: Derived from OFFA agreements, www.offa.org.uk/access-agreements/, and each university's website 2012

It is far too early to know what impact the 2012/13 reforms may have on the demand for, and supply of, part-time higher education. However, it is clear from the Browne Review and the White Paper that the government seeks to open up access to higher education for part-time students, make it more affordable, encourage more people to study part-time, and hence stem the decline in part-time higher education study. They aim to do this while reducing public expenditure on higher education. In the remainder of this chapter I assess the reforms and question their policy objectives and whether the policy goals are achievable.

The costs of the loans for part-time students

Turning to the Coalition's desire to reduce public expenditure on part-time higher education and to put part-time higher education on a financially sustainable footing. According to BIS (2010b), the reforms to part-time student finances will lead to savings in public expenditure because of the cuts in the HEFCE teaching grant for part-time students and the abolition of the existing student fee and course grants. Prior to the 2012/13 reforms, just over £400 million was paid through the funding council for 109,000 full-time equivalent part-time students. The funding council provided direct support for around 240,000 part-time students (headcount). In addition, £63 million was spent on fee and course grants plus £13.5 million on targeted support. The cost of providing loans is estimated to be £220 million by 2014/15. The net effect of the changes to funding for part-time students will be to cut public expenditure. The annual saving is estimated at £150 million in 2014–15 (BIS, 2010b)[12].

Both the money the government currently provides higher education institutions for teaching, and the part-time student grants, are counted as public expenditure and assist in the reduction of the structural deficit. However, most spending on student loans, which will replace the teaching funds, is not – apart from the loan subsidy. As Barr (2011: para 2) observes: 'Though little has changed in cash terms (since the government has to finance the upfront cost of loans), there is an apparent reduction in the BIS budget; it is not unfair to say that an accounting trick is driving deleterious policy change.' The cash needed to provide loans will be borrowed and thus add to the stock of public sector debt.

In reality, it is difficult to estimate accurately the costs of the new part-time loans because it is unclear nationally what universities are charging for their part-time courses, what proportion of part-time students are taking out the loans, what their loan repayments will be, and so what the Resource Accounting and Budgetary (RAB) charge will be – that part of a loan written off by the government that will never be recovered fully from graduate loan repayments. The RAB charge is important because it represents the government subsidy on student loans, counts as public spending (as measured by the Public Sector Borrowing Requirement) and appears in BIS's budget as current spending. Consequently, it is a cost to the taxpayer.

Numerous commentators have tried to assess these loan costs and RAB charges for full-time students and the government has provided detailed analysis too, although estimates vary considerably. But, at the time of writing, only one study has examined the costs of loans for part-time students (Million+/London Economics, 2013). Their calculations suggest that the RAB charge will be negative for part-time students who take out loans, and that part-time fee loans could actually generate income for the Treasury.

> We estimate that the removal of part-time fee and course grants between 2010/11 and 2012/13 will save the Treasury approximately £55 million, while the introduction of part-time fee loans is expected to generate £33 million from the 2012/13 cohort for the Treasury.
>
> (Million+/London Economics, 2013: 7)

The extra income will come from the positive real interest rates on the part-time loans, the smaller size of their loans[13], and because most part-time students are older and employed and have earnings in excess of the loan repayment threshold of £21,000. As Callender and Wilkinson (2011) also confirm, the higher pay levels of graduates from part-time study suggest that they are likely to repay their student loans at a faster rate than graduates from full-time study, and to pay higher interest rates. Both will benefit the Exchequer and make loans for part-timers potentially cheaper for the public purse than those for their full-time equivalents.

The London Economics study suggests an overall RAB charge for all part time students of +7.5 per cent, which means that for every £100 of student loan the government lends a part-time student, it gets back £107.5.[14] This increases to +29.8 per cent or £129.80 for male part-time students but falls to a negative RAB charge of −11 per cent or £89 for female students. It will take an average of 14 years for male students to pay off their loans and 22 years for women (Million+/London Economics, 2013: 15).

London Economics' calculations have assumed an average part-time tuition fee of £3,990 and that this fee increase will lead to a 5 per cent fall in demand. Consequently, they estimate that the gross tuition fee income for higher education institutions between 2010/11 and 2012/13 will rise from £175 million to £630 million but higher education institutions will lose £314 million in the HEFCE teaching grant so will be about £141 million better off.

While the London Economics study is to be welcomed, there is no way of knowing if the assumptions underpinning their modelling are accurate because of an absence of data. So, their calculations should be treated with considerable caution. Indeed, they warn that gains to higher education institutions could be wiped out if fewer undergraduates started their courses in 2012/13.

Similarly, London Economics' positive RAB charge for part-time students, alongside Callender and Wilkinson's (2011) conclusions depend on how many and what sort of people enrol in part-time study post-2012/13. It cannot be presumed that the profile of the part-time undergraduate student population will remain the same following the 2012/13 reforms. Namely, that part-time study will continue to attract highly qualified and fairly well paid people working full-time, or that those taking out loans will have these characteristics. Indeed, it is likely that as a result of the funding changes the composition of part-time student body will alter. Specifically, in line with the findings of Dearden *et al.* (2010) and others (London Economics, 2010), the fall in demand for part-time study is most likely to occur amongst students experiencing higher fees who do not qualify for loans and have to pay their fees upfront – those, in other words, with high level entry qualifications and higher levels jobs. Conversely, those most attracted to part-time study might be those who are eligible for loans to cover the higher fees, individuals who tend to have low entry qualifications and lower earnings. Hence, the earnings profile of part-time graduates may well change and their average earnings may well fall. Such developments would lead to a rise in the overall RAB charge of part-time loans.

In reality, the exact consequences of the 2012/13 reforms and the reductions in government spending are currently difficult to assess. They depend on the reactions both of potential part-time students and higher education institutions to the changes. Indeed, the government acknowledges that:

it is not only difficult to estimate what overall demand levels for part-time study will look like under the new system – it is also impossible to estimate the change in benefits, particularly if the composition of part-time students is going to change (and hence the average part-time premium).

(BIS, 2010b: 21)

The funding changes and demand for part-time study

The number of part-time undergraduate entrants has fallen by 40 per cent since 2010/11 – equivalent to 105,000 fewer students (HEFCE, 2013: 13). These falls are far greater than those for full-time students (UCAS, 2012a), which have been the focus of attention. Significantly, even universities that had bucked the national downward trend in part-time recruitment and had experienced a steady rise in enrolments over the past five years or more, such as the OU and Birkbeck, are reporting falls of around this magnitude for 2012/13 (NIACE, 2013). These universities account for a significant proportion of the overall decline, but 'cannot explain the scale of reductions across the sector' (HEFCE, 2013: 13).

This headline figure is of deep concern. However, one year after the introduction of the new funding regime, we still have no idea which student groups are most affected or have any insights into the socio-economic characteristics of those who are, or are not, participating in part-time higher education, as we do for full-time students. We do not have any early warning system about changes in part-time applications and enrolment patterns. Unlike full-time students, part-time students do not apply to university through UCAS, but instead apply directly to the institution of their choice. The absence of a centralized application system means we cannot assess demand nationally. Instead, we have to rely exclusively on enrolment data that reflect both the demand for, and supply of, part-time provision. Moreover, these detailed national HESA data on part-time enrolments are only released 18 months after the end of the application cycle. So we will not gain a detailed insight into the initial effects of the reforms on part-time recruitment in 2012/13 until January 2014.

In the absence of such hard data, we can only speculate about the impact of the changes. In line with the aspirations of the White Paper and the *Browne Report*, will they improve the student experience and promote social mobility by 'opening up access to higher education' (BIS, 2011: 61) and by 'ensuring that higher education in England is affordable for students' (BIS, 2011: 16)?

In turn, this raises a number of questions about why demand appears to have fallen so dramatically and whether it is associated with the changes in funding and/or other factors such as the recession. Are those who are eligible for these loans taking advantage of them? Are these particular loans a suitable funding mechanism for part-time students? Given that the majority of part-time students do not qualify for the loans, what is happening to demand among these students who face far higher tuition fees, which they have to pay themselves, upfront (or with employer support)?

Are part-time students taking advantage of the new loans? By May 2013 only 34,200 or 22 per cent of part-time 2012/13 entrants had taken out a loan, a far smaller proportion than the third predicted by the government (Hansard, 2013). However, more detailed information on the characteristics of these students is unavailable. We have very limited insights from existing research about part-time students' attitudes to loans. Some research, conducted before the rise in tuition fees, suggests part-time students have little appetite for student loans (Callender *et al.*, 2006). However, loans might be attractive to older people, those with low-earnings or incomes, or those who are retired. Such individuals would be heavily subsidized by government as they are unlikely to pay off their loans in full because the loans are income-contingent and outstanding debt is forgiven after 30 years. The average income of pensioners is well below the £21,000 income threshold for repaying the loans. Yet other potential part-time students may not take out loans, especially those who already have sizable financial commitments such as mortgages, those who are debt averse, and those who feel that paying 9 per cent of their income on their student loan repayments is more than they can manage or are prepared to pay given the uncertainties about the returns on their investment during a recession. They may not feel that the benefits of study outweigh the costs.

Research suggests that while part-time undergraduates have varied motivations for studying, their actual decision to enter higher education is not taken lightly. Like other mature students (Osborne *et al.*, 2004), they are far more likely to weigh up the costs and benefits of studying and take time to decide whether or not to do so. Going to university is not 'the normal thing to do' or next step for someone like them, unlike younger full-time school leaver students where it has become 'normalized' (Purcell *et al.*, 2008). Indeed, part-time students may well be making more 'informed choices' than their younger peers: the opportunity costs as well as the risks may well be greater for some of these potential students.

Anecdotal evidence suggests that even where potential students were well informed about funding arrangements for new study and understood the costs, they still failed to enrol and take advantage of the loans. So while investing in properly targeted communication about the new funding arrangements is important – indeed the inadequacies of the government's communication strategy on part-time funding has been heavily criticized – this cannot explain all of the fall in demand, as some would argue (NIACE, 2013). As one commentator has observed:

> It may not have been a failure to communicate, more a failure to persuade
> … Students … were not convinced that they would achieve an appropriate
> return on this increased investment … They understood the costs but were

not necessarily convinced enough about the value to enrol in 2012. ... their confidence in the value of a degree is low.

(King, 2013: 15)

Such issues might also help explain the greater falls in applications in 2012/13 from mature full-time students compared with their younger peers (UCAS, 2012b). So too might they also account for why applications into 2013/14 continue to fall amongst students in England aged 30 and over, while applications from younger students have begun to recover (UCAS, 2013) (see also chapter 6 by Wyness).

The right sort of loans for part-time students?

Until we have a better understanding of which type of part-time students have taken out loans and which have rejected them, it is difficult to propose any policy changes. However, we might consider whether these particular loans are the right sort for encouraging greater participation in part-time study.

The justification for student loans and cost sharing loan policies is predicated on the financial returns of higher education and other private benefits, and the ideology that those who benefit from higher education should contribute towards its cost. The analysis by London Economics suggests that part-time students benefit enough financially from their studies to warrant the introduction of income-contingent loans. However, other evidence from the international literature on the returns to lifelong learning is mixed (Dorsett *et al.*, 2010). A number of studies suggest graduates who delay their education receive a premium relative to those who do not (Ferrer and Menendez, 2009; Garrett *et al.*, 2010; Blanden *et al.*, 2010). By contrast, others suggest that lifelong learning is not as beneficial as conventional learning would have been to those who undertake it (Light, 1995; Holmlund *et al.*, 2008; Egerton and Parry, 2001; Jenkins *et al*, 2002). If, as some now argue, the private financial returns of part-time study are lower than those for full-time students in terms of higher earnings and employment opportunities – are the current loans an equitable or efficient option?

Ziderman (2013) demonstrates how government-sponsored student loan schemes around the world differ in the central objective pursued: objectives that are important because they have implications for the loan schemes' design and provisions. He identifies three main categories of objectives: cost sharing, social targeting, and student independence. As suggested, the loans in England can be characterized as cost sharing since they facilitate cost-recovery and the raising of tuition fees. Social targeting is explicitly and directly concerned with the accessibility of the poor while the student independence objective seeks to ease student financial burdens during study.

Arguably, if the government is committed to 'opening up access to higher education' (BIS, 2011: 61) and increasing the participation of poorer and more marginal groups, then a social targeting model may be more appropriate than a cost sharing model. Such a model offers financial incentives to poor potential students, both in terms of overcoming the financial burden of tuition fees and by offsetting fears that the benefits of higher education may not be sizeable. This may be particularly important for part-time students given the lower financial returns of part-time study, their high non-completion rates, and the negative financial returns associated with non-completion (London Economics, 2010) whereby students may end up with large student loan debts but little or no financial returns.

Ziderman (2013) argues that the most effective method of enhancing the poor's educational access is through means-tested grants for tuition fees (and living costs). These are expensive, however. Consequently, heavily subsidized loans with low interest rates to encourage borrowing are a potential solution. He does not advocate loan subsidization more generally: 'the aim should be near full loan recovery, loan schemes targeted on the poor may constitute an acceptable exception' (Ziderman, 2013: 37). However, these loan subsidies also are expensive to government:

> Since a grant offers a stronger and more direct incentive for access than does a (partially) repayable loan, the apparent advantage of loans over grants is less clear-cut. This highlights a central conundrum in loan policy: at what level of built-in loan subsidy does a grant become a more cost-effective instrument for helping the poor than a subsidized loan (with hidden grants)? This suggests that, in country settings where state budgets are constrained, a more appropriate financial aid program for the poor is likely to involve a combination of both loans and grants, with a relatively larger overt grant element for the very poor.
>
> (Ziderman, 2013: 43)

Finally, turning to the majority of potential students who do not qualify for loans under the new funding regime: they will have to pay their tuition fees upfront, as they did before the 2012/13 reforms, except now their tuition fees have increased threefold. These individuals might also think the fees are too expensive an investment, or simply unaffordable. As discussed, the extensive international research warns against upfront tuition fees without adequate financial support since they can depress participation. Moreover, given the evidence on the lower financial returns of part-time higher education, this will tend to discourage students unless the state subsidizes them.

Other research also indicates that part-time students and their employers may be unwilling or unable to meet the large increase in tuition fees introduced in 2012/13, especially given the recession and lower levels of investment in learning. Cuts in public expenditure are likely to have a disproportionate impact on opportunities to study part-time, too, since the majority of part-time students work in the public sector. Callender and Wilkinson's (2012) longitudinal study of part-time students, covering the current recession but before the introduction of the 2012/13 reforms, shows how part-time tuition fees rose by 27 per cent, well above the rate of inflation

(4.4 per cent RPI). Both students and employers shared the costs of these tuition fee increases. However, employers were less likely to pay all of students' fees, and more students were making a contribution toward their fees.

Using this survey data, Callender and Wilkinson also assessed the optimum tuition fee price for maximizing participation by using price sensitivity modelling, following Van Westendorp (1976). The underlying premise here is that there is a relationship between price and quality: you get what you pay for. At the time of the study these students' annual tuition fees were £1,467, below the £2,264 they estimated to be the average price at which part-time courses would be too expensive for them to consider taking them. If the fees increased to £2,000, between 59 per cent and 74 per cent of surveyed students reported that the course would be too expensive. If it rose to £3,200, the figure jumped to between 78 per cent and 89 per cent.

Taken together with the changes in employer behaviour and financial support, this does not bode well for new part-time entrants. Both the maximum tuition fee of £6,750 and the average tuition fees reported in Table 8.2 are far higher than students' perceived 'too expensive' threshold. More part-time students will no longer be able to rely on their employer for financial help to pay for all of their fees, and will have to pay for some or all of these themselves. Together they are likely to restrict opportunities to study part-time and depress demand. It is difficult to see how for this majority of would be part-time students, these reforms are 'opening up access to higher education' (BIS, 2011: 61) and 'ensuring that higher education in England is affordable for students' (BIS, 2011: 16).

If the government is truly committed to part-time study and its importance for economic growth in re-skilling the existing workforce – and does not want to see a fall in the demand and supply of part-time higher education – then, at a minimum, it should reconsider the current eligibility criteria for student loans. Specifically, it should extend eligibility for loans to those who already hold an equivalent level or higher qualification. If the government were to do so, the RAB charge on loans for these individuals could be lower and even positive, given their higher earnings and the higher loan interest rates they would pay. Indeed the government may make a profit out of part-time undergraduate loans, in line with London Economics' (2013) findings. There would be no excuse for budgetary constraints.

Importantly, while the private financial returns to part-time study might be low, our research suggests that the non-pecuniary returns are high in terms of improving both graduates' working and non-working lives (Callender and Wilkinson, 2013). For instance, two years after graduation, 80 per cent of those surveyed believed that their ability to do their work had improved as a direct result of their course, while 88 per cent reported greater personal development, 78 per cent more confidence, and over a half were happier. Moreover, the majority of part-time students begin to reap these benefits *before* they graduate and complete their studies (Callender and Wilkinson, 2012). Indeed, our research suggests that the non-financial returns of part-time study are potentially *relatively* greater in comparison to the private financial returns, and in turn, justify more generous state funding.

Conclusions

There continue to be significant unresolved issues regarding the funding of part-time higher education study. In part-time providers' favour, part-time student places remain uncapped, unlike the strict controls on full-time student places, which makes part-time provision a potentially attractive revenue source in an environment of restricted full-time places. It also makes market competition keener because if a university's quality drops, we would expect reduced demand and a downward pressure on price, although part-time students' limited mobility restricts their choices. Indeed, we already see greater variation in tuition fees within the part-time sector – because of its segmented nature – than we do in the full-time sector. However, it is unlikely that uncapped part-time student places will continue in the longer term.

Another important issue untouched by the White Paper, is flexible funding. In theory, student loans make moving in and out of part- and full-time study easier. However, if there is a desire to make higher education study more adaptable and attractive to a wider range of students whereby they can change their mode of study and higher education institution while pursuing a qualification, as happens in the US, then a system of funding around credit accumulation is required. For instance in the US, an estimated 38 per cent of undergraduate enrolments in degree-granting institutions were part time in the fall 2010 (United States Department of Education, 2012). Over an academic year, however, the proportion attending part time for some or all of the year is considerably higher (Chen and Carroll, 2007). Indeed, the rules associated with the receipt of loans work against such flexibility. Students have to enrol for a specific undergraduate qualification in order to qualify for one. Prior to the introduction of loans, for instance, OU students could sign up for a variety of modules and gain a qualification through credit accumulation. Now this is not possible. Nor is it easy for students to transfer to another higher education institution. The absence of modular or credit-based funding, therefore, inhibits flexible provision and delivery that can respond to the needs of students and their employers.

The aims of the 2012/13 reforms of part-time student financial support were to encourage more people to study part-time, to open up access, make part-time study more affordable, and to stem the decline in part-time undergraduate study, while at the same time reducing public expenditure. These policy objectives are welcome, but it is questionable whether such goals can be achieved through the policy instruments introduced and whether they are the most appropriate for part-time students. Indeed, these reforms are having the opposite effect. It may well be the case, therefore, that part-time higher education study continues to decline rather than grow: not what the government or the sector wanted. Part-time students and part-time study may well be one of the main casualties of the White Paper, and are certainly not at the heart of the system.

The government's part-time student funding policies are unproven, and as they admit, have unknown consequences and unforeseen unintended consequences. We will not know their outcome for several years. The type of people attracted to part-time study may change, with only those eligible for student loans or gaining employer support participating. This may be one of the unintended consequences of these reforms and would lead to a more homogeneous undergraduate student body, and arguably a less diverse higher education sector. Ultimately the government's policies for part-time students fail to heed Johnstone and Marcucci's words that 'cost-sharing is no miracle cure' (2010: 282) and 'our advocacy of cost-sharing is always an advocacy for its ability to supplement and augment government revenue, never to replace it' (2010: 283).

As the 2011 White Paper acknowledges, the changes represent a radical reform of the higher education system. They herald a retreat from the state's financial responsibility for part-time higher education with a shift towards individual universities, but especially students who are ineligible for loans carrying all of this responsibility and the risks. Implicit in this strategy is a fundamental ideological revision about the purpose of higher education, driven by economic competition and the dominance of financial values. Undergraduate higher education is not seen by government as a public good, of value to society as a whole beyond those who receive it, and so worthy of public funding, but instead as a private good with private economic returns from individual investment. Higher education's private-good functions are pitted against its public-good functions and reveal a policy mindset and political ideology where the public and private benefits are a zero-sum game. The direct non-market benefits of higher education, which McMahon (2009) argues exceed the market benefits, are ignored.

In the short term, the changes are having a destabilizing effect on the part-time higher education sector. There may be some fiscal savings but will these be at the expense of the longer term effects on quality, social equity and universities as public, civic, and cultural institutions? We need a much better understanding of what is happening across the part-time sector before recommending any reforms. Are the declines in part-time study associated with tuition fee policies, the limitations of student financial support, and/or other factors, such as the economy, occupational regulation, employer behaviour, and other government higher education policies? Most importantly, we need the political will both within the sector and the government to tackle the challenges posed by part-time study.

Notes

[1] The following discussion only relates to United Kingdom domicile undergraduates students studying in England since devolution provision for part-time undergraduates varies within the UK countries.

[2] Note this is an average figure and will vary by intensity of study.

[3] In 2011/12 students studying 50 per cent to 59 per cent of a full-time course could get a maximum of £820, those studying between 60 per cent and 74 per cent could get up to £985, and those studying 75 per cent or more can get up to £1,230.

[4] The government subsequently announced that there will be no age limit for the receipt of tuition fee loans.

[5] This is equivalent to 75 per cent of the maximum full-time fee of £9,000.

[6] For the tax year ending 5 April 2011, the median gross annual earnings for full-time employees were £26,200, for men they were £28,400, and for women £22,900 (ONS, n.d.).

[7] It is not clear how these estimates are calculated given the absence of data on part-time enrolments.

[8] For part-time new system students, the basic fee is £4,500 and the maximum fee is £6,750.

[9] This sum does not include bursaries or scholarships in cash.

[10] Each higher education institution had a minimum of 7,000 part-time undergraduates in 2009/10.

[11] Students study at different intensities of study, so to make the tuition fee comparable, the tuition fees listed are for a full-time equivalent course.

[12] These BIS calculations were undertaken before the decision to extend eligibility to loans to courses of 25 per cent or above rather than 33 per cent or above. This change will have reduced these savings by a small amount.

[13] Part-time tuition fees are lower than those of their full-time peers and part-time students are ineligible for maintenance loans.

[14] The equivalent RAB charge for full-time students, they calculate, is +39.6 per cent.

References

Barr, N. (2011) 'Assessing the White Paper on higher education'. Evidence 185–8. In House of Commons (2011) *Government Reform of Higher Education, Twelfth Report of Session 2010–12*. Business, Innovation and Skills Committee, HC 885. London: TSO.

BIS (Department for Business, Innovation and Skills) (2010a) *Interim Equality Impact Assessment: Urgent reforms to higher education funding and student finance*. Online. www.bis.gov.uk/assets/biscore/higher-education/docs/i/10-1310-interim-equality-impact-assessment-he-funding-and-student-finance.pdf (Accessed 1 December 2010).

—(2010b) *Interim Impact Assessment: Urgent reforms to higher education funding and student finance*. Online. www.gov.uk/government/uploads/system/uploads/attachment_data/file/32410/10-1309-interim-impact-assessment-he-funding-and-student-finance.pdf (Accessed 1 December 2010).

—(2011) *Higher Education: Students at the heart of the system*. London: Stationery Office.

—(2012) Government Response to the Higher Education White Paper, *Students at the Heart of the System* (URN 11/944). Online. www.gov.uk/government/uploads/system/uploads/attachment_data/file/32405/12-890-government-response-students-and-regulatory-framework-higher-education.pdf (Accessed February 2012).

Blanden, J., Buscha, F., Sturgies, P., and Unwin, P (2010) *Measuring Returns to Lifelong Learning*. Discussion paper 110. London: Centre for Economics of Education. Online. http://cee.lse.ac.uk/cee percent20dps/ceedp110.pdf (Accessed 27 May 2010).

Brown, N. and Ramsden, B. (2009) *Variable Tuition Fees in England: Assessing their impact on students and higher education institutions: a fourth report.* London: Universities UK.

Callender, C. (2011) 'Widening participation, social justice and injustice: part-time students in higher education in England'. *International Journal of Lifelong Education*, 30 (4), 507–25.

Callender C., and Feldman, R. (2009) *Part-time Undergraduates in Higher Education: a literature review.* Manchester: Higher Education Careers Services Unit.

Callender, C., Hopkin, R., and Wilkinson D. (2010a) *Futuretrack: Part-time students career decision-making and career development of part-time higher education students.* Manchester: HESCA.

Callender, C., Jamieson, A., and Mason, G. (2010b) *The Supply of Part-time Provision in Higher Education in the United Kingdom.* London: Universities UK.

Callender, C. and Wilkinson, D. (2011) *The Impact of Higher Education for Part-time Students.* London: United Kingdom Commission for Employment and Skills.

—(2012) *Futuretrack: Part-time higher education students – the benefits of part-time higher education after three years of study.* Manchester: Higher Education Careers Services Unit.

—(2013) *Futuretrack: Part-time higher education students two years after graduating – the impact of learning.* Manchester: Higher Education Careers Services Unit.

Callender, C., Wilkinson, D., and Mackinnon, K. (2006) *Part-time Students and part-time study in higher education in the United Kingdom: A survey of students' attitudes and experiences of part-time study and its costs 2005/06.* London: Universities UK/Guild Higher Education.

CBI (2013) *Tomorrow's Growth: New routes to higher skills.* London: Confederation of British Industry. Online. www.cbi.org.uk/campaigns/skills-for-growth/tomorrows-growth-report/tomorrows-growth-report-page-turner/ (Accessed 31 July 2013).

Chen, X. and Carroll, C.D. (2007) *Part-time Undergraduates in Postsecondary Education: 2003–04.* Washington: Department of Education.

Dearden, L., Fitzsimons, E., and Wyness, G. (2010) *The Impact of Higher Education Finance on University Participation in the United Kingdom.* BIS research paper no. 11. London: Department for Business, Innovation and Skills.

Dorsett, R., Lui, S., and Weale, M. (2010) *Economic Benefits of Lifelong Learning.* NIESR discussion paper 352. London: National Institute for Economic and Social Research.

Egerton, M. and Parry, G. (2001) 'Lifelong debt: rates of return to lifelong learning'. *Higher Education Quarterly*, 55, 4–27.

Eurydice (2011) *Modernization of Higher Education in Europe: Funding and the social dimension.* Brussels: Education, Audiovisual and Culture Executive Agency.

Feinstein, L., Anderson, T., Hammond, C., Jamieson, A., and Woodley, A. (2007) *The Social and Economic Benefits of Part-time, Mature Study at Birkbeck College and the Open University.* Milton Keynes and London: Open University, Centre for the Wider Benefits of Learning, Institute of Education and Birkbeck College.

Ferrer, A., and Menendez, A. (2009) *The Returns to Flexible Post-secondary Education: The effect of delaying school.* CLSRN working paper. Online. http://ideas.repec.org/p/ubc/clssrn/clsrn_admin-2009-26.html.

Garrett, R., Campbell, M. and Mason, G. (2010) *The Value of Skills: An evidence review.* London: Commission for Employment and Skills. Online. www.ukces.org.uk/evidence-reports/the-value-of-skills-an-evidence-review-evidence-report-22 (Accessed 4 April 2011).

Hansard (2013) Student loans – House of Commons Written answers for 5 Jun 2013 : Column 1162W. Online. www.publications.parliament.uk/pa/cm201314/cmhansrd/cm130605/text/130605w0002.htm (Accessed 7 July 2013).

HEFCE (Higher Education Funding Council for England) (2009) *Part-time First Degree Study: Entry and completion.* Issues paper. Bristol: HEFCE.

—(2013) *Higher Education in England: Impact of the 2012 reforms* 2013/03 Bristol: HEFCE.

HESA (Higher Education Statistics Agency) (n.d.) *Tuition fees and education contracts analysed by domicile, mode, level, and source.* Online. www.hesa.ac.uk/index.php/content/view/1146/ (Accessed 20 March 2010).

—(n.d.) *Non-continuation rates (including projected outcomes) 2008/09.* Online. www.hesa.ac.uk/index.php?option=com_contentandtask=viewandid=2064andItemid=141 (Accessed 29 August 2012).

Holmlund, B., Liu, Q. and Skans, O. (2008) 'Mind the gap? Estimating the effects of postponing higher education'. *Oxford Economic Papers*, 60, 683–710.

IRHEFSF (Independent Review of Higher Education Funding and Student Finance) (2010) *Securing a Sustainable Future for Higher Education (The Browne Review).* London: Department for Business, Innovation, and Skills. Online. www.bis.gov.uk/assets/biscore/corporate/docs/s/10-1208-securing-sustainable-higher-education-browne-report.pdf

Jenkins, A., Vignoles, A., Wolf, A., and Galindo-Rueda, F. (2002) *The Determinants and Effects of Lifelong Learning.* CEE discussion paper no. 19. London: Centre for the Economics of Education.

Johnson, C., Pollard, E., Hunt, W., Munro, M., and Hillage, J. (2009) *Student Income and Expenditure Survey 2007/08 English Domiciled Students.* DIUS research report 09 05. Nottingham: DIUS.

Johnstone, D.B. and Marcucci, P. (2010) *Financing Higher Education Worldwide: Who pays? Who should pay?* Baltimore: John Hopkins University Press.

King, T. (2013) 'Part-time matters'. *Adults Learning Extra*, 14–15. Online. http://shop.niace.org.uk/media/catalog/product/a/d/adults-learning-extra-mar2013-part-time-he.pdf (Accessed 27 February 2010).

Light, A. (1995) 'The effect of interrupted schooling on wages'. *Journal of Human Resources*, 30, 472–502.

London Economics (2010) *Review of Student Support Arrangements in Other Countries.* BIS research paper no. 10. London: Departments for Business, Innovation and Skills. Online. www.bis.gov.uk/assets/biscore/corporate/docs/r/10-670-review-student-support-in-other-countries.pdf

Long, B. (2008) *What is Known About the Impact of Financial Aid? Implications for policy.* Working paper. New York: National Center for Postsecondary Research. Online. www.postsecondaryresearch.org/i/a/document/6963_LongFinAid.pdf (Accessed 20 August 2010).

Mason, G. and Bishop, K. (2010) *Adult Training, Skills Updating and Recession in the United Kingdom: The implications for competitiveness and social inclusion.* London: Centre for Learning and Life Chances in Knowledge Economies and Societies. Online. www.llakes.org.uk

McMahon, W. (2009) *Higher Learning, Greater Good: The private and social benefits of higher education.* Baltimore: Johns Hopkins University Press.

Million+/London Economics (2013) *Are the Changes to Higher Education Funding in England Cost-Effective?* Online. www.millionplus.ac.uk/documents/cost-benefit_analysis_pamphlet_2_FINAL.pdf (Accessed 22 February 2012).

NIACE (National Institute of Adult Continuing Education) (2013) *Adults Learning Extra.* Leicester: NIACE. Online. http://shop.niace.org.uk/media/catalog/product/a/d/adults-learning-extra-mar2013-part-time-he.pdf (Accessed 27 February 2013).

OECD (Organisation for Economic Co-operation and Development) (2012) *Better Skills, Better Jobs, Better Lives. A strategic approach to skills policies.* Paris: OECD.

OFFA (Office for Fair Access) (2012a) *2013–14 Access Agreements: Institutional expenditure and fee levels.* Online. www.offa.org.uk/wp-content/uploads/2012/07/2013-14-access-agreements-institutional-expenditure-and-fee-levels.pdf (Accessed 23 August 2010).

—(2012b) *Access Agreement 2012–13: Final data including initial teacher training.* Online. www.offa.org.uk/wp-content/uploads/2012/07/OFFA-2012.06-PDF.pdf(Accessed 25 February 2013).

Osborne, M., Marks, A., and Turner, E. (2004) 'Becoming a mature student: how adult applicants weigh the advantages and disadvantages of higher education'. *Higher Education,* 48, 291–315.

Pollard, E., Bates, P., Hunt, W., and Bellis, A. (2008) *University is Not Just for Young People: Working adults' perceptions of and orientation to higher education.* DIUS research report 08 06. London: DIUS.

Pollard, E., Newton, B., and Hillage, J. (2012) *Expanding and Improving Part-time Higher Education.* BIS research paper no. 68. London: Department of Business Innovation and Skills.

Purcell, K., Elias, P., Ellison, R., Atfield,G., Adam, D., and Livanos, I. (2008) *Applying for Higher Education – the Diversity of Career Choices, Plans and Expectations: Findings from the first Futuretrack survey.* Manchester: Higher Education Careers Services Unit.

Reay, D. (2012) 'Universities and the reproduction of inequality'. In Holmwood, J. (ed.) *A Manifesto for the Public University.* London: Bloomsbury Academic.

Santiago, P., Tremblay, K., Basri, E., and Arnal, E. (2008) *Tertiary Education for the Knowledge Society.* Paris: OECD.

Swain, J. and Hammond, C. (2011) 'The motivations and outcomes of studying for part-time mature students in Higher Education'. *International Journal of Lifelong Education,* 30 (5), 591–612.

UCAS (2012a) *End of Cycle Report 2012.* Cheltenham: UCAS.

—(2012b) *How Have Applications for Full-time Undergraduate Higher Education in the UK Changed in 2012?* Cheltenham: UCAS.

—(2013) *UK Application Rates by Country, Sex, Age and Background (2013 cycle, January deadline).* Cheltenham: UCAS.

United States Department of Education (2012) *Digest of Education Statistics 2011.* Online. http://nces.ed.gov/programs/digest/d11/ (Accessed 9 March 2012).

Van Westendorp, P.H. (1976) *NSS-price Sensitivity Meter: A new approach to study consumer perception of prices.* Venice: ESOMAR Congress. Amsterdam: European Marketing Research Society.

Woodley, A. (2004) *Earning, Learning and Paying: The results from a national survey of the costs of financing of part-time students in higher education.* DfES research report RR600. Nottingham: DfES.

Ziderman, A. (2013) 'Student loan schemes in practice: a global perspective'. In Heller, D. and Callender, C. (eds) *Student Financing of Higher Education: A comparative perspective.* London: International Studies in Higher Education series.

Chapter 9

Aspects of UK private higher education

Paul Temple

Private higher education in higher education systems

In his 1983 comparative study of higher education systems across the world, Burton Clark characterized one of the major system types he had identified as 'private and public systems: multiple sectors' (Clark, 1983: 59). By this he meant that there are multiple categories of institutions, funded variously from public and private sources. The most important examples of this category were the United States and Japan, with a number of Latin American countries following them. By contrast, he placed the UK in the category of 'multiple public systems: multiple sectors', by which he meant that there were institutions funded from different public sources – notably, at that point, the universities and the polytechnics – but that institutions in each of these systems were far from homogenous: Clark noted the differentiation between the ancient universities, the civic universities, the 1960s foundations, and so on. Clark did not identify a private sector of any significance in the UK. If he were writing today, he might place the UK in his 'private and public systems: multiple sectors' group, while probably noting the small proportion of students studying in private institutions, compared to those other national cases he had identified. He would probably go on to observe, however, that since the majority of funding for university teaching, in whatever type of institution it takes place, will arguably be private money from 2012 – public money loaned to students, to be repaid on favourable terms, but not appearing as public spending in the national accounts – then the whole UK 'public' system has shifted substantially towards the private system. It could even be argued that a new category within Clark's typology, with only one national case extant, had come into existence – multiple private systems: multiple sectors.

Private higher education in the UK, as it is usually thought of, has hitherto made an insignificant contribution to the overall pattern of educational provision, as in most other European countries. In all such countries, state policies and, crucially, state funding have determined higher education policies throughout the nineteenth and twentieth centuries, the period when modern higher education was effectively created. In many continental European countries, university creation was an integral part of nation-building, nowhere more so than with Wilhelm von Humboldt's creation of the University of Berlin in 1810 – the model for the development of research universities around the world. The subtle relationship planned by von Humboldt between the university and the state was intended to prevent both political interference in teaching and research and what today would be called 'producer capture' by the professoriate (Wittrock, 2006: 112). It is apparent that von Humboldt's conception of the university as the embodiment of the unity of teaching and research, and the delicate balance of power he considered necessary to maintain this unity and everything he saw as flowing from it, could not be left in private hands.

In the twentieth century, the combination of a relatively high standard of state-backed higher education, with no or minimal tuition fees for most students, has, with other factors, relegated private sector provision (whether for-profit or non-profit) to a marginal position in European national patterns of higher education. An important exception in some European countries are denominational universities, usually Catholic ones – Belgium, France, Italy, and Spain offer examples. And we may note that the Catholic University of Lublin, in Poland, claims it continued as 'the only independent university in the Soviet Bloc' during the communist period (Slancheva, 2007: 67).

The explosive growth of private higher education institutions in central and eastern Europe following the collapse of communist power in 1989 is another special case. Here was an unmet demand for places in a public university sector where expansion pre-1989 had, in most countries, been strictly limited. The range of subjects on offer was also limited – the emphasis in most countries was on science and technology, often of a highly applied kind. After 1989, the combination of this pent-up demand, in terms of volume and breadth, with a temporary absence of formal accreditation or other quality-control processes – previously regarded as unnecessary in systems operating through detailed state regulation – made the creation of a private sector almost inevitable. Across the region, large numbers of small institutions quickly sprang up, typically relying on teaching by professors 'moonlighting' from nearby public universities (Nicolescu, 2007; Slancheva, 2007). Whatever the formal position, it seems likely that the profit motive played a large part in their development – not least by providing a second source of income for academic staff whose salaries, where they were paid at all, had been eroded by rapid inflation (Kwiek, 2008; Slancheva, 2007). It is hard to judge the long-term stability of these private sectors, even that of Poland, where currently around one-third of higher education students are in private colleges. Questions of quality and standards continue to be raised, and sharply falling birth-rates across the region may be expected to create spare capacity in the public sector in the near future, perhaps thereby siphoning-off demand in the private sector (Vasagar, 2011). It also seems that students typically prefer to pay fees to attend public universities (in countries where the public universities charge fees to lower-achieving applicants) rather than private ones – hardly surprising, as the public universities in such countries are usually historically established and have higher local reputations (Nicolescu, 2007: 212). These countries' private sectors, then, are in a dynamic equilibrium with their local public sectors, rather than operating independently of them.

When the post-war expansion of higher education began in western Europe in the 1960s, driven partly by increasing numbers of school students staying on beyond the minimum school-leaving age – and which in countries such as France led automatically to increased numbers of young people with a right to a university place – as well as by economic growth and increased demands for higher skills, it might have been assumed that private provision would have developed to help meet this new demand. Instead, everywhere in western Europe, the expansion of higher education was seen as a state responsibility, on a par with state responsibility, in the European post-war settlement, for improved health care, social welfare, modernized transport infrastructure, and so on. Even private provision supported by state financial aid, either directly to institutions or to their students (what might today be called a public–private partnership), seems not to have been an option. This did not just reflect the continental *étatisme* in the period of post-war reconstruction: when higher education's expansion was being planned in the late 1950s and 1960s in the UK, no public case was made, so far as is known, that private provision might, at least in part, have a role to play. Instead, it seems to have been taken for granted that the correct approach was one 'where the state intervened to create wholly new universities', with generous state financial support for their students, but which then left the universities alone to act 'as a kind of intellectual conscience of the nation' (Shattock, 2012: 10, 43).

Public and private in the UK: A distinction without a difference?

In the UK, the distinctive historical pattern of university development meant the public/private distinction was never so clear-cut as it was elsewhere in Europe and in most other countries. In the United States, however, the position up to the early nineteenth century was more akin to that of the UK: there, the public/private distinction was not considered significant – there was often 'a fusion of "public" and "private" concepts within the same institution' (Thelin, 2004: 71). A strong public role in the provision of higher education can be traced back to the colonial period, when the first colleges were generously supported from public funds – Harvard, for example, received a quarter of the Massachusetts Bay Colony's tax revenues in its early years (Thelin, 2004: 12) – but were not 'public' in the modern sense.

In contrast to continental Europe, UK universities, starting with Oxford and Cambridge and going on to the ancient Scottish universities, had always been private, non-profit institutions but with important links to the state – nicely exemplified in the case of medieval Oxford by a series of Royal Decrees, upholding what would now be described as the University's autonomy. Henry III, in the mid-thirteenth century, appears to have been particularly well-disposed towards the University, to the considerable annoyance of the townspeople of Oxford (Leff, 1968). Six centuries later, the origins of England's third university, the formally private, non-profit University of London, were also bound up with the government's view of higher education: the University was established in 1836 'by direct government action ... [a] paradox of being a state educational foundation in the age of laissez-faire' (Harte, 1986: 79). In these developments we see the public/private boundary blurring further, a state of affairs that continues to baffle foreign visitors to UK universities to this day: a nominally private institution being created by the central state.

The public/private boundary UK universities straddle can be appreciated by examining the funding sources of a typical pre-war university or (often) university college – that is, an institution without its own degree-awarding powers, perhaps teaching the syllabus laid down by the University of London's 'external' programme, which led to the award of London degrees (Moodie and Eustace, 1974: 32). Typically, the largest single source of funding was student tuition fees. The rest was made up from endowment income and grants from local councils and charitable foundations and – though not always – the central University Grants Committee (UGC), which made financial support available to its 'grant list' but not to all higher education institutions (Williams, 1988). To read the minutes of a provincial university governing body from the 1920s or 1930s is to see decision-making in a medium-sized, locally-based enterprise, balancing precarious income streams against carefully-watched spending and whose long-term future was anything but secure. Operationally, there would be little difference between a 'public' university of this period and a small for-profit college, validated by a university, today. Perhaps the key difference might have been that the pre-war university would be strongly rooted in its city and the recipient of practical and moral support from its business and civic communities.

In the post-war period, UK universities became dependent on increasing amounts of public money to support their growth, particularly as any endowments had been badly eroded by wartime inflation (UGC grants made up 63.9 per cent of universities' incomes by 1949/50 (Shattock, 2012: 12)), but never became nationalized concerns, at least formally. (Although there is a substantial literature on the theme of 'scholastic leadership and tradition collaps[ing] in the face of state intervention', which permitted, in this instance, 'one of [Mrs Thatcher's] most vigorous "nationalizations"' (Jenkins, 1995).) I shall refer to traditional UK universities as 'public', in inverted commas, as a reminder of this ambiguous point.

Emerging as a public–private partnership, the view of the UK higher education system as an anomaly thus became internationally entrenched. It is evident in the difficulty international studies of higher education have in classifying the UK: a 2005 UNESCO study, for example, placed the UK in its category of 'countries with a large private higher education sector (over 50 per cent of enrolments)' – ahead of the United States, which it placed in its 'countries with a medium-sized private higher education sector (between 25 per cent and 50 per cent of enrolments)'

(UNESCO, 2005: 90). Clearly, the authors of this study identified the whole of UK higher education as non-state, and then, presumably, concluded that this must mean 'private'.

The University of Buckingham was established in 1973 in the small market town of Buckingham, about 60 miles from London. It admitted its first students as a university college in 1976, and currently has around 1,000 students. It claims to be the UK's 'only independent university with a Royal Charter'. What it means by this is that it does not itself receive any direct public financial support, although, as its UK/EU students are entitled to receive student loans on the same basis as students at other English universities, the University does receive indirect support from the taxpayer via subsidized student fees. But in terms of formal governance and ownership it is no different from UK 'public' universities, if we leave aside the fact that it was established as an ideological project, by a group led by Max Beloff, who then became its first principal, to provide a counterweight to what was seen by its founders as higher education's excessive politicization. The website of the University's Centre for the Study of Liberty gives us an indication of the University's ideological position: 'But liberty is constantly under threat from governments and their apologists who seek to over-tax and over-regulate. We have thus sought to create a countervailing institution that will reinforce the value of liberty' (University of Buckingham, 2012). Despite such rhetoric, however, the basic governance and operation of the University of Buckingham is not different in kind to that of other UK universities. In 2001, one of Buckingham's academic staff unwittingly showed that the gap in the market Buckingham was intended to fill was rather small. Despite healthcare and education in the UK being 'organized under principles ... redolent of Stalinist central planning' – understating one's case clearly being frowned on at Buckingham – it was, he thought, 'disturbing [that there is still] little interest in expanding the private sector [of higher education] here' by following Buckingham's lead (Barry, 2001: 211). Or possibly, the 'Stalinist central planning' apparently characterizing the UK public sector was not as distasteful to the majority of potential students as it was to the writer in question.

However, if we can accept that Buckingham is a sufficiently different type of UK higher education institution to merit the title of private provider, then it is unique in being established with a particular political goal in mind. More recently, a small group of private providers have received degree-awarding powers: BPP University College, the College of Law, Ashridge Business School, the IFS School of Finance, and, most recently, in 2012, Regents College – all of which have restricted degree-awarding powers subject to renewal every six years; only Buckingham has unrestricted degree-awarding powers, in common, again, with 'public' universities. Of these, BPP, which obtained degree-awarding powers in 2007, was, until recently, the only for-profit institution. A holding company, BPP Holdings Ltd, controls a number of separate companies providing different types of professional education – if the

McTimoney College of Chiropractic can be so described. BPP Holdings, in turn, was acquired in 2009 by the US-based Apollo Global, owner of the online provider the University of Phoenix, and a major operator of for-profit higher education in the US and internationally. However, the College of Law has now been bought by a private equity firm, and in late 2012 gained the title of the University of Law. Its new owners will clearly expect to see a financial return on its investment, and so it may be assumed to be in the for-profit sector (Morgan, 2012c).

The cases of BPP and the College of Law show that the legal and ownership positions of private universities or colleges cannot be regarded as stable when they can be bought and sold (and presumably closed if they become unprofitable) without hindrance: the time limits on the degree-awarding powers of organizations that are not university institutions in the typically accepted sense seem a sensible safeguard. What has at times seemed an archaic mode of institutional creation, the Royal Charter, can also be seen to offer a level of permanence that differentiates an institution from a mere organization. As the 1904 Royal Charter of the University of Leeds puts it (to take a random example): 'There shall be from henceforth for ever in Our said City of Leeds a university of the name and style of "The University of Leeds", which shall be and continue one body politic and corporate with perpetual succession ... '

Typologies of private higher education

The environment for higher education, in the UK and elsewhere in Europe, has changed radically over the last few decades. The expansion of higher education and associated institutional changes in the UK since the 1980s – notably with the title 'university' now covering a wider range of institutional types than previously – have created a more fluid landscape and encouraged the growth of private providers. A range of specialist private organizations fill particular niches in an increasingly complex higher education ecology – providers of purpose-built student accommodation on or adjoining university campuses or providers of pre-sessional education for international students, for example. Globally, it has been estimated that some 30 per cent of higher education enrolments are in private, mostly non-profit, institutions (Levy, 2009), with strong growth in Latin America and Asia. In some countries whose wealth and the local higher education supply and demand situation might have indicated opportunities for private providers, strong state regulatory oversight of higher education, perhaps associated with a desire to exert political and/or religious controls, has limited what can be done. Saudi Arabia is an example, but there are now signs of change even there (Jamjoon, 2012).

There are a number of categorizations of private providers internationally. This broadly follows the one put forward in a recent study by Universities UK (2010):

- Apex, elite and semi-elite: only the US has private institutions in the 'apex' category, although in several other countries there are examples of universities in the next few steps down from the most prestigious universities. These institutions are invariably non-profit
- Identity institutions, mostly religious in orientation, again mostly non-profit
- Demand-absorbing – the most numerous category, found where public provision is inadequate in terms of quantity or quality: the UUK report divides this category further into 'dubious' and 'serious'. Both for-profit and non-profit examples are to be found in this category
- Public/private partnerships, normally between a public university and a for-profit organization: a recent UK example is the partnership between Pearson Education and Royal Holloway, University of London, under which the new Pearson College will offer a bachelor's degree in business studies validated by Royal Holloway.

Another categorization (Geiger, 1986) is based on the drivers for private provision, considered against the local context of the public sector: 'better' (elite or similar private institutions), 'more' (demand-absorbing private institutions), or 'different' (identity-based institutions, specialist niche markets, or where public institutions fail to offer some type of provision, for example). Geiger also offers a categorization into parallel, mass, and peripheral, which fulfils essentially the same purpose. It is interesting to reflect how the UK private sector might be analysed against this typology. The 'better' label clearly does not apply, as all the UK's institutions with any claim to international prestige are firmly in the 'public' sector. Given the UK 'public' system's expansion in recent decades, it is also hard to believe that the 'more' category applies in a meaningful way. And – with the exception of Buckingham's libertarian claims – in the missions espoused by most private institutions it is hard to detect much in the way of 'different', unless a focus on low-cost subjects in high demand is considered to be distinctive. The UK private sector appears, then, to be anomalous in terms of accepted typologies. To some extent, this is because the sector is located in the UK but deals mainly with non-UK students, often studying for non-UK awards. Much of it is in, but not of, the UK, in other words. Insofar as it does cater for UK/EU students, it is niche provision of various kinds – particularly part-time professional courses – that are prominent.

The 2011 White Paper and private provision in the UK

In the UK, government policies from the late 1980s have stimulated competition between existing universities, both for student recruitment and for research funding. The increasing significance, sophistication, and cost of university marketing activities – barely in existence a generation ago – is one testimony to the policies' success (Maringe and Gibbs, 2009: 29; Temple, 2011). Competition for research funds is worth particular examination, as it is readily quantifiable in cash terms (although of course excellent research and expensive research are not identical, and the focus on cash raises the profiles of universities with 'big science' departments at the expense of others), and because a major research portfolio affects the external perception of the university via league tables and publicity generally, and so feeds through into student recruitment. The first Research Assessment Exercise (to be known from 2014 as the Research Excellence Framework), intended to assess institutions' research capabilities and to allocate funds differentially as a result, took place in 1986. As a result of successive exercises in 1989, 1992, 1996, 2001, and 2008, obtaining research funding has become increasingly competitive and led to a highly concentrated distribution. In 2006/07, six institutions each received over £100 million in dual support research income (that is, research funding from the Funding Councils and the Research Councils combined), while the median figure was around £2.5 million (UUK, 2008: 44). Even this figure, modest enough in research grant terms, tails off rapidly once the median institution is passed, meaning that nearly half of all UK universities carry out only very small amounts of research, or, effectively, none at all. On the criterion of research income alone, then, UK policy over the past quarter-century to increase competition among universities has, it may be argued, been highly successful: it has led to a more diverse university system, containing institutions that have increasingly little in common other than the title 'university'. Indeed, it may even be thought that the very success of this policy has reached the point where it has the perverse effect of actually limiting competition, as a variety of factors – costly research infrastructures, existing research groups, international partnerships, and other matters – have made it very difficult indeed for a non-research-intensive university to compete with the handful of 'premier league' institutions. The football analogy is obvious, but a similar picture can be seen in other artificial attempts to create competition: in utilities, for example, where barriers to entry are so high that a small number of companies – including, in a further irony, foreign state-controlled companies – are able to manage the market.

But while the higher education market has become more competitive, the very title 'university', which effectively limits entry to this market, has become more fluid. There has been a slow but steady process over recent years of lowering the barriers to gaining degree-awarding powers and a university title. This led to a significant increase in the number of full universities in the UK: between 1992 and October 2012, in addition to the former polytechnics and their Scottish equivalents, 29 universities have been created in the UK from institutions that did not previously have the title.

The process has been accelerated under the Coalition Government which took office in 2010. In November 2012 Minister David Willetts announced that a further ten institutions would be put forward for the title of 'university'. The government's 2011 White Paper had previously set out a number of measures intended, apparently, to encourage greater private sector involvement in higher education – crucially, by making it easier to gain a university title. The requirement to have a minimum of 4,000 students – dating from the previous government's 2003 White Paper, which led to the requirement that a university should undertake research and be active in a range of disciplines being removed – has now been reduced to 1,000: about the size of the average English state-funded secondary school. The government also intended to remove any legal impediments to private companies buying existing universities. Such other changes will, the White Paper suggested, 'make it easier for [new providers of higher education] to attract private investment' (BIS, 2011: para 4.35). The implication here, though unstated, must be that these new providers will be for-profit organizations, as non-profit institutions are unlikely to be attractive to private investors (as opposed to philanthropists). It was expected that legislation to implement these and other changes would be proposed in 2012: in fact, it seems as if the government has had second thoughts about the political wisdom of at least some of these moves, despite their being strongly backed by the minister concerned, David Willetts.

A striking feature of the 2011 White Paper's approach to the encouragement of greater private provision is the absence of a clear rationale: the precise problem that private providers are expected to help solve is never set out. In its Foreword the White Paper tells us: 'Our university sector has a proud history and a world-class reputation, attracting students from across the world. Higher education is a successful public–private partnership' (BIS, 2011: 2). So quality or standards – or attractiveness to students – are presumably not the problem, and nor is the relationship between universities and government. No examples of significant failures among existing institutions are given. Instead, and to add to Stefan Collini's (2011) typology of tenses now used in official documents on higher education (mission statement present, future dogmatic), the conditional optimistic is widely deployed. So we learn that 'new entrants to the sector ... may have different strengths ... they may offer particular well-honed teaching models ... [and they] may find it easier to include an international higher education experience for their students' (BIS, 2011: para 4.5). Leaving aside the curious notion of seeking a 'well-honed teaching model' – the usual criticism of university teaching is that models are only too well-honed, through constant repetition – and the implication that existing universities lack international links – when a regular criticism is that universities spend too much time on supposedly glamorous international ventures rather than attending to domestic matters – what we see here is a breathtaking lack of specifics. The text bears the hallmarks of a writer casting around in an attempt to find vaguely plausible reasons to support a decision which has already been made on quite different grounds.

The White Paper also assumes that private providers are discriminated against by the current arrangements, and that legal and other changes need to be made to allow them to compete on equal terms with the 'public' sector. The 'level playing field' cliché makes an early appearance in the relevant chapter of the White Paper:

'To achieve [wider] choice for students, all higher education providers, whatever type of course they offer, must be able to compete on a level playing field' (BIS, 2011: para 4.7). However, a level playing field implies that neither end slopes. At present, public sector institutions have certain duties laid upon them that private colleges do not have, including being subject to the Freedom of Information Act (FOI) and the decisions of the Office of the Independent Adjudicator (OIA) in respect of student complaints. Both involve costly and time consuming processes, potentially involving awkward or otherwise undesirable (from the institution's point of view) disclosures. Moreover, it is hard to believe that a commercial organization such as BPP would be willing to make available the kind of internal documents public institutions are routinely required to produce under FOI and OIA requests. The private sector currently benefits from such advantages over public institutions since they do not receive public funding, even if some of their students do – this argument is a less than compelling one, however, as the FOI applies equally to university activities that are not publicly funded, such as research or consultancy projects for private clients. The funding arrangements for undergraduates from 2012, however, will erode this distinction, if not completely remove it, and it is the logic of the White Paper's position, in any case, that the public and private sectors should be 'treated on a more consistent basis' (BIS, 2011: para 4.10) and thus be subject to the same regulatory requirements.

Neither the supposed weakness of the current arrangements are set out, nor are the concrete benefits of an alternative approach described. It is hard to avoid the conclusion that increasing the number of private providers was set as an ideological goal and a policy framework (if that is not too grand a title) was put together to support such an objective.

It is worth pausing here to reflect on the significance of profitability because in the UK, as I have shown, the public/private divide that would be significant in many other countries has little real relevance if non-profit institutions – of the Buckingham model, say – are what are being considered as 'private'. The recent growth of for-profit institutions in the UK raises new considerations. In economics, the notion of profit is usually seen as having theoretical benefits by signalling opportunities for investment and for indicating where innovation may generate high returns. Both could potentially lead to increased wealth for the economy in question. So, in principle, why should profitability not have a role to play in providing higher education? The argument that education is 'too important' to be left to the vagaries of the profit motive is not compelling: there seems to be little controversy in most countries about the supply of food being determined by judgements of profitability by food producers, distributors, and retailers.

There are several reasons why profitability is a difficulty in education, however – and in higher education in particular. One has to do with externalities (or spillover effects): the benefits of education are felt well beyond the individuals directly involved in learning. Just as the construction of an urban subway line might be shown to be profitable if the increases in property values and the economic activity that it generates could be represented on the subway authority's balance sheet, so a university receiving a public subsidy might be shown to be profitable if the increased incomes of its graduates, and the economic value-added and wider social benefits that they generate over their lifetimes, could be captured in the university's financial accounts. While the argument applies most strongly to basic education – the returns to the whole society of near-universal literacy and numeracy are huge – it also applies to higher education since the benefits of high skills are also experienced widely. But if educational provision depended on the profitability of individual enterprises, it is likely that provision would be less than optimal since these externalities would not figure in calculations of profitability.

Supply could be increased through public subsidies to students and/or institutions but this would then create a set of perverse incentives that are hard to manage in an educational setting. Running a profit-making enterprise is problematic when your customers are both your raw material and your finished product: as with most other enterprises, you want to maximize the quantities of both – which sets up tensions in an educational institution. In countries with both non-profit and for-profit higher education institutions, this helps explain why it is the former that tend to be of the higher status, while the latter focuses on standardized courses in technical or professional fields. It also means that for-profit institutions have 'an ambiguous relationship to the question of civic and community engagement' (Watson *et al.*, 2011: 11), which further limits their roles in creating educational value.

A large number of private institutions actually do provide higher education in the UK. There are certainly over a thousand of them, although no comprehensive register exists – and it would in any case become immediately out of date. Most are very small, typically teaching international students, often for non-UK awards. The business model of many of these institutions is puzzling to an outside observer: they seem to have no distinctive academic or professional expertise or a marketing proposition that would not be available, at a similar price, in more established, better-known institutions that are themselves degree-awarding bodies. They certainly do not have a recognized brand to offer. One conclusion must be that they are teaching students who would not be admitted to a mainstream university on attainment grounds, whether in terms of academic ability or English language competence. It might be that the government's new, more restrictive, visa regime, in the teeth of opposition from the entire university sector, will put some of these small colleges out of business. It would be deeply ironic if one strand of the current government's ideology – restricting immigration, even when the people affected are not immigrants at all in the usually accepted sense of the term – undercut another ideological objective, that of enlarging the private higher education sector.

Meanwhile, in the United States, a devastating critique of for-profit higher education was made in 2012 by Senator Tom Harkin, chairman of the Senate Health, Education, Labor, and Pensions Committee. 'In this report', Senator Harkin was reported as saying, 'you will find overwhelming documentation of exorbitant tuition, aggressive recruiting practices, abysmal student outcomes, taxpayer dollars spent on marketing and pocketed as profit, and regulatory evasion and manipulation' (Lewin, 2012).The widely syndicated *Doonesbury* cartoon strip made this a storyline in summer 2012 in which the president of a less-than-stellar private but non-profit college, of which many of the strip's characters are alumni, considers turning it into a for-profit organization. As his provost tells him: 'Remember, for-profits take any warm body with federal aid. They're all about enrolment, not completion.'

Similar cases appear to be emerging in the UK, where a lightly-regulated for-profit sector is now able, as in the US, to gain access to public funds. UK/EU students at private colleges are able to apply for student loans on courses designated by the government department responsible (currently, BIS), which gives the colleges access to tuition fee income from the Student Loans Company. The number of students at private colleges receiving this support more than doubled in 2011/12 compared with the previous year, involving £100 million in loans (Morgan, 2012b). While such provision appears to have encouraged their growth, problems apparently similar to those uncovered in the Harkin report in the US are now emerging. In a recent case, Guildhall College in London (not to be confused with the long-established Guildhall School of Music and Drama) was found to be registering students on courses designated for student support, when in fact the students concerned wished to study on courses that were not so designated. The College benefitted by some £750,000 before designation was withdrawn (Morgan, 2012a). It is difficult to see how, in practice, abuses of this kind can be prevented in a systematic way if there are hundreds of such colleges, each with relatively small numbers of students: it is unrealistic to expect BIS to police a system like this, constantly in flux, and likely to become even more fluid once opportunities for large-scale, low-risk fraud become more widely appreciated.

The changing ecology of UK higher education

The ecology of UK (or at least, English) higher education is changing. The private, for-profit and non-profit sectors are expanding and gaining highly prized degree-awarding powers, once reserved for a relatively small number of well-established, publicly-funded institutions. Another niche in this ecology is being filled by further education colleges, which are expanding their higher education provision. Under the new tuition fee system, colleges have been allowed to expand their higher education offer at lower fee levels than most universities – even, sometimes, when that university is the validating partner for the college in question. Government market-oriented policies are, again, pointing to a more diverse pattern of provision (Parry *et al.*, 2012). As noted, a range of private for-profit firms are playing an increased role in providing ancillary services – as a glance at any issue of the glossy magazine *University Business*, established in 2006, will show.

I therefore see a more complex pattern of higher education developing, with intersecting fields of public and private provision and a wider range of overlapping institutional types. While the two sectors remain largely self-contained, there might be more interactions in the future – most perhaps involving larger non-profit colleges (of the Regents College type, for example) with research ambitions. But it must be open to question to what extent we can still speak of a single higher education 'system' or 'sector' if it contains such diverse organizations. Even the term 'institution' seems inappropriate for for-profit providers, which are bought and sold in the way ordinary businesses would be: they cannot possess anything of a university's stability or values as such terms are normally understood.

References

Barry, N. (2001) 'Privatizing university education'. In Tooley, J. (ed.), *Buckingham at 25*. London: Institute of Economic Affairs.

BIS (Department for Business, Innovation and Skills) (2011) *Higher Education: Students at the heart of the system*. London: BIS.

Clark, B. (1983) *The Higher Education System: Academic organization in cross-national perspective*. Berkeley: University of California Press.

Collini, S. (2011) 'From Robbins to McKinsey'. *London Review of Books*, 33 (16), 9–14.

Geiger, R. (1986) *Private Sectors in Higher Education: Structure, function and change in eight countries*. Ann Arbor: University of Michigan Press.

Harte, N. (1986) *The University of London 1836–1986*. London: The Athlone Press.

Jamjoon, Y. (2012) 'Understanding Private Higher Education in Saudi Arabia: Emergence, Development and Perceptions'. Unpublished PhD thesis, Institute of Education, University of London.

Jenkins, S. (1995) 'The lady who turned to nationalisation'. *Times Higher Education*, 20 October.

Kwiek, M. (2008) 'Accessibility and equity, market forces, and entrepreneurship: developments in higher education in Central and Eastern Europe'. *Higher Education Policy and Management*, 20 (1), 89–110.

Leff, G. (1968) *Paris and Oxford Universities in the Thirteenth and Fourteenth Centuries*. New York: Wiley.

Levy, D. (2009) 'For-profit versus non-profit private higher education'. *International Higher Education*, 54 (Winter 2009).

Lewin, T. (2012) 'Senate Committee report on for-profit colleges condemns costs and practices'. *New York Times*, 29 July.

Maringe, F. and Gibbs, P. (2009) *Marketing Higher Education: Theory and practice*. Maidenhead: McGraw-Hill/Open University Press.

Moodie, G. and Eustace, R. (1974) *Power and Authority in British Universities*. London: George Allen & Unwin.

Morgan, J. (2012a) 'College loses designations over "registration malpractice" to gain funding'. *Times Higher Education*, 1 November.

—(2012b) 'Public-backed funding to private college students shoots up to £100m'. *Times Higher Education*, 6 December.

—(2012c) 'The revenues look good, but are the customs sound?' *Times Higher Education*, 30 August.

Nicolescu, L. (2007) 'Institutional efforts for legislative recognition and market acceptance: Romanian private higher education'. In Slancheva, S. and Levy, D. (eds), *Private Higher Education in Post-communist Europe: In search of legitimacy*. New York: Palgrave Macmillan.

Parry, G., Callender, C., Scott, P., and Temple, P. (2012) *Understanding Higher Education in Further Education Institutions*. London: Department of Business, Innovation and Skills.

Shattock, M. (2012) *Making Policy in British Higher Education 1945–2011*. Maidenhead: McGraw Hill/Open University Press.

Slancheva, S. (2007) 'Legitimating the difference: private higher education institutions in central and eastern Europe'. In Slancheva, S. and Levy, D. (eds) *Private Higher Education in Post-communist Europe: In search of legitimacy*. New York: Palgrave Macmillan.

Temple, P. (2011) 'University branding: what can it do?' *Perspectives – Policy and Practice in Higher Education*, 15 (4), 1–4.

Thelin, J. (2004) *A History of American Higher Education*. Baltimore: Johns Hopkins University Press.

UNESCO (2005) *Towards Knowledge Societies*. Paris: UNESCO Publishing.

Universities UK (2008) *Patterns of Higher Education Institutions in the UK (Eighth report)*. London: Universities UK.

—(2010) *The Growth of Private and For-profit Higher Education Providers in the UK*. London: Universities UK.

University of Buckingham (2012) University Mission Statement. Online. www.buckingham.ac.uk/international/beloff (Accessed 2 September 2012).

Vasagar, J. (2011) 'Poland's students go private in force'. *The Guardian*, 6 April.

Watson, D., Hollister, R., Stroud, S., and Babcock, E. (2011) *The Engaged University: International perspectives on civic engagement*. New York: Routledge.

Williams, G. (1988) 'The debate about funding mechanisms'. *Oxford Review of Education*, 14 (1), 59–68.

Wittrock, B. (2006) 'The legacy of Wilhelm von Humboldt and the future of the European university'. In Bluckert, K., Neave, G., and Nybom, T. (eds) *The European Research University: An historical parenthesis*. New York: Palgrave Macmillan/IAU.

Chapter 10

Postgraduate education: Overlooked and forgotten?
Geoff Whitty and Joel Mullan

The importance of both research and postgraduate education is neglected in the White Paper (BIS, 2011). Indeed, its very title – *Higher Education: Students at the Heart of the System* – gave an unfortunate message about the nature of the English higher education system in so far as it seemed to understate the importance of research to our understanding of modern universities. The previous government's framework for higher education, *Higher Ambitions* (BIS, 2009), which effectively brought about the Browne Review and prefigured some of the current government's policies, did at least contain a whole chapter on research, innovation, and knowledge exchange.

It might be argued that the UK's global standing in research is exceptional and may not therefore be in need of urgent attention to the same extent as universities' teaching functions. Indeed, a report commissioned by the government from Elsevier recently described the UK as a 'leading research nation' and 'a world leader in terms of article and citation output'. However, it also pointed to some 'potential areas of vulnerability' and suggested that 'its leadership position may be threatened by its declining share of researchers globally, and by its declining share of global spending' (2011: 5). Another recent report by the Prime Minister's Council for Science and Technology stated that 'the UK's position needs to be strengthened if it is to remain competitive in research' (2010: 18). In this situation, one might have reasonably expected a major White Paper on future higher education policy to have had considerably more to say about research and its supply line[1].

Nevertheless, it would be fair to say that the Coalition Government has protected existing public funding levels for research to a greater extent than might have been anticipated given its general approach to public spending. Even so, to those on the ground the small print on capital spending and research councils has made initial claims about ring-fencing seem rather hollow and, of course, the extent of protection for research spending in the future remains unclear. The effects of recession and public expenditure cuts on other parts of the economy have also limited the amount of research funding coming to universities from other sources. This has been particularly evident in fields such as education, where much of the contract research funding has come from government departments in the recent past (BERA/UCET, 2012).

Meanwhile, there has been increasing concentration of public research funding through greater selectivity in the distribution of the so-called QR (quality related) core funding to universities for research and in the allocation of research studentships. The former comes from the Higher Education Funding Council for England (HEFCE), which distributes this funding to universities on the basis of the outcomes of a periodic Research Assessment Exercise (soon to be replaced by the Research Excellence Framework). The latter increasingly come via Doctoral Training Centres established by the UK Research Councils. While there may be strong arguments for these developments, the failure of the government to consider in any depth their implications for the relationship between research and teaching, except to encourage the development of teaching-only universities including new private sector providers, is to be regretted. Furthermore, as Sir Peter Scott, former vice-chancellor of Kingston University, has pointed out 'it would be "naïve" to assume that the research funding landscape would not be affected by the changes to teaching funding in "substantial but unpredictable ways"' (Jump, 2012: 8).

But even if, given its title, this particular government White Paper was understandably focused on students, it also marginalized two increasingly important groups of students themselves: taught postgraduates (PGT) and research students (PGR). The Browne Review of higher education funding (IRHEFSF, 2010), despite having postgraduate funding explicitly included in its terms of reference, used only one of sixty-odd pages in its Report to deal with the funding of postgraduate courses. Even the White Paper itself devoted only nine paragraphs to the issue in an 80-page document.

Initially, the government seemed to accept the *Browne Report*'s assumption that, not only was there no need to extend the proposed undergraduate student support package to postgraduates, existing core funding to institutions for most taught Master's courses could cease on the same basis as for undergraduate courses. Ministers claimed that withdrawal of funding for courses would be offset by an increase in public funding for student support. Yet no new support package for postgraduate students similar to that being introduced for undergraduates was being proposed.

Even when the government did acknowledge a potential problem, it referred it to the HEFCE, which instigated a temporary fix by maintaining existing levels of core funding for postgraduate teaching in higher cost subjects. Meanwhile, the Department for Business, Innovation and Skills (BIS), the central government department responsible for higher education policy, reactivated an earlier working party, and both BIS and the HEFCE initiated some useful fact finding exercises. So far, though, the government has failed to provide any real leadership on the issue and, as recently as September 2012, the minister responsible, David Willetts, was reported as having appealed for people with ideas about how to address the problem of funding for postgraduate students to 'make themselves heard' (Jump, 2012: 8).

To be fair to the government, the higher education sector itself was slow to recognize the issue. Indeed, Willetts has even suggested that one of his problems in getting postgraduate education higher up the government's agenda was that there 'isn't a particularly lively debate in the sector' about it (Jump, 2012: 8). It is certainly true that at meetings of vice-chancellors in the immediate aftermath of the *Browne Report*, voices concerned with the issue got lost among what were seen as more pressing matters involving undergraduate provision under the proposed new fees regime. At first, it was largely the leaders of postgraduate institutions for the arts and social sciences who led efforts to highlight the dangers, but subsequently there has been a wider recognition that the consequences of not getting postgraduate education right could be considerable. The 1994 Group of smaller research intensive universities addressed the issue directly in its own report *The Postgraduate Crisis* (1994 Group, 2012), and given the high concentration of postgraduate provision in London, London Higher, the regional consortium of higher education institutions in the capital, has taken a particular interest in the issue.

As for a wider constituency, there has been relatively little discussion of postgraduate education in debates on higher education in parliament or in the press. However, influential bodies, such as the British Academy, picked up the issue (Roberts, 2010; British Academy, 2012) and an unofficial cross-party parliamentary body, the Higher Education Commission (HEC), instigated an inquiry into the future of postgraduate education, the work of which is discussed in some detail below.

Why postgraduate education matters

While we do not know what impact the Coalition Government's new regime for undergraduate fees will have, we can anticipate how potential postgraduates might respond to the prospect of adding debt to the tens of thousands they will have already accumulated as undergraduates. As a result, demand for postgraduate education could well fall, which would be of concern for a number of reasons.

First, any threat to the future of postgraduate education could have a serious impact on universities. Quite apart from specialist postgraduate institutions, around half the intake of some comprehensive universities is now postgraduate in one way or another. Aside from any direct detriment to institutional income from falling postgraduate recruitment, the concern within the Academy itself has related particularly to the impact of a decline in postgraduate numbers on the future strength of UK research and scholarship. As British Academy President, Sir Adam Roberts (2010), put it, 'if fees reform puts graduates off postgraduate study, where will academia find its new blood?'

Even Browne himself accepted a need to monitor the impact of higher undergraduate fees on postgraduate recruitment but took undue comfort from the fact that, under previous arrangements, overall enrolments at postgraduate level had increased significantly between 2002–03 and 2008–09. Yet the rate of increase for home students was significantly lower even then. UK postgraduate education is highly thought of elsewhere in the world and full-time courses in many subjects attract far more international than home students. Most of the growth in postgraduate student recruitment in this country has been from non-EU countries. Even though home recruitment began to rise significantly between 2008 and 2010 – and some people suggested that, as some of those students were already repaying undergraduate loans, there was clearly no problem – that increase seems now to have stalled particularly in relation to STEM subjects (Willetts, 2012). So, despite a short-term increase in the numbers and proportion of home students during two years of recession, home student recruitment to both PGT and PGR remains a matter of concern. Given that there is evidence from Futuretrack, a major longitudinal survey of existing undergraduates (Purcell *et al.*, 2012), that debt already deters students from undertaking postgraduate study, increased debt under the post-Browne arrangements could take us into dangerously uncharted territory.

Second, postgraduate education is essential to the UK, not just in terms of the income it brings from international students, but also to the health of our own economy. David Willetts has acknowledged that 'it would be clearly detrimental to this country if we saw a big fall in postgraduate numbers' (Willetts, 2011). He therefore asked Sir Adrian Smith, then director general for knowledge and innovation in BIS, to review the future of postgraduate study in the new funding environment, although it is unclear whether this review led to a report, and the main emphasis to date has been on monitoring impact.

In the context of globalization – however we understand it – the pressures on the economy, industry, and jobs are likely to intensify and postgraduate skills will be of vital importance to future economic success. In his report for the previous government, Smith argued that the skills of postgraduates are 'critical for tackling major business challenges and driving innovation and growth' (2010: 5). He pointed out that postgraduates are 'innovation catalysts', bridging the gap between ideas and business, and adding capacity to the UK's research and development workforce.

Disturbingly, a recent Bologna process report shows that substantially fewer UK students move on to 'second cycle' education, typically at Master's or doctoral level, than in other European countries. The UK is one of only three countries with a progression rate of less than 10 per cent within two years, alongside Andorra and Kazakhstan (Eurydice Network, 2012). Globally, emerging economies have also recognized the important role of postgraduate skills, with Brazil and China, for example, investing huge sums on educating their citizens to postgraduate level, many of them – at least for now – at foreign institutions including our own. In the longer term, these countries will substantially increase their own home provision. Since 2003, China has already more than doubled its new postgraduate enrolments to nearly 600,000 per year, and its Ministry of Finance has recently announced a system of National Graduate Scholarships for both Master's and doctoral students (Luo and Yang, 2012).

A failure to increase – let alone stem any decline in – the flow of UK students coming properly equipped to provide British industry with what it needs could have serious economic consequences. The inventor Sir James Dyson has, for instance, often pointed to a crisis of recruitment of UK-based postgraduate engineering students. He claimed that, in 2008, only 70 out of 3,825 additional postgraduate engineering students were from the UK. More recently he cautioned about the huge impact this could have on the economy and called for more government grants to enable UK students to study at postgraduate level (Richardson, 2011). If companies are struggling to find the skilled staff they need they are likely to at least start considering relocation. Other postgraduate skills shortages have been identified by Sir John Beddington, former government chief scientific advisor in fields such as cybersecurity and the nuclear sciences (Beddington, 2011).

Third, although it has been relatively neglected in the debate so far, there is the contribution that postgraduate education makes to the wider cultural health of the nation. While some of this can be – and often is – expressed in economic terms of supporting the 'creative industries', there is surely still a case to be made for postgraduate education in its own right. The failure to consider this is part of a wider emphasis on instrumentalism in the policies of all recent governments and a lack of serious discussion about the role of universities in our society (Collini, 2012; Furlong, 2013).

Fourth, there is the specific contribution that postgraduate study makes to the professions. For example, the government itself has noticed that school teachers in high-performing countries are educated to Master's level. Yet, while encouraging more teachers to take such courses, it has stopped funding a scheme that enabled them to do so (Noble-Rogers, 2011).

Fifth, there is a social justice and access argument for thinking about how to support postgraduate education. Thus, in addition to the overall supply issues identified above, there are major concerns about fairness, equity, and opportunities for social mobility.

For example, even after the government's reforms, fees for home undergraduate students will remain regulated. At postgraduate level, with some exceptions, they are not. Average fees for a one-year Master's course for a home student rose to £4,000 in 2011, while an MBA cost an average of £12,000 (Tobin, 2011). Fees for non-subsidized subjects are likely to rise significantly following the tripling of undergraduate fees from 2012, as many universities will be reluctant to price postgraduate courses below undergraduate courses. Fees for higher cost subjects that continue to receive some core funding may also rise. Indeed, there are reports that such rises are already happening in some places (Reddin *et al.*, 2011; Morgan, 2011).

Yet compared with provision for undergraduates, financial support for postgraduates is 'hit or miss'. The UK Research Councils' programme of studentships for research postgraduates provides support to only 22 per cent of those studying full time and just 1.4 per cent of those studying part time. Taught postgraduate students are eligible to apply for Professional and Career Development Loans – although only 44 per cent of loan applicants were successful in 2011/12, down from 59 per cent in 2009/10 (HEC, 2012). A small number get support from their employers, most notably part-time students on taught courses, but many more fund themselves. Cost sharing is already widespread at postgraduate level, but the removal of any state subsidy for many students has made the extent of a student's own means to contribute increasingly important.

Browne (IRHEFSF, 2010) himself quoted figures that showed that private school students are already more likely than their state school peers to undertake postgraduate study. They are significantly over-represented in the postgraduate population, accounting for 17 per cent of all postgraduates, despite being drawn from only 7 per cent of the population.

Table 10.1: The backgrounds of postgraduates and undergraduates

	Privately educated	State school educated
Postgraduate population	17%	83%
Undergraduate population	14%	86%
Total population	**7%**	**93%**

Source: IRHEFSF (2010), drawn from Sutton Trust, itself drawing on DLHE data

In arguing for 'fairer financial support for postgraduate students', Alan Milburn (2009) suggested that a lack of postgraduate funding for access to the professions had serious implications for social mobility. Evidence from other countries confirms that as undergraduate qualifications become the norm, postgraduate study is an increasingly important social sorting mechanism. Speaking more recently, Milburn, as the Coalition Government's social mobility tsar, warned that access to postgraduate education was 'a real time-bomb in terms of social mobility', saying that:

> Everyone agrees that nobody should be barred from undergraduate education because they can't afford fees, and yet we completely accept this barrier when it comes to postgraduate education. The fact is, postgraduate education is not a luxury for the individual, it is a necessity for our economy and wider society.

> (Milburn, 2012a)

Paul Wakeling and Chris Kyriacou (2010) have shown that rates of progression to postgraduate research degrees are higher among students at Russell Group universities, which tend to have more privileged intakes than most other universities.

More generally, working-class students are somewhat less likely than others to progress to postgraduate study immediately after a first degree, but rates of progression to higher degrees by social class after three years show sharper social class differentiation. Wakeling (2012) attributes this to the use of postgraduate study as a 'second chance' by those who can draw upon familial resources to facilitate further study. There is a real danger, then, that postgraduate education will become the new frontier of widening participation or, if we get it wrong, a new arena for the perpetuation of privilege.

Finally, there is a risk of 'market failure' in some specific fields of postgraduate study. Terence Kealey (2011), the vice chancellor of the University of Buckingham, has claimed that 'the UK market in taught postgraduate courses has long been liberalized, so its fees are correspondingly high, yet demand rises inexorably'. He, like Browne, may have been unduly influenced by buoyant recruitment for Business School MBAs and similar courses, which are associated with high subsequent earning premiums. For, while higher degrees as a whole do bring benefits to individuals and the Exchequer, not all subjects can command high fees, nor do they all produce impressive returns for the student. Smith showed that recent postgraduates earned on average £23,500 six months after graduating – a postgraduate premium of around 24 per cent (Smith, 2010). However, business and administrative studies postgraduates earned 36 per cent more than first-degree holders, while languages and engineering students gained only an 11 per cent premium (O'Leary and Sloane, 2005).

Clearly, in this situation some parts of the sector are more likely to thrive in the market place than others. It would therefore be a 'hard sell' to argue that there is a strong case for the government to intervene in the MBA market. There are, however, other parts of the sector that are not as healthy, particularly in terms of UK recruitment. In these areas we can anticipate market failure taking place, to the detriment of individuals and society, if remedial action is not taken.

There are thus a number of specific 'at risk' areas of study, some of them with high public benefits but low private returns. In some arts subjects, individual financial benefits from study at this level could be minimal, despite its wider social benefits, something future funding options will need to take into account. Furthermore, the majority of home postgraduate students are part-time and unless things change they will face the triple disincentive of increased undergraduate debt, higher postgraduate fees, and no student support package. There are also particular concerns about some post-qualification courses in education, health, and social care, where public expenditure cuts have affected both salaries and the availability of support from employers. If we want to ensure that we have high standards of professional education in these fields, some intervention and investment from government might be required there as well.

Towards a topography of postgraduate education

One of the reasons why the visibility of postgraduate education is limited is the relative paucity of data about it. Both BIS and the HEFCE have now recognized this as a problem and are seeking to establish a better database to inform future policy deliberations. For example, the 2010 Smith Review recommended that the sector should advise government on what additional information was needed to inform policy decisions on widening access to postgraduate study, and in a letter to the HEFCE in January 2012 the responsible ministers at BIS, Vince Cable and David Willetts, expressed support for the work the Funding Council was doing to understand more about the purpose, characteristics, and outcomes of postgraduate study.

Having said that, postgraduate education is a notoriously difficult concept to define. Postgraduate education can be defined as courses that are more advanced than undergraduate courses, usually studied by those who already hold undergraduate degrees (Sastry, 2004). However, as such, it is something of an umbrella term, encompassing a diverse array of provision – from short certificate courses to four-year PhD research projects to professional doctorates studied largely in the workplace. The key distinctions are between postgraduate taught courses (PGT) in a wide range of disciplines, postgraduate courses specifically designed as professional training and development (PGP), and postgraduate research degrees (PGR), including many professional doctorates.

However, as the British Academy (2012) points out, the line between PGT and PGR provision is sometimes blurred. The same is true of the line between PGT and PGP, especially in respect of what counts as Continuing Professional Development (CPD).

The HEC, which we discuss below, mapped existing HESA student data onto this new typology (Table 10.2), although the mapping is not exact. It has not been possible, for example, to disaggregate professionally-oriented Master's degrees from the 'taught Master's' category. It does, however, provide a rough overview of the current size and structure of the postgraduate sector.

Enrolment onto postgraduate courses has increased steadily over the last decade with research enrolments rising by 20.5 per cent and taught enrolments by 34.3 per cent between 2002 and 2010. As indicated earlier, the rise is predominantly due to rapid increases in uptake by international students. The trend is particularly marked in PGT, where international enrolments increased by 105.8 per cent compared to an increase of 15.8 per cent in home enrolments. Uptake of PGR courses by international students over the same period increased by 26.8 per cent, compared to a 14.1 per cent increase in domestic uptake. In a handful of disciplines at PGT level, rapid increases in international enrolments have actually masked a decline in the number of domestic enrolments (HEC, 2012: 34).

Table 10.2: A typology of postgraduate provision

PG Taught	PG Professional	PG Research
Postgraduate **diploma** and **Master's** courses, extending an individual's knowledge or allowing them to convert to a new discipline	**Professional certificates and diplomas**	**Research Master's –** e.g. MRes: includes methods training and often used as a stepping point to a PhD; Mphil: sometimes used as a PhD exit point
Integrated Master's such as Meng	**PGCE** (Initial Teacher Training) and similar licences to practice	Traditional model **PhD**
Postgraduate **modules,** e.g. Open University courses	**Vocational Master's courses** – either as CPD or preparing individual for a particular profession	**'New route' PhD** – with larger taught elements and wider skills training
	MBA	Some **professional doctorates** – that count in REF (Research Excellence Framework)
	Some **professional doctorates** – where required as licence to practice but not included in REF	

Source: Adapted from the Higher Education Commission, 2012

Over half of PGT students in the UK study part time, with around 60 per cent of students aged 26 or over – although the number of young, full-time students has increased steadily in the last few years (Bell and Chester, 2011). By contrast, only 29 per cent of PGR students in England study on a part-time basis.

There is a degree of concentration of postgraduate students in certain subject areas. Bell and Chester report that over 60 per cent of all taught postgraduate students are studying in just four subject areas: business and administrative studies, education, subjects allied to medicine, and social studies. As can be seen from Table 10.3, there are significantly more students studying towards research degrees in science subjects than in the arts, humanities, and the social sciences. It should also be noted that 69 per cent of Research Council funding for postgraduate research is focused on science disciplines.

Table 10.3: Summary of all postgraduate students at UK HEIs in 2010–11

		Arts	Sciences	Combined subjects	Total
PGR	PhD	35,535	52,245	5	87,780
	Mphil	8,185	7,290	5	15,475
	Total – PGR	**43,720**	**59,535**	**10**	**103,255**
PGT	Taught Master's	198,775	107,690	110	306,575
	Other at taught Master's level	6,900	3,075	0	9,970
	Integrated Master's	4,050	63,190	0	67,245
	PG diplomas, certificates and institutional credit	52,250	27,680	1,925	81,850
	Total – PGT	**261,975**	**201,635**	**2,035**	**465,640**
PGP	Professional/regulated PG	25,300	6,390	140	31,820
	MBA	26,345	380	0	26,720
	PGCE (Initial Teacher Training)	28,530	0	0	28,530
	Total – PGP	**80,175**	**6,770**	**140**	**87,070**

Source: HEC, 2012: 24

In a number of areas our understanding of the postgraduate landscape remains inadequate. These include, but are not limited to, a lack of comprehensive and consistent applications data owing to the absence of a common application system, a lack of consistent and reliable data on the socio-economic backgrounds of the postgraduate cohort, and limited data on longer-term employment outcomes for postgraduate students. Information in all three fields, and the latter two in particular, is vital to inform deliberations on how far a new approach to funding postgraduate education in the UK is needed.

Even in the area of fees and finance for postgraduate education, crucial to the current policy debate on funding, the data are limited. However, the following figures 10.1 and 10.2 show the main sources of funding currently available to home and EU PGT and PGR students:

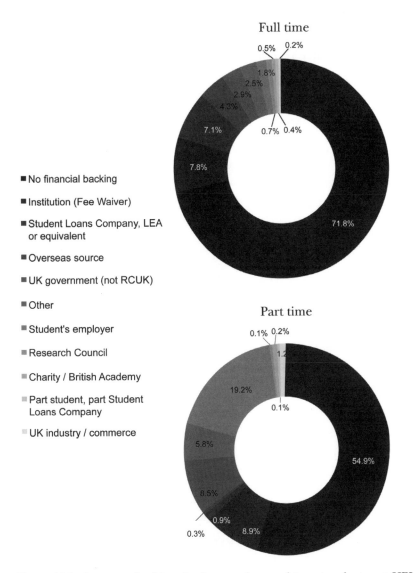

Figure 10.1: Sources of tuition fee income for taught postgraduates at HEIs in England

The majority of home PGT students receive no financial support towards the cost of their tuition – although this category includes students who receive a small interest rate subsidy from the government through state-supported Professional and Career Development Loans. HESA data from 2010–11 suggest that 8.4 per cent of all PGT students were supported by their institution through fee waivers or similar. Only 0.4 per cent were supported by the Research Councils, whose financial support for taught postgraduate study has increasingly been phased out. Part-time PGT students are more likely than full-time students to have funding from an employer (HEC, 2012:

56). The 10.8 per cent of all PGT students who have such funding may, however, be an underestimate, as those students who pay their own tuition fees directly to their institution and later receive reimbursement from their employer might go undetected.

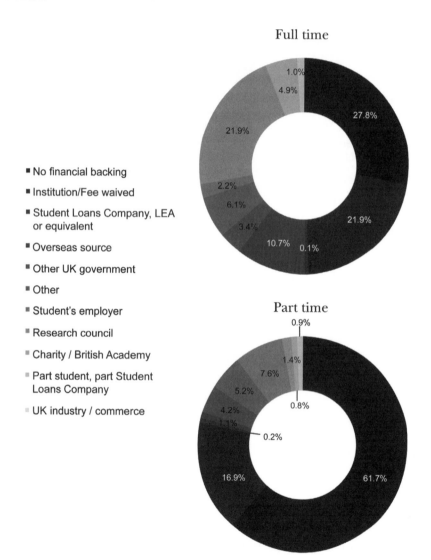

Full time

- No financial backing
- Institution/Fee waived
- Student Loans Company, LEA or equivalent
- Overseas source
- Other UK government
- Other
- Student's employer
- Research council
- Charity / British Academy
- Part student, part Student Loans Company
- UK industry / commerce

Part time

Notes: The population is restricted to students registered at HEIs in England, and includes students in all years of study (rather than just entrants)

Figure 10.2: Sources of tuition fee income for research postgraduates at HEIs in England

By contrast, a significant proportion of home PGR students receive funding towards the cost of fees and living costs either from the Research Councils (16 per cent of all such students in 2010–11) or from their institutions (20.5 per cent in 2010–11). A further 3.7 per cent of all PGR students are funded by charitable organizations. HESA data suggests that only 3.7 per cent of all research students are funded by their employer, though here again this is likely to be an underestimate due to shortcomings in the reporting method. Nevertheless, 37.6 per cent of all postgraduate research students appear to be completely self-funded – particularly amongst those studying in the arts and humanities. Part-time students are more likely to be self-funded, with 61.7 per cent receiving no financial backing (HEC, 2012: 50).

The work of the HEC

The HEC was formed in 2011 by a group of parliamentarians who thought there was a need for a platform for a more nuanced, informed, and reflective debate on higher education policy. The Commission brought together 20 leaders from the education sector, the business community, and the three major political parties. It took a Select Committee-style approach to its work – holding inquiries, taking evidence, and producing written reports with recommendations for policymakers.

Owing to some of the aforementioned concerns, the HEC decided, for its first inquiry, to address the issue of postgraduate education. It took evidence from a large number of organizations and individuals – holding five evidence sessions in Westminster, a roundtable with the Wellcome Trust on postgraduate education in the life sciences, and a half day of workshops at the annual conference of the UK Council for Graduate Education. It also made visits to four campuses (at Oxford, Cranfield, and Greenwich Universities and the National Film and Television School), which consisted of meetings with heads of institution, academics, and students. In these sessions, members spoke directly to 11 vice chancellors and nearly 40 students and early career researchers. In addition, the Commission received 54 written submissions.

The Commission looked at postgraduate education in three timeframes. It sought to understand more about the nature of the sector now and the state of postgraduate education in British universities today; it looked at the likely state of the sector in 2015, when the cohort beginning their undergraduate programmes in September 2012 under the new fee regime will come to consider entering postgraduate study; and finally, to the nature of the sector beyond 2015 – considering what the UK's long-term vision for the postgraduate sector should be.

Possible approaches to funding

Perhaps one of the most urgent and difficult issues the Commission had to confront was that of funding, particularly for fees and/or living expenses for home students on postgraduate taught courses. As indicated earlier, there is a prospect of students facing increased postgraduate fees and other expenses and repaying them in the context of rising undergraduate debt – and at a time when, as we have noted, existing

Professional and Career Development Loans seem to be drying up. While the HEFCE teaching grant funding remains available for some courses, the arrangement is only temporary at present and does relatively little to offset the costs to the student as fees rise. Unless the funding issue is addressed, Don Nutbeam, vice-chancellor of Southampton University, may well be right to claim that 'the alternative is a system in which UK universities continue to operate in a global market place ... from which our own students become increasingly excluded' (Nutbeam, 2011).

There are different views about the best way to finance postgraduate education in the future and some of the main ones were summarized in the Commission's following report:

POSSIBLE WAYS TO FINANCE POSTGRADUATE EDUCATION

A single loan scheme for undergraduate and postgraduate education

The Australian government provides student loans to cover the costs of postgraduate fees under the Higher Education Loans Programme (HELP). Repayments, made through the tax system, are progressive – with those earning more repaying back a greater proportion of their income each month. The total costs of the scheme are controlled through a lifetime cap of AUS $116,507 (£75,273) for medical students and AUS $93,204 (£60,217) for other students. The scheme is available for most, though not all, postgraduate courses. The HELP system covers only fees, which are lower in Australia than the UK.

The Australian model was presented to the Commission by Southampton University Vice Chancellor Don Nutbeam. Rather than replicating the Australian model exactly through creating a second separate loan scheme for postgraduates, Nutbeam proposes creating a single loan scheme which home students can draw on to cover both undergraduate and postgraduate learning. He contends such a system could be established without major changes to the current arrangements for student financial support for undergraduate education.

An income-contingent loan of £10k for masters degrees

In a report for CentreForum published in late 2011, Tim Leunig proposed that government should offer income-contingent loans of £10,000 to prospective postgraduate taught students in order to cover maintenance costs.

Loan repayments would be made through the tax system, with graduates repaying 9 per cent of any income between £15,000 and £21,000. Repayments would not be taken from earnings over £21,000, as that is the point at which undergraduate student loan repayments will begin under the new student finance regime. Those earning over £21,000 would thus pay off £540 of their postgraduate loan each year.

An interest rate would be applied, ranging from inflation to inflation plus 3 per cent on a progressive scale with outstanding debt forgiven after 30 years. Leunig proposes that loans should be available for any postgraduate taught degree, with eligibility restricted to those with first class or upper second class honours degrees.

Risk-sharing by students and universities

In oral evidence to the Commission Professor Nicholas Barr argued for extension of the undergraduate student loan system to postgraduates. Noting that '*student loans are designed to make a small loss, protecting those with low lifetime earnings from repaying the entire sum*', he argued that the key question for public policy was who carried this loss. Instead of the loss risk being placed on taxpayers – which would inevitably mean controls on student numbers – it could instead be shifted to the cohort of students and the universities through risk premiums.

A long-term private bond

One idea put to the Commission envisaged universities collectively leveraging investment from capital markets to provide a long-term loan facility for UK students. Universities could be an attractive prospect for financial markets given the predictability of their revenue streams and the longevity of their business models.

Corporate bonds could be issued via a Special Purpose Vehicle (SPV) composed of a number of universities – potentially also including their alumni, private investors, industry, business, and other stakeholders – with government acting as guarantor. Each bond issuance would provide a facility for students at participating institutions to draw down loans for postgraduate study. The targeting of loans would be established as part of the lending criteria of the SPV, and this in turn would be a repayment risk insured against by each institution. This could provide a scalable, postgraduate funding solution which offers less risk exposure for individual institutions and removes the need for risk-selecting students. As a contingent liability, the bond is accounted for outside of the Public Sector Net Credit Requirement and offers students a cheaper repayment alternative to existing commercial loan schemes.

Alumni borrowing – the Prodigy Finance model

Prodigy Finance connects alumni with students attending the top universities in the world – 'creating a community of investors and borrowers'. Alumni purchase bonds which cover an entire class of students at a particular university. Investors can choose to only invest in their own alma mater or to spread the funds among multiple universities. Prodigy structure the bonds to ensure a balanced and diverse portfolio of students in each issuance. The return to investors depends on the repayment performance of students – though to date there have been no defaults. There are however questions about the scalability of this model beyond MBAs and other high-return degrees.

Tax incentives for employers

A number of contributors to the review advocated the establishment of tax credits for employers contributing to the cost of postgraduate education for their employees. Birkbeck College, University of London, stated that '*Financial incentives to employers to pay for their staff to undertake part-time postgraduate studies should be considered seriously, as many employers are keen to do so but have limited resources.*'

A research review of international tax incentives (CEDEFOP, 2009) identifies a need to avoid deadweight costs, especially among large enterprises, who may invest regardless of incentives. In designing a potential incentive system there may be a case for restricting eligibility to small and medium sized businesses. The CEDEFOP report also acknowledges that it is difficult to make informed policy decisions about tax incentives, noting the '*scarcity of quantitative and qualitative information*' and that '*comprehensive public evaluations of them are practically non-existent*'.

Source: Adapted from HEC, 2012: 67–9

A key question concerns how targeted or otherwise any such funding scheme should be. The Commission identified three principles for prioritization.

The first and perhaps most important principle is maximizing the value added of the loan scheme. The scheme's design should seek to minimize deadweight cost and should not crowd out existing streams of funding.

Secondly, the scheme might wish to target loans in areas where we are currently underinvesting and which are strategically important to our future competitiveness. The House of Lords Science and Technology Committee, for example, recommended that the government 'extend the student loan scheme currently available to undergraduates to cover STEM Master's degrees' (House of Lords, 2012). However, there are a number of other subject areas, such as modern foreign languages and quantitative social science, which are as vital to competitiveness and as important to maintain. There may well be arguments in relation to other vulnerable subjects, whether or not strategically important.

Thirdly, the scheme may look to prioritize funding allocations on the basis of improving access to the professions. This could involve targeting loans at courses which are de facto requirements for entry into employment. An alternative approach would be to target funding at individuals, removing the barriers to participation faced by particular credit-constrained subgroups of society. In a written submission to the

HEC inquiry, Universities UK suggested that the government might 'perhaps identify those students that were eligible for maintenance grants at undergraduate level or through the use of other indicators ... identify students that may not otherwise pursue postgraduate study' (UUK, 2012).

After the HEC had reported, the National Union of Students made a further proposal of a way in which loans might be introduced for postgraduate students with minimal additional costs to the Exchequer (McVitty and Wright, 2012). This involved three specific schemes: one for fees and maintenance loans for those from hitherto poorly represented groups seeking access to the professions, another employer-backed scheme for those studying for any postgraduate professional development qualification alongside employment, and finally a fees-only loan of around £6,000 for well qualified Master's students in any field. The loans would be available through the Student Loans Company but on different terms to undergraduate loans and there would be a limited number of them in the first instance.

The Commission's recommendations

Although the HEC report reinforced the criticism of the White Paper for neglecting postgraduate education and made a strong case for state-backed student loans to be introduced for segments of postgraduate provision where the financial markets have failed to provide competitive sources of finance, it did not itself propose a new funding scheme. However, it did establish a need for one and recommended that the government should immediately establish a taskforce to examine the feasibility of a postgraduate student loan scheme and develop policy options by December 2013.

Alongside its advocacy of increasing the enrolment of home students on postgraduate courses, the Commission also noted that the very availability of such courses was threatened by a potential decline in international students as a result of changes in UK immigration rules. It is thus not clear that the buoyant international recruitment noted earlier will continue indefinitely. Indeed, subsequent figures suggest that 2012–13 has already seen a contraction in the total number of international students coming to the UK from some key markets. The enrolment of Indian students has already fallen by 24 per cent (HESA, 2013) and there is some recent survey evidence that even Chinese students are now becoming less likely to consider the UK as the preferred destination for their studies (ExEd, 2013).

The Commission also made a number of other important recommendations, including better collection of data on the postgraduate landscape and improved understanding of employers' needs for postgraduate skills, changes to the relevant immigration regulations, greater national and corporate investment in research and development, and the setting up of a joint working group to consider the issue of quality and international competitiveness in research degrees.

Conclusion

In the same month as the HEC reported on postgraduate education, Alan Milburn's latest report on how universities can advance social mobility (Milburn, 2012b) also recommended a new loan system for postgraduate students. His report argued that the 'risk that the ability to pay upfront, rather than an individual's potential, will increasingly become a determining factor in who can access postgraduate education … poses an unacceptable threat to the long-term health of the UK higher education sector' (2012b: 6).

Taken together, these two reports mounted significant pressure on the government to address this neglected issue as a matter of urgency. Support has also been received from Bright Blue, an influential group within the Conservative Party, with Director Ryan Shorthouse imploring the government to turn its eyes to postgraduate study and extend government loans to postgraduates (Shorthouse, 2013). Further pressure came from 11 English vice-chancellors who wrote to the government about the funding crisis facing postgraduate education (Boffey, 2013a). Meanwhile, Minister David Willetts announced that he was holding a roundtable with interested parties 'to discuss the emerging evidence of a problem and to consider potential solutions in the current difficult economic climate' (Boffey, 2013b: 21).

If no decision is made on an appropriate funding scheme for home students in the near future, some urgent interim measures will need to be put in place before students begin to emerge with increased undergraduate debt. Among those floated have been maintenance of teaching funding for postgraduate courses at least until any new funding scheme is in place. It may also prove necessary to extend such core funding to subjects currently excluded from it. Philanthropic support might also be sought for a specific endowment fund to support 'need-blind' entry for home students in some subjects. Other possibilities might include repayment 'holidays' for those returning to study part-time while repaying their undergraduate debts. For key professions like health, social work, education, and defence, the state could act as a surrogate employer and provide incentives for students to enrol on postgraduate courses, as already happens in the case of pre-service teacher training courses, for example.

Beyond that, there is, of course, a need for a serious debate about the meaning and importance of graduate skills and the nature and quality of postgraduate education, as well as about the balance to be struck between undergraduate and postgraduate provision. However, such a debate should take place in a context where access to postgraduate education is a realistic possibility for those who can benefit from it. A 'one-stop shop' for information on courses and funding for postgraduates would also help here.

All this is urgent. It would indeed be ironic if the new undergraduate arrangements introduced by the Coalition Government were to prove more equitable than their critics fear, only to find that inequities are reintroduced via that part of the system that has so far been relatively neglected in the funding debate. As Graham Spittle, chief technology officer at IBM and chair of the HEC inquiry into postgraduate education that has informed this chapter, has concluded:

> The UK government should recognise that their responsibility for higher education does not stop with undergraduates. We need to take a holistic whole-system view of education – and that must include postgraduates.
>
> (Spittle, 2012: 42)

If we do not, then not only postgraduate education itself, but the standing of British universities and their research, as well as the future health of the economy and society, could well be at stake.

NOTE: In July 2013, just as this book was going to press, the HEFCE published two reports on the state of postgraduate education (HEFCE, 2013a; 2013b). At the same time, £75 million of public investment in improving postgraduate finance was announced. The HEFCE will earmark £25 million from the Catalyst Fund for pilot projects that stimulate progression into taught postgraduate education and a further £50 million, from the National Scholarship Programme budget, will be made available from 2015/16 onwards. Sector organisations and commentators continue to press for a more systematic approach to tackling the postgraduate funding challenge, with the Social Mobility and Child Poverty Commission describing as 'very disappointing' the government's apparent decision not to commission an independent report looking at the issue of postgraduate access (SMCPC, 2013).

Note

[1] The Coalition Government did however publish a separate research and innovation strategy six months later in December 2011. See www.gov.uk/government/uploads/system/uploads/attachment_data/file/32450/11-1387-innovation-and-research-strategy-for-growth.pdf

References

1994 Group (2012) *The Postgraduate Crisis.* Policy report 12. London: 1994 Group.

Beddington, J. (2011) Letter from the government chief scientific advisor to Sir Alan Langlands. 21 July 2011. Online. www.hefce.ac.uk/media/hefce/content/whatwedo/knowledgeexchangeandskills/strategicallyimportantsubjects/govscience.pdf (Accessed 28 October 2012).

Bell, L. and Chester, J. (2011) *Analytical Briefing: Taught postgraduate funding and finance.* London: Universities UK.

BERA/UCET (2012) *Prospects for Education Research in Education Departments in Higher Education Institutions in the UK.* London: BERA.

BIS (Department for Business, Innovation and Skills) (2009) *Higher Ambitions: The future of universities in a knowledge economy.* London: BIS.

—(2011) *Higher Education: Students at the heart of the system.* London: BIS.

Boffey, D. (2013a) 'Universities warn of crisis for postgraduates'. *The Observer,* 6 January.

—(2013b) 'State school graduates "fail to reach job potential"'. *The Observer*, 13 January.

British Academy (2012) *Postgraduate Funding: The neglected dimension*. Position statement. London: British Academy.

CEDEFOP (2009) *Using Tax Incentives to Promote Education and Training*. Luxembourg: Office for Official Publications of the European Communities.

Collini, S. (2012) *What are Universities For?* London: Penguin.

ExEd (Exporting Education) (2013) 'High spending Chinese students shun UK'. London: ExEd. Online. http://exeduk.com/news/ (Accessed 21 January 2013).

Elsevier (2011) *International Comparative Performance of the UK Research Base*. London: BIS.

Eurydice Network (2012) *The European Higher Education Area in 2012*. Bologna process implementation report. Brussels: Education, Audiovisual and Culture Executive Agency.

Furlong, J. (2013) *Education: An anatomy of the discipline*. London: Routledge.

HEC (Higher Education Commission) (2012) *Postgraduate Education: An independent inquiry by the Higher Education Commission*. London: Policy Connect.

HEFCE (Higher Education Funding Council for England) (2013a) *Trends in Transition from First Degree to Postgraduate Study: Qualifiers between 2002–03 and 2010–11*. Bristol: HEFCE. Online. www.hefce.ac.uk/pubs/year/2013/201313/

—(2013b) *Postgraduate Education in England and Northern Ireland: Overview report 2013*. Bristol: HEFCE. Online. www.hefce.ac.uk/pubs/year/2013/201314/

HESA (Higher Education Statistics Agency) (2013) 'Press release 184 – non UK domicile students'. Online. www.hesa.ac.uk/index.php?option=com_content&task=view&id=2663&Itemid=161 (Accessed 16 January 2013).

House of Lords Science and Technology Committee (2012) *Higher Education in Science, Technology, Engineering and Mathematics Subjects*. London: House of Lords.

IRHEFSF (Independent Review of Higher Education Funding and Student Finance) (2010) *Securing a Sustainable Future for Higher Education (The Browne Report)*. London: Department for Business, Innovation, and Skills. Online. www.bis.gov.uk/assets/biscore/corporate/docs/s/10-1208-securing-sustainable-higher-education-browne-report.pdf

Jump, P. (2012) 'We'd welcome ways to solve the postgraduate funding puzzle'. *Times Higher Education*, 20 September.

Kealey, T. (2011) 'Free the market: take the cap off tuition fees'. *The Times*, 29 March.

Leunig, T. (2011) *Mastering Postgraduate Funding*. London: CentreForum.

Luo, W. and Yang, Y. (2012) 'Surge in postgrads puts pressure on advisers'. *China Daily*, 23 October.

McVitty, D. and Wright, A. (2012) *Steps Towards a Fairer System of Postgraduate Taught Funding in England*. London: National Union of Students.

Milburn, A. (2009) *Unleashing Aspiration: The final report of the Panel on Fair Access to the Professions*. London: Cabinet Office.

—(2012a) 'Social mobility in higher education'. *Graduate Market Trends*, Spring.

—(2012b) *University Challenge: How higher education can advance social mobility*. A progress report by the Independent Reviewer on Social Mobility and Child Poverty. London: Cabinet Office.

Morgan, J. (2011) 'Postgraduates "priced out of the market" by sharp fee increases'. *Times Higher Education*, 21 July.

Noble-Rogers, J. (2011) 'Why teachers need to carry on learning'. *The Independent*, 24 March.

Nutbeam, D. (2011) 'Postgraduates need financial support'. *The Guardian*, 1 February.

O'Leary, N. and Sloane, P. (2005) 'The return to a university education in Great Britain'. *National Institute Economic Review*, 193 (75).

Prime Minister's Council for Science and Technology (2010) *A Vision for UK Research*. London: Council for Science & Technology.

Purcell, K., Elias, P., Atfield, G., Behle, H., Ellison, R., Luchinskaya, D., Snape, J., Conaghan, L., and Tzanakou, C. (2012) *Futuretrack Stage 4: Transitions into employment, further study and other outcomes*. Warwick: Warwick Institute for Employment Research.

Reddin, M., Penny, C., and Kingston, B. (2011) *National Survey of UK Tuition Fees 2011–2*. Online. www.thecompleteuniversityguide.co.uk/higher-education-staff/mike-reddin-public-goods (Accessed 16 January 2013).

Richardson, H. (2011) 'Lack of top researchers could harm UK plc, warns Dyson'. BBC News website. Online. www.bbc.co.uk/news/education-12464204 (Accessed 15 February 2011).

Roberts, A. (2010) 'It's hard to go on'. *Times Higher Education*, 23 December.

Sastry, T. (2004) *Postgraduate Education in the United Kingdom*. Oxford: HEPI.

Shorthouse, R. (2013) 'A bright future: accelerating education reform'. In Shorthouse, R. and Stagg, G. (eds.) *Tory Modernization 2.0: The future of the Conservative Party*. London: Bright Blue.

SMCPC (Social Mobility and Child Poverty Commission) (2013) *Higher Education: the Fair Access Challenge*. London: HM Government.

Smith, A. (2010) *One Step Beyond: Making the most of postgraduate education*. London: Department for Business, Innovation, and Skills.

Spittle, G. (2012) 'An economic necessity: putting postgraduates at the heart of the system'. In Coiffait, L. (ed.) *Blue Skies: New thinking about the future of higher education*. London: Pearson.

Tobin, L. (2011) 'Will a master's get you a job?'. *The Guardian*, 15 February.

Universities UK (2012) Written submission to the Higher Education Commission inquiry into postgraduate education. Unpublished.

Wakeling, P. (2012) 'Contribution of Evidence'. Evidence presented to the Higher Education Commission's postgraduate education inquiry. Unpublished.

Wakeling, P. and Kyriacou, C. (2010) *Widening Participation from Undergraduate to Postgraduate Research Degrees: A research synthesis*. Swindon: NCCPE and Economic and Social Research Council.

Willetts, D. (2011) Speech to meeting of Universities UK, 25 February 2011. London.

—(2012) Parliamentary answer, House of Commons, 22 October 2012. London.

Chapter 11

Leading the British university today: your fate in whose hands?
David Watson

Introduction

At the time of writing UK higher education is going through one of its more 'manic' periods. Recent policy decisions, allied to the government's austerity programme (which has yet fully to reach publicly funded higher education), as well moral panics about graduate employability, have created a storm which, if not 'perfect', has made the sector and its leadership twitchy to an extent that has not been experienced since the late 1970s.

The policy framework

To demonstrate the regularity of government intervention in the system as a whole, below I set out the main landmarks of reform in the UK since the early 1960s. To put the point crudely, for every third entry of a cohort into the system since then, the system has been thrown up into the air by a government claiming it is fixing the sins of the previous administration – including, sometimes, its own party. In international terms this degree of legislative hyperactivity is extraordinary (Watson and Bowden, 2005).

UK government higher education initiatives 1963–2012

1. The *Robbins Report* (1963): creation of 'new' universities, plus the 'ability to benefit' criterion
2. The Woolwich speech and the creation of the Polytechnics (1965)
3. The *James Report* (1972): reorganization of teacher education and 'diversification'
4. Withdrawal of the overseas student subsidy (1980), public expenditure cuts (1981), and the White Paper proposing a smaller and rationalized system (1985)
5. Creation of the National Advisory Body for Public Sector Higher Education (NAB), centralizing the former local authority responsibility for higher education outside the universities (1985)
6. White Paper endorsing the expansion and incorporation of the Polytechnics, Central Institutions, and large Colleges (1987), achieved in the Education Reform Act (1988)

7. White Paper on the ending of the binary line (1991), achieved in the Further and Higher Education Act (1992), along with Funding Councils for the devolved administrations; creation of the 'new new' universities

8. The *Dearing Report* (1997): opens the way for undergraduate fees, legislated for in the Teaching and Higher Education Act (1998)

9. White Paper (2003) leads to 'variable' fees, the establishment of the 'new new' universities (without research-degree awarding powers), and to potential foundation-degree awarding powers for further education institutions in the Higher Education Act (2004)

10. White Paper, *Higher Ambitions: The future of universities in a knowledge economy* (2009)

11. The Browne Review (2010) leads to proposals for higher undergraduate fees, and a revised graduate contribution scheme

12. White Paper, *Higher Education: Students at the heart of the system* (2011): replacing Funding Council grants to institutions with a higher level of fees (up to £9,000) to be advanced by the Student Loans Company and recovered through fees (Watson, 2011).

This might not matter so much if there were a well-understood direction of travel, or a consistently articulated final goal. Instead, we have seen violent 'mood swings' on issues like the size of and provision for the sector, both within and across governments of differing stripes. Meanwhile, in addition to political tinkering, the biggest part of this story has to be missed targets. Prime Minister Tony Blair boldly announced a target of 50 per cent of 18–30-year-olds in higher education at the Labour Party Conference in 1999: we are stuck in the low forties and are likely to go backwards (Gill, 2008). *The Learning Age* wanted a fully-functioning credit transfer system by 2000 (DfEE, 1998: para 6.18). *The Future of Higher Education* saw all higher education teachers as having an accredited qualification by 2006 (DfES, 2003: 50). To the frustration of successive ministers, the central government policy writ runs small, except in relation to fees and funding.

At the time of writing (October 2012) the Coalition Government, whose parties entered the 2010 election with diametrically opposed policies on higher education, is struggling with the implementation of the policies in *Students at the Heart of the System* (BIS, 2011).

Broadly, this White Paper represents the eleventh new 'framework' for UK higher education since the *Robbins Report* of 1963. It exhibits the characteristic mixture throughout this half-century of reform of brittle certainty, uncertainty, and evidence-free gambling on the outcomes.

Some things in the Paper provided confirmation of prior announcements, including a broken-backed response to Browne on fees. Fees are capped at £9,000 (Browne had suggested removing the cap entirely) and a proposed redistributive levy has been dropped. Further interventions attempt to make a curious kind of market, where at one end students with high qualifications – initially AAB at A-level, now ABB – can almost demand entry to a range of so-called elite institutions (whether or not these have the capacity to respond), and at the other, institutions will be encouraged to undercut each other on price. At the same time the Office for Fair Access (OFFA) will have its teeth sharpened.

A second category of proposals – mostly those where the Coalition initially disagreed – were put out for 'consultations', now largely concluded. These included: post-qualification admissions (PQA): flatly rejected – probably now for a considerable time; upfront payment of fees (where the Liberal Democrats lost out to the Conservatives in allowing this apparent undermining of the progressive intentions of the fee repayment scheme); criteria for degree-awarding powers (largely aimed at making entry easier for private providers; reduction or removal of VAT for shared services (finally approved); and another attempt at devising a regulatory system that is both lighter-touch and more interventionist (BIS, 2012).

In contrast are the evidence-light leaps of faith, where clearly no further research would be welcome. These include: the robustness of data about the student experience, the lighter-touch 'regulation' of standards and awards (surely counter-intuitive after the post-expansion moral panics about what constitutes a degree anyway), and the cavalry over the hill of the 'for-profit sector' (with no acknowledgement of the US evidence about how the same companies can fleece and distort a generous system of public support for deserving students [see Stratford, 2012]).

Most serious of all is the likely effect on public finances. Upfront payment will simply increase costs (and at the same time, perversely, dampen demand). Over time, and not least because of EU-wide obligations, the returns look wildly optimistic (HEPI, 2012a). Perhaps the most significant piece of whistling in the dark is the blithe confidence that 70 per cent of the funds advanced on students' behalf will come back through the loan system.

As a result the system currently faces at least five interrelated and unresolved pressures:

1. The fee arrangements have suppressed demand, but not to the extent that some feared (HEPI, 2012c). The exceptions are part-time and mature enrolments, which have dropped like a stone (HEFCE, 2013: 3–4)

2. The government's other market interventions (in particular, those that allow institutions to recruit as many of the most highly – but traditionally – qualified students) may be cutting against their 'social mobility' goals of diversifying the intake into 'top' universities

3. There are fears that the next spending review will open up (again) the question of protection for research funding. Nervousness here is compounded by the prospect of the Research Excellence Framework (REF) exercise at the end of 2013

4. The prospects of a more 'liberated' (i.e. less regulated) private sector blow hot and cold. This arena is also complicated by the goal of a more 'risk-related' regulatory regime, with an uncertain demarcation between the Funding Council (HEFCE in England) acting as a regulator and the Quality Assurance Agency (QAA) consulting on its new 'quality code' (for the UK as a whole)

5. Devolution in general poses another set of uncertainties, also wound up by the prospect of the referendum on Scottish independence in 2014 (HEPI, 2012b).

In aggregate, this set of strains is exacerbated by the Coalition's reluctance to table a Higher Education Bill, and hence provide a further lightning-rod for internal division and external opposition. Without primary legislation, number controls cannot be reformed, the regulations necessary for 'liberating' the private sector remain out of reach, and in an ironic way the position of the Funding Councils (especially the HEFCE) as 'buffer' bodies has strengthened, not diminished.

Institutional choices and trajectories

All over the world governments seek disciplined mission specificity for their higher institutions: they would like identifiable groups of universities and colleges, doing different things, and on expectations of different levels of funding. All over the world institutions won't behave, largely because their 'academic' employees won't behave – they are basically chasing similar (subject and professional) measures of esteem.

Such a drive often gets connected with the notion of a 'binary system': when a set of 'traditional' or 'academic' institutions is contrasted with another designed to deliver a more local (and locally accountable), vocational, accessible, and responsive service. There is a related international pathology. States with binary systems often feel that the rigidities of the framework are holding them back (the UK is an example). Some without them feel this is the only way forward (Austria is considering reforms of this type). Sometimes those who have made the move get disenchanted and want to move back (like Australia, who may be followed by South Africa). Herein lies another rule: in policy terms the grass is always greener on the other side of the fence (or somebody else does it better).

In these circumstances it is unsurprising that despite the strength of calls to differentiate their missions, the majority of institutional leaders have chosen to preserve the full range of their activities and to keep their options open. Analysis of undergraduate prospectuses reveals, for example, the very limited range of claims of distinctive or exceptional performance. These (almost) always include: a research environment (on a scale from 'intensive' to 'informed'); attention to teaching and learning (much more likely to be about infrastructure – like 'world-class learning resources' – than to pedagogy itself); graduate destinations (including the ubiquitous 'employability' claim); an 'international' community; and the social and recreational environment (the latter has receded a little lately in favour of the first four – not many lead any more, as they once did, on nightclubs). Nor do the main voluntary interest groups (or 'gangs') make much sense in terms of objective performance. There are currently five (as follows – numbers are as on websites on 11 November 2012), although the situation is increasingly fluid, and it is very hard to make sense, for example, of the Russell Group on any objective measures:

- The Russell Group of self-proclaimed 'research intensive' institutions (24)
- The '94 Group of smaller 'research intensives' (12)
- 'Million+', claiming to educate over a million students and made up chiefly of former Polytechnics and Scottish Central Institutions (21)
- Guild HE – the representative group of pre-1992 Colleges of Higher Education (25)
- The University Alliance, a group formerly called 'non-aligned!' – perhaps better termed the Groucho Marx Group (25).

In particular, it is clear that institutional status (and 'gang' membership) have very little to do with sound and responsible management, which is found (or not) in all types of institutions. In an attempt to show how specious many of these claimed boundaries are, Brian Ramsden and I created in 2007 the 'Association of Seaside Universities'. We were able to get convincing contributions to our manifesto from all 14 eligible universities (Watson, 2009: 105–13).

Another familiar illusion is that of 'academic drift' by the so-called new universities, most recently claimed by Stefan Collini, who calls it 'the flow of emulation' (Collini, 2012: 5, 54). Since 1992 there has been a popular view that the post-92 institutions began meekly to imitate their 'old university' counterparts. In fact, as Rachel Bowden and I demonstrated in an analysis of the first ten years of the 'new new universities', if anything the reverse was true (Watson and Bowden, 2002). The former PSHE institutions by and large stuck to their own traditional business (of professional and vocational higher education, and through part-time and mixed-mode as well as full-time study). What did begin to happen was that traditional universities, seeing this sort of development as in tune with the times, began instead to move across this unfamiliar field themselves (not least by founding Business Schools).

Among the main drivers towards this convergence or isomorphism, five stand out in particular.

1. There are the *policy* uncertainties set out above. The vice-chancellor of the University of Central Lancashire was speaking for the community when he stated that the biggest risk faced by his institution is Her Majesty's Government.
2. The student market poses another set of problems. What students want and need can confound the most sophisticated policy frameworks, where spokespersons react to what they regard as irrational choices by prescribing more and

decreasingly plausible 'information'. Look at the ways in which student demand led the systems of the 'developed' world towards meeting the needs of the cultural, creative, and service economies. Their ICT requirements (where they are normally ahead of their teachers) compound this. The UK system provides ample evidence of how (despite political voices to the contrary) a market does exist. Indeed student choices – of subjects, of institutions, and of mode of study – could be said very substantially to have moulded the system as we have it today. That is why so many supply-side STEM (science, technology, engineering, and mathematics) initiatives have failed (the same is not true in the developing world [Nuffield Foundation, 2008]). That is why there is a slow but inexorable move towards studying closer to the family home. And that is why institutions (like the UK Open University), which hold out the prospect of earning while learning, are increasingly popular.

3. Inherited and accumulated *resources* (of all kinds) can limit freedom of manoeuvre.

A good device for taking a cold-eyed, objective view of the relative position of any institution starting out on the process of mapping its future is to use the 'prosperity index'. This elementary league table, invented by Rachel Bowden and myself at the end of the last century, aggregates all of the income received by UK higher education institutions from all sources in the year and divides the amount by the full-time equivalent number of students they taught in that year (Watson and Bowden, 1999). It is a crude proxy for what those students might expect in terms of the quality of the infrastructure, staffing, and services. In the terms of today's discourse, these are the resources available to support the 'student experience': teachers and administrators, libraries and laboratories, buildings and gardens (the Aristotelian *peripetaea*), partnerships and networks, and the 'cloud' effect of research and intellectual capital. It has the useful side effect of strongly predicting the rank orders established by much more dubious multi-factorial league tables in newspapers and magazines. The original 'prosperity table' predicted the *Times* league table with a correlation of 0.92. In that sense it was, of course, a circular measure: the institutions had 'performed' in various ways to gain these resources. It does, however, operate as a significant reality check for a number of institutions for whom modesty rather than self-aggrandizement is indicated.

Table 11.1 shows the top ten of the 162 institutions in 2010–11. In order to correct for volume and breadth of activity I have assumed a cut-off at 10,000 FTE students, so the list begins at number 4 (the top three on the full list are small, highly successful specialist institutions: the London School of Hygiene and Tropical Medicine, Cranfield University, and the London Business School).

Table 11.1: Prosperity Index (total income over FTE students) 2010–11 for the top ten large (10k+ FTE) institutions

1. Cambridge (4)	£65,836
2. Imperial College (8)	£48,819
3. Oxford (9)	£46,817
4. UCL (11)	£37,608
5. Edinburgh (16)	£27,769
6. LSE (17)	£26,235
7. Kings's College London (19)	£25,874
8. Bristol (22)	£23,850
9. Liverpool (23)	£23,474
10. Warwick (27)	£22,173
Notes: Actual position in brackets	

Source: HESA

It is immediately significant that all of these, apart from LSE, have Medical Schools, confirming the fact that medicine makes a huge difference to relative income. As for separating the 'apex' from the 'clingers-on' the fault line after number 4 is palpable, validating the concept of a 'golden triangle' between Oxford, Cambridge, and London (several others of the smaller London Colleges are in roughly the same zone, but not included because of their size; for example the London School of Hygiene and Tropical Medicine is at number 3 on the overall list, at £115,603). If College income were included, Oxford and Cambridge would be even further out on their own.

Table 11.2 shows the other end of the spectrum. One human reaction, comparing the bottom to the top, is to ask what possible advantage could be gained by fining these institutions for the further support of those at the top (consider, for example, the enormous contribution made to the sector by the OU – with roughly one tenth of the resources per FTE student of Cambridge)

4. Then there is the question of *performance*. It is striking how many institutional strategies are driven by a desire to be at or near the top of rankings and league tables, the statistical merits of which make the professional cringe and whose implicit goals are naïve in the extreme. How many 'apex' institutions are there are there in a given country, and how many could there be (see point 5 below)? The tempting vice-chancellor-like answer is 'my institution, and every one above me'

Table 11.2: Prosperity Index (total income over FTE students) 2010–11 for the bottom ten large (10k+ FTE) institutions

1. Open University (162)	£6,098
2. Edge Hill (161)	£7,054
3. West of Scotland (157)	£7,913
4. Leeds Metropolitan (156)	£7,933
5. Huddersfield (152)	£8,103
6. Glasgow Caledonian (151)	£8,107
7. Bournemouth (150)	£8,184
8. Bedfordshire (149)	£8,222
9. Plymouth (147)	£8,321
10. De Montfort (144)	£8,442
Notes: Actual position in brackets	

Source: HESA

5. Such issues all build up to the question of *reputation*. Each institution will maintain a separate 'reputational reservoir', and the larger it is the more easily the university will be able to ride out pressures and problems (especially those that attract the media (Watson and Maddison, 2005: 142–52).

　　Empirically, nearly every national system of higher education has one, two, or not more than a very few 'apex' institutions (the term was coined by Robert Cowen (Cowen, 2007)). These are internationally and nationally recognized and prized. In the UK Oxford and Cambridge would fall into this category. Juliet Chester and Bahram Bekhradnia have explored the detail of their exceptional qualities (HEPI, 2009) and, as an important new book by David Palfreyman and Ted Tapper identifies, these institutions have, and generally act upon, a sense of responsibility for the higher education sector as a whole (Palfreyman and Tapper, 2008). The retiring Vice-Chancellor of Cambridge, Alison Richard, put the point well: 'Cambridge occupies a distinctive and distinguished place among universities, but our future health and that of UK higher education as a whole are interdependent' (Richard, 2009).

Views like this tune in well with the historical commitment in the UK to a 'controlled reputational range' of institutions (Watson, 2006). With strong mutual commitments to academic enlargement, to quality assurance (through, for example, external examining), and to collective promotion (through Universities UK), there has been a sense that UK higher education is a collaborative exercise, in which each end of a reputational pecking order knows about the other and has something bound up in its success. The undermining of this precious quality may be the most damaging effect of UK higher education policy over the past decade (roughly since 2003).

Meanwhile, the brittle assertion of 'world-classness' itself may be a mirage: what counts in the tables (like research citations and self-evaluation by members of academic fields) is the opposite of most of the features governments say they want from 'their' institutions (like high teaching quality, contributions to social justice, and entrepreneurialism).

The 'zone of freedom of action'

In response, sound institutional intelligence can assist with at least the following ten features of effective strategic leadership and management:

1. The first is balancing ambition and realism – ensuring that strategic goals are not only stretching but attainable. (Objectives that are simply out of reach prompt cynical reactions from groups inside and outside the institution)
2. The second is getting matters in proportion – for example, 'right-sizing' that section of a research strategy focused on the Research Assessment Exercise (RAE) and its successor, the Research Excellence Framework (REF).

   The most secure measure of 'research intensity' shows the same gap between the apex and the aspirants. Table 11.3 ranks the same ten institutions as Table 11.1 by their position on the league table of research funding as a proportion of teaching and research funding from the Funding Councils.

Table 11.3: 'R' funding as a proportion of 'T+R' 2011–12: selected institutions

1. Oxford (4)	68%
2. Cambridge (5)	68%
3. LSE (6)	66%
4. Imperial College (7)	63%
5. UCL (8)	62%
6. Edinburgh (12)	51%
7. King's College London (16)	45%
8. Bristol (21)	43%
9. Warwick (22)	43%
10. Liverpool (40)	34%
Notes: Position in overall rank in brackets	

Source: HESA

Once again there is a natural gap (after rank 5). Also again, on the overall table the big hitters are interspersed with all sorts of smaller players, giving the lie to the fact that size rules in research performance (this time the Institute of Cancer Research is 1st, the London Business School 2nd, and the London School of Hygiene and Tropical Medicine 3rd). In this rank, the lowest Russeller (Exeter) is at number 51 (with 27 per cent) and the lowest 94-Group institution (East Anglia) is above it at number 50 with 28 per cent. The highest '94-Grouper is SOAS, at the dizzy heights of number 13 (50 per cent). The Alliance joins in at number 63 (Bradford, 18 per cent) and Million+ at number 83 (the Guildhall School of Music and Drama, 9 per cent)

3. Thirdly, there is the permanent challenge of contextualizing league tables – most of which are profoundly misleading (especially the newspapers' 'multi-factorial' variants; 'single-issue' and standardized tables, like the National Student Survey, can be more useful). It is striking how many institutional strategies are driven by a desire to be at or near the top of rankings and league tables, the statistical merits of which make the professional cringe and whose implicit goals are naïve in the extreme

4. This does not preclude bench-marking for challenge as well as for comfort – as in testing performance against institutions from different as well as the same parts of the sector

5. Meanwhile, inside the institution it is important to probe course and departmental granularity – in other words, getting below the tyranny of whole-institution averages (like the Funding Council 'bench-marks') to see how they are built up, and hence being able to tackle issues locally and in detail

6. Then there is the challenge of reassuring stakeholders – as well as building cases for partnership and other support

7. Leaders also have to learn to deal effectively with the counter-intuitive – when the evidence provided by institutional research does not fit the managers' preconceptions

8. The golden rule is about getting the money right – a necessary but not sufficient condition of institutional success

9. Connected with this is the increasing salience of information systems, and their integration (JISC, 2009)

10. All of this leads up to the task of establishing and maintaining the institution's unique 'zone of freedom of action', where temporary, creative cross-subsidy is probably the institutional manager's most powerful device (Watson, 2009: 140).

Managing the future

If there is a moral in this story, it is that institutional leaders can only manage the future if they are serious and successful about managing both the past and the present condition of their universities and colleges. Leadership has to be about extrapolation from a well-understood institutional history, as well as about correcting the course, and, where appropriate, about fresh starts. Except in the case of heavily pump-primed private higher education, approaches based on 'Cambodia Year Zero' are non-starters. Knowing the real condition of your institution – where it came from, how it is performing, how well it could perform, and at what – is an absolute prerequisite for facing the future with both ambition and realism (Sayers and Kubler, 2010: 45–7).

A more important issue is the reality check this offers those institutions wishing to associate themselves with a largely fictional wider elite in the slipstream of the apex, largely, it seems because they have banded together in private clubs for the purpose. As the analysis above suggests, such clubs seem to have little really to do with relative significance across the wider sector; other 'clusters' could be much more powerful and helpful to policymakers. They also make a significant category mistake: for almost all funding decisions in the UK system the university is not the unit of analysis: it is the performance of subsidiary elements (researchers, courses, subjects, teams, and departments – which can of course be aggregated, sometimes misleadingly). At a cruder level, one leadership illusion that works all the way down the reputational pecking order is that 'all our geese are swans' (or everybody here is 'world-class', or at least 'excellent').

It is very easy for institutional leaders to take credit for whatever goes well and to blame others for what goes wrong. We are now entering another one of those periods (the late 1970s and early 1980s were the last) when we need to be a smarter system. We are certainly facing another powerful – if not necessarily perfect – storm: of national policy confusion (exacerbated by devolution), of funding uncertainty, and of diminished public confidence. Survival and prosperity will once again only securely be achieved – as it has been in the past – by understanding and adapting in a framework of enduring principles. If there is a single lesson from the forty-year history leading up to the current confusion about the future for UK higher education, it is that survival (and occasional prosperity) has largely come from within. Our fate is in our own hands.

References

BIS (Department for Business, Innovation and Skills (2011) *Higher Education: Students at the heart of the system*. London: BIS.

—(2012) Government Response to Higher Education White Paper, *Higher Education: Students at the heart of the system* and *A New Regulatory Framework for the HE sector*. London: BIS.

Collini, S. (2012) *What Are Universities For?* London: Penguin.

Cowen, R. 'Comparing and transferring: vision, politics and universities'. In Bridges, D., Juceviciene, P., Jucevicius, R., McLaughlin, T., and Stankeviciute, J. (eds) (2007) *Higher Education and National Development: Universities and societies in transition*. London and New York: Routledge.

DfEE (Department for Education and Employment) (1998) *Higher Education for the 21st Century: A response to the Dearing Report.* London: HMSO.

DfES (Department for Education and Skills) (2003) *The Future of Higher Education: Creating opportunity, releasing potential, achieving excellence.* Norwich: Stationery Office.

Gill, J. (2008) 'Labour concedes that it won't deliver its 50% target on time'. *Times Higher Education,* 17 April.

HEFCE (Higher Education Funding Council for England) (2013) *Higher Education in England: Impact of the 2012 reforms.* Report 2013/03. Bristol: HEFCE.

HEPI (Higher Education Policy Institute) (2009) *Oxford and Cambridge: How different are they?* Oxford: HEPI.

—(2012a) *Universities and Constitutional Change in the UK: The impact of devolution.* Oxford: HEPI.

—(2012b) *The Cost of the Government's Reforms of the Financing of Higher Education.* Oxford: HEPI.

—(2012c) *The Impact on Demand of the Government's Reforms of Higher Education.* Oxford: HEPI.

JISC (Joint Information Services Committee) (2009) *Organizational Leadership, Management and Strategic Planning in UK HE.* Briefing paper for the Joint Information Services Committee. Online. www.jisc.ac.uk/media/documents/aboutus/strategy/david%20 watson%20essay.pdf

Nuffield Foundation (2008) *Science Education in Europe: Critical reflections.* London: Nuffield Foundation.

Palfreyman, D., and Tapper, T. (eds) (2008) *Structuring Mass Higher Education: The role of elite institutions.* London: Routledge.

Richard, A. (2009) 'Deliberate diversity'. *CAM,* 58 (Michaelmas), 41.

Sayers, N. and Kubler, J. (2010) *Research into the Future of Higher Education: Implications for leadership and management.* London: Leadership Foundation for Higher Education.

Stratford, M. (2012) 'Senate report paints a damning portrait of for-profit higher education'. *Chronicle of Higher Education,* 30 July. Online. http://chronicle.com/article/A-Damning-Portrait-of/133253/ (Accessed 30 July 2012).

Watson. D. (2006) 'Who killed what in the quality wars?' No 1. in series *Quality Matters.* Cheltenham: QAA.

—(2009) *The Question of Morale: Managing happiness and unhappiness in university life.* Maidenhead: Open University Press.

—(2011) 'Cassandra and the politicians: higher education and policy memory'. *Educational Review,* 63 (4), 409–19.

Watson, D. and Bowden, R. (1999) 'Now take a look at our figures'. *Guardian Education,* 16 November.

—(2002) *The New University Decade.* Brighton: University of Brighton Education Research Centre.

—(2005) *The Turtle and the Fruit-fly.* Brighton: University of Brighton Education Research Centre.

Watson, D. and Maddison, E. (2005) *Managing Institutional Self-Study.* Maidenhead: Open University Press.

Chapter 12

Conclusions

Claire Callender and Peter Scott

Introduction

Any analysis of the White Paper *Higher Education: Students at the Heart of the System* faces a number of difficulties. Although it was published at a particular moment, June 2011, it was only one stage in a policy process that had begun with the publication of the *Browne Report* nine months before and is continuing to unfold. Although Lord Browne spoke, rather incautiously perhaps, of a 'paradigm shift' when he introduced his Report, the current reforms of English higher education can be traced back well into the period of New Labour rule between 1997 and 2010 (or even earlier), as Michael Shattock demonstrates in his chapter on the historical antecedents to the current reform. These reforms have also been substantially elaborated since the White Paper's publication. Some of its strands have been significantly revised, others have not been pursued, and new elements have been introduced. As the Greek philosopher Heraclitus pointed out long ago, it is impossible to step into the same river twice. It is the same with any analysis of a complex policy process such as that represented by the 2011 White Paper. All that can be offered by way of conclusion, therefore, is a set of preliminary reflections and provisional assessments, all subject to change.

There is a temptation to describe the White Paper, the document itself and also its pre-history and subsequent evolution, as a 'shambles' – or an 'omni-shambles', in current political *argot*. But that would perhaps be unfair and certainly unwise. All policy processes reflect the dynamic between short-term political choices and long-term structural changes. The former are inherently ephemeral and volatile, adding to the impression of improvisation and inconsistency. The latter may appear inexorable and inevitable, giving an equally strong impression that 'there is no alternative' (in effect, there are no political choices to be made with regard to overall direction, only of timing – and, possibly, implementation). But both impressions are misleading. Politicians genuinely aspire to make strategic choices, even if they are often fiercely constrained by tactical considerations (especially so in the case of the White Paper because it was produced by a coalition government). Real choices also continue to be available, although they may require a degree of political will and courage that is often lacking (and which may be difficult to exercise within an increasingly mediatized political environment). In other words, there is nothing inevitable about the policies outlined in the White Paper, even if there is nothing surprising either, because the dominance of neo-liberal market ideology, although shaken by the unfolding financial and economic crises, has not (yet) been shattered.

In this conclusion two issues will be explored. The first is how best to interpret the reforms of English higher education of which the White Paper is the centrepiece – in terms of continuity or rupture? The second is the reforms' collateral effects, or unforeseen and unintended consequences, on a range of issues including student demand, access and equity, part-time study, postgraduate education, and new providers.

Interpreting the reforms

There can be little doubt that the majority of higher education leaders view these reforms as a 'cruel necessity', as indeed they did the substantial increase in tuition fees by the Labour Secretary of State for Education, Charles Clarke, in 2004 (UUK, 2011). In their view a gap has opened up between the funding required by institutions – in particular, 'world-class' research intensive universities – and the resources the state is willing, or able, to provide. They recognize, with varying degrees of regret, that the essence of a welfare state has been fundamentally challenged by the new neo-liberal global order, and that the constrained public funding that is available is likely to be focused increasingly on health, pensions, and welfare. They accept that further downward pressure on public expenditure in general, and expenditure on higher education in particular, has been applied by the Coalition Government's determination to reduce the deficit by 'shrinking the state'. As a result they see no alternative to some form of 'cost sharing' between taxpayers and students (and graduates), of whom the former will contribute less and the latter more to the overall cost of higher education. A minority, of course, has actively welcomed the radical – and, they hope, irreversible – shift from grants made to institutions to tuition fees paid by students. Naively perhaps, they regard the shift as likely to enhance their freedom of action. A small number eagerly anticipate the development of a full-blown market in higher education.

In the short term the reforms will deliver the additional funding that is their primary justification in the eyes of the majority:

- First, ministers have themselves publicly stated that total funding (direct grants made to institutions by the Higher Education Funding Council for England (HEFCE) and the loans made available by the Student Loans Company to students to pay increased tuition fees) will increase – while failing at the same time to explain how this increase can be reconciled with the government's overarching aim to reduce the deficit. Vince Cable, the Secretary of State for Business, Innovation and Skills, told the Universities UK annual conference in September 2011 that total expenditure on higher education by his Department would increase from £9 billion in 2011–12 to £10 billion in 2014–15 (Cable,

2011) – and that figure did not include the rising bill for student loans. This increase is partly transitional (and so temporary) – as one funding regime is phased out and a new regime phased in – and partly structural (and therefore potentially permanent), although it is difficult on current evidence to determine their respective weights

- Secondly, although there has been a lively debate about the likely level of the so-called RAB (resource accounting and budgeting) charge – the degree of continuing public subsidy required to compensate for the fact that many graduates will never pay back the full amount of their loans – there is no doubt that the amount will be substantial (Bekhradnia and Thompson, 2012a). Ministers insist that the charge will be 33 per cent (3 per cent higher than the RAB charge figure originally given in the White Paper), while their critics, using the government's own model, calculate that it could be much higher – perhaps more than 50 per cent. However, even if the government's lower figure is accepted, there will be little, if any, reduction in the total of publicly provided funding available to higher education (as opposed to nominal public expenditure).

However, this optimistic funding scenario must be qualified for two important reasons:

1. The transition from the old to the new funding regime has created higher levels of uncertainty, and produced greater turbulence. Although overall funding has increased, these gains have not been spread equally across the system. Some institutions have enjoyed substantial increases, while others have experienced losses. Such an uneven pattern has been only partly attributable to shifts in the preferences of students now empowered by increased performance data from institutions in the form of key information sets (KIS), although that would fit the White Paper's market-oriented logic. In fact, there is little evidence of any significant shifts in student preferences – so far. The main reason appears to be the variable capacity of institutions, and of departments and courses within them, to manage the new funding environment – and, in particular, the complex tripartite system of student number controls. Whatever the cause, the effect is to produce substantially increased turbulence. Optimists hope this will be a relatively short-lived phenomenon, the inevitable pains of transition. Pessimists fear it may become a more endemic phenomenon, arguing that greater turbulence is a logical (and desired) outcome of the development of a more marketized system of higher education. In the past public policy was designed to reduce turbulence – for structural reasons, because both graduate life cycles and academic development and research timescales are long (like procurement cycles for defence or major infrastructure projects); but also for normative reasons, because as key civil society institutions universities needed to be insulated to some degree from the immediate pressures of politics and the market place. The

HEFCE, and its predecessors, created a range of policy instruments to smooth transition and reduce turbulence. The prophylactic of such protection is now being progressively reduced – with unknown consequences.

2. The planned increase in publicly provided resources for higher education may be, literally, too good to be true. In his 2013 Budget the Chancellor of the Exchequer, George Osborne, announced an across-the-board 2 per cent squeeze on the budgets of all Whitehall departments. Although the details of this latest round of reduction were not scheduled to be available until after the publication of this book, expenditure on higher education is such a large fraction of the Department of Business, Innovation and Skills' (BIS) budget that it is almost impossible for it to remain unscathed. In the longer term the next Spending Review is likely to pose a further threat to funding levels that are regarded as generous (and are, in the sense that they represent real increases at a time when most other publicly funded services are suffering often catastrophic declines). As an opening shot in the spending review war, Danny Alexander, chief secretary to the Treasury, wrote to ministers in March 2013 warning them to prepare for cuts of 10 per cent in their departmental budgets. The difficulty of cutting expenditure on higher education, of course, should not be underestimated. The continuing indirect public subsidy represented by the RAB charge could only be reduced by toughening the repayment regime for student loans, while direct public expenditure is increasingly focused on research – Quality Research (QR), as determined by the outcomes of the forthcoming Research Excellence Framework (REF) – and higher-cost STEM courses (those in science, technology, engineering, and medicine) and SIVS (strategic and vulnerable subjects). But the strong sense that planned levels of public support on higher education are highly vulnerable, combined with increased levels of turbulence in the system, detract from any feelings of optimism that the reforms of English higher education, and the new fees-based funding regime, has helped deliver the resources needed to fill the funding gap.

As a result it is difficult to interpret these reforms. On the one hand they represent continuity because they have protected, however temporarily and precariously, the funding base of English higher education, and they represent the latest instalment in a policy process, as Peter Scott described in more detail in chapter 3, dating back to the reintroduction of direct student fees by New Labour following the *Dearing Report* (if not the replacement of maintenance grants by loans in the 1990s). On the other hand they represent rupture, because they have created much higher degrees of turbulence that institutional leaders are struggling to manage but also because they do not appear to have established a sustainable funding regime such as the *Browne Report* aspired to produce. Not only do they appear to be unsustainable in terms of what is known about the Coalition Government's intentions with regard to reducing overall public expenditure and 'shrinking the state', they also appear to be unsustainable because inconsistencies (and even contradictions) within the reform process are undermining their effectiveness. Some of these inconsistencies reflect failures of implementation, others may represent more fundamental flaws in design.

Unintended consequences – and collateral damage?

All reforms are incomplete – in the double sense that they cannot cover every issue and that, even in the case of those issues they do, they rarely offer entirely satisfactory solutions – logically or logistically. The reform of English higher education is no exception. However, some reforms are more incomplete than others. The question, therefore, is whether the reform formally triggered by the *Browne Report* and codified in the White Paper (and subsequent policy iterations) is an example of an especially incomplete reform. To be able to offer even a provisional assessment two different aspects need to be considered. The first is an internal test: whether the different elements within a reform package are reasonably consistent and also whether the package is sufficiently comprehensive. The second is an external test: of the reform package's resilience and, in particular, its capacity to absorb the impact of subsequent political (and economic) 'events' and other factors that could not have been reasonably anticipated (or, at any rate, reliably factored into it). Such external factors have been most vividly described by the former US Secretary for Defense Donald Rumsfeld in his infamous reference to 'knowns, known-unknowns and unknown-unknowns'.

Both tests can be applied to the reform of English higher education under five headings. Four – student demand, access and equity, part-time study, and postgraduate education – are different aspects of the reform's impact on levels of participation and patterns of study (in short, student-related aspects of the reform). The fifth – new and alternative providers – relates to its impact on the shape of the system and on institutions. Finally, the powerful, if indirect, impact of the *Browne Report*/White Paper reform on institutional priorities, organizational cultures, and the orientation (and ethos) of English higher education also needs to be considered.

Student demand

As an earlier chapter pointed out, the recommendations made in the *Browne Report* were a recipe for expansion. The lifting of the fees cap, plus the tapered 'taxation' of fee income beyond £6,000, was designed to avoid the need to restrict (or even reduce) student numbers at a time when public expenditure would need to be cut. The other alternative, reducing the unit-of-resource (funding per student), was dismissed by the Browne Committee. In practice the number of applications fell sharply following the government's decision to set a £9,000 cap (in other words, a tripling of fees). According to the University and College Admissions Service's (UCAS) *End of Cycle Report 2012*, 13 per cent fewer full-time students in England were admitted in 2012–13 than in the previous year. Full-time applications for 2013–14 were initially sharply down even on the reduced levels for 2012–13 but recovered to end up slightly ahead at the time of UCAS's January deadline. The number of students admitted will not be known until the autumn of 2013.

There has been a lively debate about the extent to which higher fees have been mainly or entirely responsible for the decline in applications, and different views have been expressed about whether this decline is simply a temporary 'blip' (such as occurred when fees were raised from £1,000 to £3,000 in 2006) or evidence of a more sustained decline in demand overall. Other factors are now likely to make it more difficult to determine the isolated impact of higher fees: notably, the decline in the number of 18- to 21-year-olds in most English regions and the deterrent effect of a tighter visa regime on international student recruitment. Although student applications were barely affected by a similar demographic slump in the late 1970s, conditions then were very different; UK higher education then recruited about a fifth rather than almost half of the relevant age group. As a result, demographic decline could bite more deeply. Nor is the socio-cultural 'protectionism' that has grown in reaction to the liberalization of the global economy likely to be a short-lived, or particularly an English, phenomenon. In the future the recruitment of international students, therefore, will most likely have to be undertaken in a colder climate – whatever the fate of the current visa regime and immigration targets. However, one thing is clear: the reform package is no longer designed to fund significant growth, as the *Browne Report* had originally intended and which was implicitly endorsed in the White Paper. Whether it will result either in consolidating or reducing student numbers is still unclear.

Access and equity

A major criticism of the central plank in the reform of English higher education – the raising of the fees cap to £9,000 – has been that potential students from more disadvantaged backgrounds would be disproportionately discouraged, as Anna Vignoles discussed in her chapter on widening participation (chapter 7). So far the evidence from UCAS statistics does not support this criticism. This conclusion has been broadly endorsed in a report from the Higher Education Policy Institute (Bekhradnia and Thompson, 2012b). In fact, the number of applications from such students fell by (slightly) less than average in 2012–13. However, that number did decline nonetheless and the relative chances of students from disadvantaged and advantaged social backgrounds continue to remain unchanged. Further progress towards more equitable access, a major policy preoccupation of New Labour governments under the general label of 'widening participation', appears to have stalled.

Also the Coalition Government's original hope that fees would be truly variable has proved to be in vain, an issue discussed in greater detail by Gill Wyness in chapter 6. Instead the great majority of institutions has decided to charge up (or very close) to the £9,000. The decision following the White Paper to encourage institutions to charge lower fees by allowing those with average fee levels of £7,500 or less to bid for additional places (the so-called 'core and margin') produced disappointing results. Only a limited number of institutions bid for the additional places and they did so mainly by reducing their average fee levels by substituting fee waivers (future debt reducing) for (cash-in-hand) bursaries. In the event, many of the allocated places remained unfilled. Such a policy failure appears to have stemmed from the price insensitivity generated by the way the new fees regime has been implemented – and, in particular, the rather generous (and leaky) repayment regime.

However, the major factor determining the impact of these reforms on access and equity is the response of institutions to the new funding environment. Any reduction in overall student numbers would tend to squeeze out more 'marginal' students (of all types). There is also already evidence of institutions 'trading up' by increasing entry tariffs, in the hope that this will improve their market (or, at any rate, their league table) position, which would have a similar effect. Finally, the substitution of the narrower 'fair access' agenda for the much broader 'widening participation' agenda, already well under way before the 2010 election, is likely to have a profound effect on institutional priorities and behaviours, despite – or perhaps because of – the proliferation of high-profile scholarships and bursaries. The emphasis has switched from wider interventions, designed to produce more equitable – and equal – outcomes to the promotion of social mobility, in the restricted interests of the 'deserving poor' (i.e. the tiny minority of well-qualified applicants from poor homes).

Part-time study

Both the *Browne Report* and the White Paper attempted to embrace part-time students in the reform of English higher education. Indeed the members of the Committee and ministers may deserve some credit for not confining their attention to full-time students. For the first time (some) part-time students have become eligible for loans to pay their tuition fees, the assumption no longer being that all part-time students are either employed or else well able to fund their own higher education. However, this positive measure has been more than cancelled out by another – unintended perhaps but nevertheless inevitable – effect of the funding reform: the decision made by many institutions to increase part-time fees *pro rata* with full-time fees. Part-time students have thus been provided with a powerful disincentive, which has produced a precipitate fall in the number of applications for part-time study. To the extent that institutions have not increased part-time fees to match the rise in full-time fees, the effect has been to make part-time students less 'valuable' – and, therefore, to reduce the incentive to recruit them. So the overall impact of the reform for part-time students has been negative.

The problem, as Claire Callender points out in chapter 8, is twofold. First, the distinction between full-time and part-time study is an administrative construct, designed for purposes of data collection and (in particular) to determine fee status and therefore eligibility for various forms of financial support. It lacks any particular academic logic. Moreover, part-time study is defined in different ways for different purposes, which compounds the confusion. Secondly, part-time study is defined in relation to full-time study that is still regarded as the normal, or standard, pattern. So part-time students are calibrated in terms of the number of contact hours, expressed as a fraction of the – notional – standard contact hours for full-time students. 'Notional' because studies have revealed wide variations in both contact and study hours for full-time students – not only between disciplines, which can be plausibly explained, but also within disciplines, which are more difficult to justify (Bekhradnia, 2012). In any case the development of mass higher education has tended to make the distinction between full-time and part-time study increasingly 'fuzzy' – most 'full-time' students now have substantial term-time jobs (a trend that will be further encouraged by higher fees), while up to a fifth of 'part-time' students are not employed; they are unemployed, on 'career breaks', dependent on support by their partners, or otherwise outside standard employment and may be earning substantially less than their 'full-time' peers. Of course, full-time and part-time students still remain discrete groups in terms of other characteristics.

This 'fuzziness' is likely to increase with the rise of work- and community-based study and of MOOCs (massive open online courses). Private providers are also likely to encourage non-standard patterns of study, to control costs as well as to enhance their attractiveness in the market. Indeed it may not be an exaggeration to conclude that in a very few years not only will the distinction between 'full-time' and 'part-time' study become more problematic, so too might the very definition of who is a 'student'. Yet the reform of English higher education depends on these distinctions and definitions. Indeed within the managed market that it aims to stimulate, entry conditions, and eligibility criteria, are likely to become even more important. It is difficult to escape the conclusion that the equal treatment of full- and part-time students cannot be produced by resort to conventional funding mechanisms within the higher education domain. Instead it would require the imaginative use of the wider tax and benefit systems.

New providers

The White Paper anticipated that a significant number of new providers would enter the higher education market, an issue explored by Paul Temple in chapter 9. Indeed without significant change in the institutional architecture of the system, it is difficult to see how higher levels of competition can be generated. From the start there has been a risk that the cartel-like instincts of existing institutions would be difficult to overcome, that they would 'price' up to the new £9,000 cap, and that the publication of KIS and the impact of league tables would only gradually modify deep-rooted institutional behaviours. As Temple writes in chapter 9, two different processes for opening up English higher education to new types of new provider were anticipated:

1. The first was that further education colleges would increase their stake in higher education. At present most higher education provision in further education colleges is essentially complementary to the provision in universities and other higher education institutions; most is at Higher Certificate/Diploma and Foundation Degree level and many courses are franchised from or validated by universities. There is little evidence so far that many colleges would prefer to develop more stand-alone provision, in competition with courses in mainstream higher education, as research commissioned by BIS itself has demonstrated (Parry *et al.*, 2012). Nor is there much evidence that colleges are anticipating substantial growth in higher education student numbers, which has been largely borne out by their failure to recruit the additional students awarded under the HEFCE's 'core and margin' initiative. However, a shift from complementary and competitive provision and a step-change in the volume of higher education provision in further education colleges would both be required to free up the market.

2. The second process was that new providers, both not-for-profit charities and for-profit corporations, would compete with existing 'public' institutions. So far progress has been slow. Two providers – the College (now the University) of Law and Regents College now Regents University London – have been granted full university status. Four others have been given degree-awarding powers, including BPP University College (now owned by the Apollo Group, a United States for-profit corporation that also operates the University of Phoenix). A number of reasons appear to explain why alternative providers are reluctant to enter the English higher education market. One is continuing uncertainty about the regulatory regime, in particular the arrangements for monitoring academic quality and standards but also other performance measures (for example, completion and graduation rates and other efficiency measures), and also about how eligible students are for loans. Private providers appear to be unconvinced that this regime will continue to be based on a 'public' model of higher education. They also believe that establishing joint ventures and other forms of collaboration with existing institutions offers a better business model than cut-throat competition. This alternative model is being pursued by some of the most active private providers such as INTO, Study Group, and Kaplan. As a result, there appears to be a limited prospect that the English system's institutional architecture is going to be substantially modified, although a secondary effect of loosening the rules for achieving university status has been to allow a number of smaller monotechnics to become universities (such as the Royal Agricultural College).

Postgraduate education

The Browne Committee, like most previous enquiries into higher education, was largely focused on undergraduate students. Although this focus on undergraduate students had not been mandated by its remit, this remit was to make recommendations on 'student fees and funding'. Rightly or wrongly this produced an assumption that these students were undergraduates and that funding was also subordinate to fees, i.e. its funding recommendations should be designed to accommodate any new fees regime rather than to design a funding system from first principles. In fact the Committee stretched its remit and, as has already been said, Lord Browne himself claimed that its recommendations set out a new 'paradigm' for English higher education. But the focus on undergraduate students remained. The White Paper did not significantly expand the scope of the reform. Its sections on research and postgraduate education were brief – no new policies were unveiled, apart from the standard rhetoric about excellence and concentration (assumed to be essentially synchronous). It is perhaps worth noting that Research Councils, which have a significant stake not only in research but also in postgraduate education, are UK-wide bodies. As such they cannot easily be corralled into the narrower reform of English higher education, an accidental but perhaps important effect of devolution.

The neglect of postgraduate education is a serious flaw in the reform package, as Geoff Whitty and Joel Mullan argue in chapter 10. One reason is that, as with full-time and part-time students, the distinction between undergraduate and postgraduate education is becoming fuzzier. In many professional disciplines it has always been a contrived demarcation. So-called 'undergraduate' Master's courses have proliferated. Many postgraduate courses are 'postgraduate' in time but not 'postgraduate' in level, often serving as conversion courses or elements in wider programmes of continuing professional development. A second reason, again as with part-time students, is that the increase in undergraduate fees has produced pressure to increase fees for postgraduate courses – and for very similar reasons. But no attempt has been made, as there has been with part-time students (however feebly and unsuccessfully), to articulate the two processes. In effect, the reform package is silent on postgraduate education. A third reason is that this silence feeds the uncertainty about the impact higher undergraduate fees (and correspondingly higher graduate debt) will have on the propensity of students to continue on to postgraduate courses. There is particular concern that, among students in comparatively low-pay occupations, higher undergraduate fees may have a significant deterrent effect. A similar concern regards postgraduate courses that do not appear to boost future earnings. In short, the reform of English higher education has served, no doubt unintendedly, to turn postgraduate education into *terra incognita* as well as the future frontier for widening participation.

Conclusion

Reforms do not need to succeed to succeed. In many, perhaps most, detailed respects the reform of English higher education triggered by the *Browne Report* and codified by the White Paper (and subsequent policy interventions) has failed to produce the changes desired by ministers – so far.

- The reform package has delivered additional resources to institutions – but in a random and unpredictable manner. In any case this increase appears to have been an unintended consequence of the financial arrangements for the transition from the old to the new fees and funding regime, the caution of institutions (and general restrictions on pay increases), and the generous student loan repayment regime introduced to 'sweeten the pill' of higher fees. As a result, levels of overall funding are regarded as precarious and temporary, likely to be reversed by additional cuts to core budgets in forthcoming Spending Reviews.
- Fees are not variable in any meaningful sense. Instead institutions have 'priced' to the cap, partly because they fear charging lower fees will be seen as a lack of confidence in their own standards (and standing) and partly because the generous repayment regime has produced low-price sensitivity. It is hardly a simplification to say that the majority of institutions have either charged the maximum £9,000, or, if they had poor recruitment records or simply wished to demonstrate their commitment to widening participation and social justice, have charged slightly less. But the differential is of little consequence within the total burden of graduate debt.
- As a result, a market has failed to develop: there is little evidence that student preferences have significantly changed – between more and less popular subjects, and between institutions arranged in their familiar 'pecking order' – despite the publication of KIS and the often elaborate – and confusing – packages of bursaries, scholarships, and fee waivers on offer. Efforts to open up the market, at least for well-qualified applicants, have probably served to reduce student diversity.
- A reform package designed to allow for expansion in student numbers – in the eyes of the Browne Committee at any rate – has produced the opposite effect. In the first year of the new fees regime, applications, and admissions, plunged. While applications by full-time students have since recovered, they remain below the levels reached under the old tuition fees and funding regime. If the impacts of demographic decline and the chilling effects of the new visa regime and anti-immigration sentiment on international student recruitment are taken into account, it seems unlikely that the current reduction in student numbers will be a short-term 'blip'.

- The institutional landscape has remained essentially unchanged and there are few signs that it is likely to alter in the short and even medium term. Further education colleges, with a few exceptions, have shown little appetite for expanding their stake in higher education, even if market conditions allowed. Alternative providers have been slow to enter the market, preferring collaboration with existing providers to cut-throat competition. As a result, there is little downward pressure on fee levels.
- The collateral effects of the reform of (full-time undergraduate) tuition fees and funding have been to produce significant shortfalls in applications by part-time students and to generate high levels of uncertainty about the future size and shape of postgraduate education. Finally, much unfinished business remains, particularly with regard to the regulation of institutional status and academic standards.

Hardly an impressive achievement. And yet … It is possible that, although a failure in terms of detailed policies, the reform of English higher education may achieve its overall objective: to change the culture of the system. The cumulative effect of these measures is likely to have an important impact on both institutional priorities and organizational cultures. Resources could well be diverted from 'front line' teaching and research into marketing and 'customer care'. In future academic leadership may be valued less highly than the 'business planning' skills needed to manage the new fees and funding environment. The changing context within which institutional leaders must operate is the subject of David Watson's contribution to this book (chapter 11). Collegially determined (and largely self-policing norms), rooted in trust, could be replaced by performance measures and management targets, one aspect of what Ron Barnett describes as the (damaging) shift from 'mystery' to 'explicitness' in chapter 5. Two points deserve to be emphasized in this respect. The first is that the drift towards such behaviours is already well established. Policy insiders and institutional managers are perhaps less aware of it – partly because they derive advantages from it and partly because they have become routinized by its effects through daily exposure – than critics such as the Campaign for the Public University (2013) and the Council for the Defence of British Universities (2013). The second point is that such corporate behaviours can flourish in the absence of true markets, just as collegial and mutualist behaviours can flourish in commercial environments. The reform of English higher education may not be successful in producing the market university, but it is certainly likely to provide a powerful stimulus to the development of the managerial university.

References

Bekhradnia, B. (2012) *The Academic Experience of Students in English Universities.* Oxford: Higher Education Policy Institute.

Bekhradnia, B. and Thompson, J. (2012a) *The Cost of the Government's Reform of the Financing of Higher Education.* Oxford: Higher Education Policy Institute.

—(2012b) *The Impact on Demand of the Government's Reforms of Higher Education.* Oxford: Higher Education Policy Institute.

Cable, V. (2011) Speech to Universities UK annual conference, 8 September. Online. www. gov.uk/government/speeches/universities-uk-annual-conference–2

Campaign for the Public University (2013) Online. www.publicuniversity.org.uk

Council for the Defence of British Universities (2013) Online. www.cdbu.org.uk

Parry, G., Callender, C., Scott, P., and Temple, P. (2012) *Understanding Higher Education in Further Education Colleges.* BIS research paper no. 69. London: Department of Business, Innovation and Skills.

Universities UK (2011) Government Response to the Higher Education White Paper, *Students at the Heart of the System.* London: Universities UK. Online. www.universitiesuk.ac.uk/highereducation/Documents/2011/ResponseToTheWhitePaper.pdf

Index